American Catholics in the Protestant Imagination

American Catholics
in the Protestant Imagination

Rethinking the Academic Study of Religion

MICHAEL P. CARROLL

The Johns Hopkins University Press
Baltimore

This book has been brought to publication
with the generous assistance of the J. B. Smallman Publication Fund
and the Faculty of Social Science of The University of Western Ontario.

The Johns Hopkins University Press
2715 North Charles Street
Baltimore, Maryland 21218-4363
www.press.jhu.edu

Library of Congress Cataloging-in-Publication Data

Carroll, Michael P., 1944–
American Catholics in the Protestant imagination : rethinking the
academic study of religion / Michael P. Carroll.
    p.   cm.
Includes bibliographical references and index.
ISBN-13: 978-0-8018-8683-6 (hardcover : alk. paper)
ISBN-10: 0-8018-8683-X (hardcover : alk. paper)
1. Catholics—United States—History. 2. Catholics—United States—
Historiography. I. Title.
BX1406.3.C375 2007
282'.73—dc22   2007006282

A catalog record for this book is available from the British Library.

Special discounts are available for bulk purchases of this book.
For more information, please contact Special Sales at 410-516-6936 or
specialsales@press.jhu.edu.

CONTENTS

By their nature, books take a relatively long time to write; and during that period an author, unless he or she is incredibly arrogant, inevitably harbors concerns about what works and what does not work in the text being created. For that reason, it is important to receive feedback from informed commentators while a book is in progress. With that in mind, I would like to thank Donald Akenson, Jeff Burns, Fred Gardaphe, Eugene Hynes, Bill Issel, Timothy Matovina, Sal Primeggia, and Thomas Tweed, all of whom very graciously took the time to read and comment on preliminary drafts of particular chapters. A book is always the sole responsibility of the author, but this book is certainly better than it would have been without their comments.

The research in this book was made possible by a grant from the Social Sciences and Humanities Research Council of Canada (SSHRC), and SSHRC's continuing and very generous support of scholarly investigation is something for which everyone in the Canadian academic community must be thankful. Publication of this book was also aided by a grant from the J. B. Smallman Publication fund administered by the Faculty of Social Science at the University of Western Ontario.

An earlier version of Chapter 1 appeared in *Religion and American Culture: A Journal of Interpretation* (Carroll 2006) and an earlier version of Chapter 4 appeared in *Studies in Religion* (Carroll 2003). A portion of Chapter 6 (mainly, the section on the upstart sects) is derived from an article published in *Religion* (Carroll 2004).

I love being an academic for many reasons, but primary among these is the fact that I have the freedom to go where my intellectual curiosity leads me. Acquiring such an ideal career would not have been possible without the very real sacrifices of my parents, Olga Ciarlanti and William Carroll, who for years put long hours into jobs they often did not enjoy and who also were a constant source of encouragement to me and my brothers.

Finally, I must acknowledge Lori, the love of my life and the person who, more than anyone else, sustains me in all that I do.

This book is about several different things at once. Most chapters are concerned with some variant of American Catholicism, and one goal certainly is to provide new insight into the several Catholic traditions that have flourished in the United States over the past two centuries. But every chapter also seeks to identify some historigraphical puzzles in the study of American religion. Thus, we will encounter staunch Irish Presbyterians in the colonial era who weren't very staunch, Irish Catholic Famine immigrants who came to America in the wake of Ireland's devotional revolution who weren't very devout, Italian Catholics clinging to the saints and madonnas they knew in their natal villages who didn't really cling very hard, Cajun Catholics whose Catholicism may be something quite different from what it appears to be, a strongly matricentered Hispanic Catholicism that turns out not to be matricentered at all, and more. As will become clear, the master puzzle in all this is why American scholars studying religion have accepted some claims about American Catholics (and sometimes about American Protestants as well) when those claims have little or no empirical support and why these same scholars have simultaneously ignored clues that point to interpretations of the American Catholic experience that allow for less passivity and more creativity than the interpretations that have prevailed. When all the bits and pieces of my response to this puzzle are put together, it will be apparent that this book is as much about the conceptual frameworks that American scholars past and present have brought to the study of American religion as it is about Catholics, and even more specifically, it is about the continuing influence of a "Protestant imagination" in studying American religion.

I like to think (though I suspect I'm romanticizing the research process) that this book represents the latest stage in an intellectual journey that began in the Church of Saints Peter and Paul (SSPP) in San Francisco's North Beach area. The full history of this church will be discussed in Chapter 3. For now, it is sufficient to say that SSPP was designated an Italian national church in 1897 and has always been emblematic of Italian American Catholicism in the San Francisco Bay area, even though for quite some time most of its parishioners have been Chinese Americans. I have a personal connection to SSPP, because ancestors on my mother's side were Italians who settled in North Beach over the period 1870 through 1915. Pasqualina Demartini (1819–1894), my third great-grandmother, emigrated from Italy in the 1840s, settled originally in Washington D.C., and— if family tradition is to be believed—headed west to San Francisco in the early 1870s, literally walking most of the way. My great-grandfather Raffaele Ciarlanti (1859–1913) decided to emigrate to San Francisco in late 1906, figuring that the devastation caused by the Great Earthquake would make it easy to set up a general store (which is precisely what he did). My mother, Olga Ciarlanti, was born and raised in North Beach. Although my parents (and I) joined the post–World War II exodus of Italian Americans out of North Beach into other neighborhoods in and around the city, we returned to North Beach on a regular basis because my mother's father owned a restaurant on Grant Avenue. On those Sundays when I was brought to the restaurant and left to amuse myself, I often visited SSPP, one of the few places open on Sunday afternoons in North Beach.

At the time, what most caught my eye at SSPP were the statues, displayed in an abundance that would soon become unfashionable in the wake of Vatican II. Some of the statues in the nave of the church might be found in any Catholic church, for instance, the Infant of Prague, the Immaculate Conception, St. Joseph, and St. Anne. Other statues depicted saints who were more distinctively Italian, like Teresa Mazarello, Gemma Galgani, and Don Bosco. But what I always found most interesting were the statues and other holy images in the three small chapels at the back of the church, where you enter the building.

The images in those back chapels were clearly *different*. My favorite was a plaster diorama showing Our Lady of Mt. Carmel sitting above a sea of blood-red flames (Purgatory) and holding out a rosary toward a dozen or so suffering souls engulfed by those flames. This particular image, unfortunately, was removed sometime in the early 1990s, presumably because it was a little too graphic for modern Catholic sensibilities. Also in those chapels were a cramped recreation of the grotto at Lourdes showing Mary talking to Bernadette, and images of St. Rocco showing the plague sore on his leg to his dog, the Madonna della Guardia talking to the seer Benedetto Pareto, and several other madonnas tied to certain specific regions or villages in Italy. One of the things that made those back chapel images so interesting, I think, was that they were colorful and "active" in a way not true of statues found elsewhere in the church. I always had a vague interest in finding out more about the sort of Catholicism associated with those back chapel madonnas and saints but did not act on it at the time.

My own parish church was dedicated to St. Emydius, patron saint of earth-quakes (a connection that was always good for a laugh in San Francisco), and both the parishioners and the pastors at St. Emydius were overwhelmingly Irish. My suspicion is that most of the sisters who taught us in the parish school were also Irish American, but it was less obvious. Unlike the horrific priests and sisters so often portrayed in plays and books written by ex-Catholics, the ones I knew were for the most part quite likable. They were strict, certainly, but they also had a sense of humor (and my memories of that humor are among the clearest I have of that period in my life), and it was obvious that they truly believed that by helping us to become better Catholics they were helping us become better human beings. What "helping us to become better Catholics" meant, most of all, was fostering devotion to Christ and to Mary and making us aware of the overwhelming importance of the sacraments (and in particular, Holy Communion).

My personal commitment to Catholic practice and the Catholic Church persisted through the experience of a Catholic high school (where the teaching brothers were a little stricter than the sisters at St. Emydius, but not by much) and only began to falter when I went to Stanford. My departure from the church, however, was not the result of being exposed to a secular education. Quite the contrary, my Catholic education provided me with a knowledge of church history that allowed me to become something of a Defender of the Faith in my first year Western Civ class, and there was no shortage of professors in the arts and humanities at Stanford who were quite sympathetic to Catholicism and the Catholic intellectual tradition. No, my departure from the church was the result of something more mundane. As I took to sleeping in on Sundays and skipping mass, I simply found that I did not miss the experience and so simply drifted away from Catholic practice. Vatican II was at the time effecting a revolution in the church, but the final result was a beige Catholicism (to borrow a term from Andrew Greeley) that seemed even less appealing than what I had known, and so eventually the split became complete. When I did return to Catholicism, it was as a scholar not as a practitioner.

As soon as tenure afforded me the opportunity to investigate what I chose, I turned to studying Catholic devotions and beliefs. Partly this was because so few social scientists seemed interested in the lived experience of the Catholicism that had been so important to me, and partly it was because this provided me an opportunity to revisit familiar things. And the methodological template that I consistently brought to bear on the material I studied was borrowed from someone whose work I had stumbled across quite accidentally and whom I regard as one of the most undervalued resources in the academic study of European Catholicism: Herbert Thurston.

Thurston (1856–1939) was an English Jesuit who wrote extensively on Catholic devotions and on Catholic mystics. He contributed more than 170 entries to the old *Catholic Encyclopedia* and was a regular contributor to *The Tablet* and *The Month*. Overall, a list of his publications (which can be found in Crehan 1952) runs to nearly 800 items. Generally, Thurston's work is appealing, even now, because of the fearlessness and erudition that he brought to bear on a range of devotions that were (and are) dear to many Catholics. He turned a cold analytic eye on claims concerning the antiquity of the rosary, the Stations of the Cross, the Brown Scapular, and the like, and usually found evidence that these devotions had emerged much more recently, and under far more prosaic circumstances, than devotional accounts suggested. He also looked carefully and critically at reports of mystical phenomena—like the stigmata, living without food, apparitions of Mary, and tokens of mystic espousal—and usually found either that the evidence attesting to these phenomena evaporated upon close inspection or that the reported behavior was susceptible to more than one interpretation.

Thurston was not a social historian; he was little concerned with explaining why certain devotions and certain forms of mysticism became popular in particular cultures at particular times. Nevertheless, his work impressed on me the need for skepticism in evaluating the claims made both by religious practitioners *and* by historians studying religion, and also the need for careful investigation of the historical record even (indeed, especially) in the case of claims about religion that are usually taken for granted.

My very first foray into the study of popular Catholicism was a study of the Mary cult (Carroll 1986). In this case, a Thurston-like attention to the historical record made it clear that this cult had for the most part been absent from the church during the first few centuries of the Christian era and had only emerged as a popular cult with the social transformation of the church's membership base when Christianity became the only official religion in the Roman Empire. Recognizing this linkage, in turn, provided the basis for a sociological understanding of just *why* this cult became popular. Similarly, in a later work (Carroll 1989), careful attention to history in the case of devotions like the rosary, the Brown Scapular, and the Stations of the Cross (and here I borrowed heavily from Thurston's own work) also revealed patterns that pointed the way to a new understanding of why and where these devotions had first become popular.

Increasingly, however, I was drawn to the study of Italian Catholicism. Partly this reflected a growing appreciation of the role that Italian Catholicism had played in shaping the devotions which the Roman church had promoted throughout the Catholic world. But partly too, or so I like to think, it reflected a desire to learn more about the Catholicism I had encountered briefly in the back chapels of SSPP. This led to two extended investigations of popular Catholicism in Italy (Carroll 1992; 1996).

What I discovered in the Italian-language literature on Italian Catholicism was that, from the 1970s onward, Italian scholars like Gabriele De Rosa had increasingly abandoned an older perspective that depicted Italian Catholicism as reflecting the fusion of pagan and Catholic traditions and had moved toward a more "dialectical" model. This newer model suggested that popular religion in Italy was best seen as resulting from the interaction between Tridentine Catholicism and a range of local groups, each pursuing different political, religious, and economic goals.

Certainly, what I found in my own investigations was that many of the popular practices that defined the lived experience of Italian Catholicism during the early modern era had emerged only in the relatively recent past. Cults organized around miraculous images of madonnas, for example, or around liquefying blood relics and the incorrupt bodies of saints proliferated in the century or so following the Council of Trent (1545–1563), even though many historical accounts have given the impression that these were "medieval" cults that Trent had tried to suppress. The Italian Catholics who were emerging in my analysis, in other words, were not mindless peasants clinging tightly and uncritically to semipagan superstitions but rather people who were embracing new forms of religious practice that could be seen as relatively creative responses to changing social conditions.

My next projects were concerned with popular Catholicism in pre-Famine Ireland (Carroll 1999) and—in what can be regarded as the first step in my intellectual return to the United States—Hispano Catholicism, the sort found in northern New Mexico (Carroll 2002). What I found in both cases was an existing body of scholarly literature that had not as yet been shaken by the sort of revolution that De Rosa and others had induced in Italy. In the Irish case, for instance, it was still common to suggest that holy well cults—which were such an important part of popular Catholicism in the three centuries before the Famine—were an archaic inheritance incorporating pre-Christian Celtic traditions into Irish Christianity. The fact is, however, that there is little or no evidence indicating that holy well cults had been an important part of Celtic religion in Ireland, and little or no evidence suggesting that such cults had been popular during the Middle Ages. Similarly, the Penitente *cofradías* that had come to predominate in the Hispano villages of northern New Mexico during the nineteenth century were routinely depicted in most scholarly accounts as deriving from a tradition of Hispanic piety that dated from the earliest years of Spanish settlement there. And yet, here too, a careful examination of the historical evidence revealed little support for this interpretation.

Eventually, in both the Irish and the New Mexican cases, I suggested that, as in the Italian case, the forms of popular Catholicism involved could be seen as a creative response by local populations to changing social conditions. As will become clear, the analyses in this present book are very much the logical outgrowth of the concerns and conclusions reached in all these earlier works.

As with most academic books, the ordering of chapters in this book does not reflect the order in which the analysis proceeded. Strictly speaking, the critical chapter is Chapter 3, on Italian American Catholicism. Partly, this is because as I examined the literature on Italian American Catholicism it became apparent that the "fusion of paganism and Catholicism" model, which had gone out of fashion in Italy itself, was still very much in vogue among virtually everyone who wrote about the Catholicism that Italian immigrants had brought with them to America. But what was likely even more critical in setting in motion the investigation that led to this book was something very specific: the fact that I finally got around to looking more closely at the history of those back chapel madonnas that had fascinated me as child.

During a visit to San Francisco, I obtained permission to scrutinize the material in SSPP's parish library; and what I discovered, quite to my surprise, was that these madonnas—which all commentators on San Francisco's Italian community had associated with the immigrants who had arrived in the late 1800s—in fact had only become the focus of popular cults at SSPP during the 1920s and 1930s, after the great age of Italian immigration had come to a close. What had produced this relatively late explosion of localized madonnas at SSPP, and why had so many scholars been blind to the timing of this pattern? The specific answers I eventually gave to these two question are discussed in Chapter 3. The point is only that my experience with the literature on Italian American Catholicism and its problems led me, in turn, to look critically at what American scholars have said about Irish American Catholics, Cajun Catholics, and Hispanic Catholics.

The Organization of This Book

The material in Chapter 1 is presented first mainly because so much of it deals with religion in the American colonies and in the early Republic. Even so, the chapter starts with something that is very current: for more than two decades now, sociologists have known that most Americans who self-identify as Irish Americans are Protestant, not Catholic; yet the popular, and even scholarly, assumption is that most Irish Americans have always been Catholic. My goal in this first chapter is to demonstrate that the story of *how* Protestants became a majority among Irish Americans is more complex than first appears. And in telling that more complex story, I advance three interrelated claims. The first is that our understanding of Irish American religion and religiosity has been warped by at least two historiographical biases, one having to do with the so-called "Scotch-Irish" in America *before* the Famine and the other having to do with Irish Catholics in America *after* the Famine. The second claim is this: if we correct for these biases, then what emerges from the historical record, albeit dimly, is a story about the Irish contribution to the rise of evangelical Christianity in America that has been largely ignored by earlier commentators. Finally, I will be arguing that this new story about the Irish in America provides us with a basis for understanding the finding reported above, namely, the persistence of an Irish identity among so many American Protestants.

Chapter 2 is concerned mainly with the Irish who settled in the United States in the wake of the Famine of the 1840s. Everyone knows that most Famine immigrants were Catholic and that in the post-Famine period Irish American Catholics became the mainstay of the American Catholic Church, and indeed, came to set the standard for what being a "good Catholic" meant in the United States. Against this background, the purpose of this chapter is twofold. First, I want to demonstrate that arguments offered previously to explain why the Irish became good Catholics in America—explanations which have pointed to Ireland's devotional revolution, nativist hostility, and the increasing tie between Catholicism and Irish nationalism—are either inconsistent with the historical evidence or (at best) explanations that might explain why the Irish maintained a Catholic identity but not why they became such devout Catholics. A second—and more positive—goal, however, is to develop a new perspective on *why* the Irish became good Catholics, by looking carefully at their experience in America (not Ireland) and at the ways in which Irish immigrants were different from other European immigrants. This new perspective leads directly to an argument suggesting that ultramontane Catholicism (the form of Catholicism promoted by the American church in the mid-nineteenth century) would have had a special appeal to Irish American females and that this was the critical step in ensuring that the Irish generally (both female and male) became the gold standard in the American Catholic church.

Chapter 3, as I have indicated, is about Italian American Catholicism. The chapter starts by considering the "Standard Story" that scholars—themselves mainly Italian American—have told and continue to tell about this variant of Catholicism. According to the Standard Story, the first Italian immigrants to the United States were strongly attached to the folk Catholicism they had known in Italy, which was a syncretic religion pervaded with pagan beliefs and practices and centered on the strongly localized saints and madonnas who had protected the home villages that these immigrants had left behind. By staging the festas associated with these familiar saints and madonnas, the Standard Story continues, these immigrants were able to ease their transition from Italy to America. A final part of the Standard Story suggests that the attachment of Italian immigrants to this "pagan Catholicism" impeded their conversion to the sort of Catholicism favored by an American church dominated by the Irish.

One of the goals of Chapter 3 is to demonstrate that this Standard Story is problematic for at least two reasons. First, a careful examination of the historical evidence suggests that the earliest Italian immigrants were less characterized by *campanilismo* (attachment to the culture of their natal villages) than the Standard Story declares, *especially* in matters having to do with religion. Second, contrary to what the Standard Story leads us to expect, the experience in the San Francisco Italian community was not atypical; in other communities as well, some of the best-known and most popular festas centered on strongly localized saints and madonnas emerged not in the period 1880 to 1920 (the great age of Italian immigration) but in the 1920s and 1930s. Another goal in this chapter is to present an explanation that sees this upsurge in festas organized around localized saints and madonnas as a creative response by Italian Americans to their experiences in America, not Italy.

But if the Standard Story told about Italian American Catholics is so easily seen to be problematic, causing scholars to overlook patterns that hint at cultural creativity on the part of Italian Americans, why has that story retained such a grip on the scholarly imagination in the United States? Answering that question will lead directly to another major theme in this book: the continuing influence of Protestant metanarratives in the academic study of American religion.

Chapter 4 deals with the Acadian/Cajun Catholic tradition. There are few in-depth studies of Acadian/Cajun Catholicism, and what literature does exist is usually written from the perspective of the institutional church. Even so, it is common to find commentators saying—if only in passing—that the Acadians and their Cajun descendants in Louisiana were deeply attached to the Catholic tradition. Since this Cajun attachment to Catholicism is assumed to be a continuation of an Acadian attachment to Catholicism, the apparent pattern is a familiar one: as in the case of Irish American Catholics and Italian American Catholics, Cajun Catholics are constructed as clinging tightly to traditions formed outside the United States. And yet, close inspection of the available data indicates that (1) there is really very little evidence that supports the stereotype of the Acadians and Cajuns as devout Catholics and (2) the few bits of data that might seem to support this stereotype can be explained in other ways. The final section of Chapter 4 uses a feminist formulation relating to "gender performance" to develop a new interpretation of the folk Catholicism that emerged in rural communities in Louisiana that did not have resident priests.

Chapter 5 is about the academic study of Hispanic Catholicism in the United States. The central claim being advanced in this chapter is that a careful examination of what we "know" about Hispanic Catholicism reveals that many commonly accepted claims are, in fact, not supported by the available evidence. As a first step in demonstrating this, we look at something very specific: academic discussions of the shrine at Chimayó, New Mexico, which is routinely characterized as the most popular Catholic pilgrimage site in the United States. What emerges from the analysis is that the history of this shrine and the behavior of the Hispano pilgrims who go to the shrine have been constructed in ways that (1) are not consistent with the historical record, (2) show the clear influence of Anglo stereotypes about Hispanics, and (3) function to divert scholars from empirical patterns that would seem to allow for more creativity on the part of Hispano Catholics.

The last two-thirds of Chapter 5 examines a broader subject: the social scientific literature that purports to discuss Hispanic Catholicism in America generally. Here too, however, as in the more limited Chimayó case, we encounter commonly made claims that do not stand up to scrutiny. These include the claims that Hispanic Catholicism has a "matriarchal core" and that massive numbers of Hispanic Catholics are converting to Pentecostalism. In explaining why so much of what we "know" about Hispanic Catholicism is illusory, the discussion—in the concluding section—builds upon the argument relating to the continuing influence of Protestant metanarratives.

Chapter 6 starts by considering the ways in which the academic study of religion in America during the nineteenth and early twentieth centuries was shaped by an implicit Protestant norm. For the most part, this is familiar ground, but whereas other commentators believe that Protestantism is no longer the hidden norm guiding the academic study of religion in the United States, my goal in the remainder of this chapter is to show that this judgment is—at best—premature. I attempt to do so by examining three bodies of scholarly literature on American religion.

I first examine the literature associated with the new "multiple narratives" approach to the study of American religion. Although studies in this tradition undeniably treat the wide diversity of religious experiences in North America, the fact that Catholics continue to emerge as a "non-American Other" is evidence of the continuing influence of Protestant metanarratives. Next, I look at three psychological measures of religion—the Intrinsic/Extrinsic Scale, the Quest Scale, the Faith Maturity Scale—that are especially popular in the psychology of religion. Here again, it is easy to detect an underlying Protestant influence by looking carefully at what these scales emphasize and what they ignore. Generally, these scales show evidence of what David Tracy and Andrew Greeley have called "the Protestant imagination." The chapter concludes by considering recent theoretical developments in the sociology of religion, in particular, the increasing popularity of the theory of religious economies. Here too, we find clear evidence of the Protestant imagination and evidence that it has diverted the attention of sociologists from otherwise important issues in the study of American religion.

The book ends with a brief Epilogue that provides an overview of how the claims being made here might be used, if readers were so inclined, to revitalize the academic study of American religion.

American Catholics in the Protestant Imagination

CHAPTER ONE

How the Irish Became Protestant in America

During the 1970s and 1980s, when studies of "white ethnics" were very much in vogue, several national surveys quite independently turned up a surprising finding: most Americans who thought of themselves as "Irish" were *Protestant*, not Catholic. Donald Akenson's (1993, 219–220) review of these surveys reports that anywhere from 51 to 59 percent of respondents (depending on the survey) who identified themselves as Irish were Protestant, about a third were Catholic, and the rest were "non-Christian" or professed no religion. This pattern has not changed. In the General Social Survey, conducted by the National Opinion Research Center at the University of Chicago over the period 1990–2000, of the 1,495 respondents who identified themselves as "Irish," 51 percent were Protestant and 36 percent were Catholic (see Table 1). Just who are these Irish-American Protestants?

For Akenson, as well as for Andrew Greeley (1988), the answer was clear: today's Irish Protestants are largely the descendants of those Irish—mainly Protestant, but including Catholics who converted—who settled in America before the great Irish Potato Famine of the 1840s. And certainly, the regional distribution of today's Irish American Protestants lends support to this view. In the *South*, an area heavily settled by the pre-Famine Irish and little affected by the post-Famine Irish immigration, which was largely of Catholics, fully 73 percent of all respondents who identify themselves as Irish are Protestant (see Table 1, column 1). By contrast, outside the South (and so in areas *more* affected by post-Famine Irish immigration) Irish Catholics outnumber Irish Protestants by a slim margin (column 2).

I now want to argue that the story of how Protestants became a majority among Irish Americans is a more complex one than usually thought. In telling that more complex story, I will be advancing three interrelated claims. The first is that our

TABLE I
Geographical and Religious Distribution of Americans Identifying Themselves as Irish

Religious Affiliation	South		Non-South		Total U.S.	
Protestant	73%	(388)	39%	(375)	51%	(763)
Catholic	19%	(101)	45%	(436)	36%	(537)
Other	2%	(9)	3%	(29)	3%	(38)
None	7%	(35)	13%	(122)	10%	(157)
Total	101%	(533)	100%	(962)	100%	(1,495)

SOURCE: General Social Survey (1990–2000), National Opinion Research Center.

understanding of Irish-American religion has been warped by two historiographical biases, one having to do with the so-called Scotch-Irish in America *before* the Famine and the other having to do with Irish Catholics in America *after* the Famine. The second claim is this: if we correct for these two biases, then what emerges from the historical record, if only dimly, is a story about the Irish contribution to the rise of evangelical Christianity in America that has been largely ignored by earlier commentators. Finally, I will be arguing that this new story about the Irish in America provides us with a basis for understanding the persistence of an Irish identity among so many American Protestants, *despite* the fact that their ancestors left Ireland centuries ago and *despite* the fact that centuries of intermarriage with other groups has provided the opportunity for other ethnic identifications.

The Scotch-Irish Myth: "If St. Brendan Really Did Discover America, Well Then, He Must've Been Scotch-Irish"

By the last decades of the nineteenth century, it was common for American historians to suggest that the Scotch-Irish—Ulster Presbyterians who had settled in America during the colonial period and their descendants—were different from the other sorts of Irish who had come to America. First, the Scotch-Irish were seen as possessing a special character. At the Third Congress of the Scotch-Irish Society of America, one presenter (Bryson 1891, 102) summed up the elements of that character thusly:

> Always and everywhere they are the fearless and unflinching advocates of liberty, the determined and unfaltering foe of oppression. They are by nature a bold, courageous and aggressive people.

A few years later, at a meeting of the American Antiquarian Society, Samuel Swett Green (1895, 35) came up with a similar, though slightly expanded, list:

The Scotch-Irish emigrants to this country were, generally speaking, men of splendid bodies and perfect digestion. . . . They were plain, industrious and frugal in their lives . . . self-reliant and always ready to assert themselves, to defend their own rights and those of their neighbors, and courageously push forward.

These character traits, in turn, were seen as having given rise to something else that made the Scotch-Irish special: their support for the American Revolution and the role they had played in securing the Revolution's success. Charles Hanna (1902/1968, 2) laid out a common version of this argument with clarity:

[T]he position of the Scotch-Irish in the New World was peculiar. They alone, of the various races in America were present in sufficient numbers in all the colonies to make their influence felt; and they alone . . . had experienced together the persecution by State and Church which had deprived them at home of their civil and religious liberties; and were common heirs to those principles of freedom and democracy which had developed in Scotland as nowhere else.

Henry Jones Ford (1915, 526), professor of politics at Princeton, would later make the same point: "remembering that they [the Scotch-Irish] were all hot for independence while everywhere else there were streaks of cold or lukewarm feeling, there can hardly be any question as to where lay the decisive influence." Ford also suggested that the movement of the Scotch-Irish into frontier areas had been decisive in building the new nation, both because it contributed to the process of national expansion (p. 599) and because Scotch-Irish settlers brought with them legal and political institutions that ensured stability in the newly settled regions (p. 537). Given this view of the Scotch-Irish, which was widely shared in Protestant academic circles, it is hardly surprising that this group was seen as having supplied a goodly number of American political leaders in the early Republic— Andrew Jackson, John C. Calhoun, James Buchanan, James K. Polk, and so on.

This recurring historiographical emphasis on the special contribution the Scotch-Irish had made to America's rise to greatness infuriated many Irish American scholars of Catholic extraction (who were often working outside university settings), mainly because they felt it diminished the contribution that the Irish *generally* had made to the rise of the Republic. "If we can prove that St. Brendan was the first discoverer of America," bemoaned James Jeffrey Roche (1899), an editor at Boston's *The Pilot*, "and that a seaman named Patrick Maguire was the boat-oar who first set foot on the strand of the New World from the boat of Columbus [then] some clumsy forger will come forward and at once declare that Brendan was a Scotch-Irishman and Maguire an Anglo-Saxon." Roche's example was fanciful, but given that some promoters of the Scotch-Irish were at the time claim-ing the likes of Thomas Jefferson and Abraham Lincoln for their ranks (McKee 2001, 73), without making any attempt at substantiation, Roche's complaint seems quite reasonable.

The most sustained attack on the "Scotch-Irish myth" was mounted by the Irish-born historian Michael O'Brien (1870–1960) (see Figure 1). In literally hun-dreds of articles, most published in the *Journal of the American Irish Historical Society,* and in seven books, the best-known of which was *A Hidden Phase of Amer-ican History* (1919/1971), O'Brien attacked the myth on two fronts. He searched a wide range of documents—including newspaper accounts of passenger ships from Irish ports disembarking in America, muster rolls, early accounts of settle-ment in Virginia, Kentucky, Pennsylvania, and elsewhere, and so on—in an effort to show that Irish Catholics had been more numerous in the colonial period than previously acknowledged. Indeed, in several places he seems close to making the claim that Catholics had been the largest group among the colonial Irish (for example, O'Brien 1914; 1923).

O'Brien's second line of attack on the Scotch-Irish myth was more subtle. Basically, he argued that distinguishing between the Scotch-Irish and "other Irish" on the basis of religion created an artificial division between groups that were more similar than different because of their common Irish background. The following remarks are typical. They were made in response to a commenta-tor whom O'Brien saw as downplaying the role the Irish had played in support-ing the Revolution.

> It is true, of course, that many Protestants and Presbyterians also came from Ire-land, and that most [during the colonial period] were from the Province of Ulster. But surely Professor Hart knows better to claim that these people were not "Irish" because they professed a different faith from the majority of their countrymen. They were natives of Ireland; their forebears came to that country in the Plantation of Ulster (1611); through intermarriages with the Old Irish they became *Hibernos ab Hiberniores,* "as Irish as the Irish themselves." (O'Brien 1927, 27)

To buttress his argument, O'Brien was fond of pointing out that in Ireland many of the leaders most involved with promoting Irish nationalism had been Protes-tants. Moreover, he argued, in America, the so-called Scotch-Irish had given their settlements Irish names, had founded "Irish" (not "Scotch-Irish") societies, and had routinely celebrated St. Patrick's Day, Ireland's national festival (see espe-cially O'Brien 1914; 1925). The strong similarities between the Scotch-Irish and other Irish of the colonial period, O'Brien argued, were precisely why contem-

Fig. 1. Michael O'Brien (1870–1960). This Irish-born historian's attack on the Scotch-Irish myth in American academic circles was undervalued in his lifetime but has been validated by more recent research. Courtesy of the *Journal of the American Irish Historical Association.*

porary newspaper accounts as well as hostile English Americans used the single term *Irish* to describe all Irish immigrants and their descendants.

O'Brien's first argument is now generally rejected, mainly because much of the evidence he presented in support of a large Irish Catholic presence in the colonial period rests upon dubious assumptions linking particular surnames to a Catholic background (see Jones 1991; Rodechko 1970). His second argument, by contrast, has fared much better. Indeed, over the past few decades several lines of research have converged to suggest, as O'Brien claimed, that prior to the Famine Irish Catholics and Irish Protestants were not nearly as different in terms of their cultural beliefs and behaviors as they would later become in the popular imagination.

Take the matter of Irish nationalism. Although there was a time when scholars quite matter-of-factly took the tie between Catholicism and Irish nationalism to be centuries old (see, for example, Shannon 1960), it is now generally recog-

nized that the tight link that now exists between Catholicism and Irish nationalism was forged in the early nineteenth century and grew stronger as that century
progressed (Maume 1998). Akenson (1993, 221) and others have pointed out that
Daniel O'Connell, the Great Liberator, was central to this process:

> Daniel O'Connell was not merely one of the greatest persons in modern Irish his-
> tory but one of the shrewdest. He understood that to be successful, he had to unite
> in one crucible, Irish nationalism, Irish cultural identity, and Roman Catholics. In
> this he succeeded. . . . [B]y 1840 when a person in Ireland talked of "Ireland for the
> Irish" everyone knew he meant the Catholics.

The point is that prior to the nineteenth century, things had been quite different. Indeed, during the eighteenth century (just as Michael O'Brien pointed
out) a great many of the scholars and activists who had sought to establish a distinctly Irish national identity were Protestant. During the 1790s, for example, the
radical Society of United Irishmen strove for a united Ireland that embraced both
Catholics and Protestants and for the elimination of English control. The Belfast
chapter of this society was largely Presbyterian, while the Dublin chapter was
evenly split between Catholics and Protestants (Curtin 1998). Many of the best-
known nationalist leaders of the period were Protestant. Robert Emmet, whose
"Let no man write my epitaph" speech shortly before his execution in 1803 would
make him a nationalist icon, had been born into a well-to-do Protestant family in
Dublin. Theobald Wolfe Tone, killed in the revolution of 1798, and the Irish par-
liamentary leader Henry Grattan (1746–1820) were also Protestant. Politics
aside, Protestant scholars like George Petrie (who would become central to the
activities of the Ordnance Survey in the 1830s) played leading roles in the
nineteenth-century campaign to recover and preserve Ireland's Gaelic past so
that it could be used as the basis for an Irish national identity (Doherty 2004).

Investigators working with American materials have also undermined the
sharp distinction previously drawn between the Scotch-Irish and Catholic Irish
by pointing out that the term *Scotch-Irish* is itself a product of the nineteenth century. Although the word does occasionally appear in the eighteenth century, most
scholars now believe that the *Scotch-Irish* label came into widespread use in the
United States only around the time of the Famine and was then mainly used by
established Irish Protestants to disassociate themselves from the largely poor and
Catholic Famine immigrants who were coming over in such great numbers (Fitzgerald 2003; Keller 1991; K. Miller 2000, 141–142). More recently, Kerby Miller
and others (2003, 447–448) have advanced a slightly different explanation—that
use of the *Scotch-Irish* label dates to the early 1800s, and was tied to an attempt

by conservative Irish Presbyterians in the U.S. to disassociate themselves from those Irish, whether Presbyterian or otherwise, who embraced ultra-democratic ideals. Nevertheless, while the matter of precisely *when* in the nineteenth century *Scotch-Irish* came into widespread use might be debatable, everyone agrees it was *not* a term that was commonly used during the eighteenth century. Then, the Irish were—again, just as Michael O'Brien pointed out—usually called simply "the Irish" (Eid 1997).

Still other scholars have eroded the emphasis on Scotch-Irish distinctiveness by doing what O'Brien did not do: identify in some precise way the similarities between Irish Catholics and Irish Protestants. Leroy Eid (1986), for example, has marshaled much evidence that Ulster Irish communities in America exhibited the same preference for pastoralism and the same rejection of intensive agriculture that was typical of a great many Ulster Scotch communities in the north of Ireland and a great many "native Irish" communities in the south. In this same vein, Donald Akenson's (1988, 28–38) careful reanalysis of the available data (admittedly meager) relating to rates of premarital sexual behavior and illegitimate births among Catholics and Protestants in pre-Famine Ireland indicates that the two groups were less different on these measures than generally supposed. Basically, Akenson finds, both groups were characterized by relatively high rates of premarital sexual activity and relatively low rates of illegitimate births. Finally, both Eid and David Doyle (1981, 79–80) point out that the character traits that were stereotypically associated with the Ulster Irish in colonial America—including boisterousness, assertiveness, lack of discipline, conviviality—were the same traits stereotypically associated with the "native Irish" living in Ireland and in America. That the popular stereotypes were much the same for these different groups is yet more evidence—like use of the single term *Irish* to describe all these groups—that contemporary observers saw little difference among them.

Not only did outsiders blend all the Irish into a single category; so did the Irish themselves. Although the Irish American benevolent societies that formed in major American cities were started by well-to-do Protestants, these organizations did not impose a religious test for membership. The rules of the Society of the Friendly Sons of St. Patrick in New York (1786, 7), for example, said simply that "the Descendants of *Irish* Parents by either side in the first degree, and the Descendants of every Member, *ad infinitum,* shall have a natural Right of Application to be admitted Members of this Society." It is notable, though, that while the society imposed no religious test, it used distinctively Catholic imagery to depict St. Patrick. On the gold medal that each member was required to purchase (and which is described in the rules of the society) he is shown trampling on a snake, holding a cross, and dressed in his full bishop's regalia. The absence of a religious test in the case of this New York society was not unusual. The *Constitution of the St. Patrick Benevolent Society of Pennsylvania* (1804), a mutual benefit society based in Philadelphia which provided assistance to members suffering from "sickness, a bodily hurt, or other unavoidable misfortune" (p. 5), was also open to "Irishmen or the sons of Irishmen" (p. 1) with no mention of religious affiliation. It was precisely because these Irish benevolent societies were open to all Irishmen that the membership base changed over time, reflecting the changing patterns of Irish emigration. Thus, as Cronin and Adair (2002, 12–13) point out, increasing Irish Catholic immigration in the early 1800s meant that Catholics came to form the majority of members in Irish American charitable societies that had been overwhelmingly Protestant during the colonial period.

The patterns and evidence reviewed in the preceding paragraphs do not imply that there were *no* differences between Irish Catholics and Irish Protestants in the colonial period. There are identifiable subgroups within the Irish Catholic population whose concerns and behavior distinguished them from the Scotch-Irish. The Penal Laws in Ireland, even granting that they were not always rigorously enforced in the eighteenth century, certainly placed restrictions on the ability of Catholics to own or inherit land or transmit it to heirs. That such laws might someday be adopted in the American colonies was a possibility very much on the minds of American Catholic landowners, which comes through clearly from Ronald Hoffman and Sally Mason's (2000) study of the Carrolls of Maryland. Then too, as Dolan (2002, 14–28) points out, a great many educated American Catholics living in major cities (for Dolan, the publisher Mathew Carey of Philadelphia is the prototypical example) embraced a well-defined variant of Catholicism that merged traditional Catholic belief with an emphasis on interiorized piety and with Enlightenment thought. On the Scotch-Irish side, David Hackett Fischer (1989, 605–782) has marshaled much evidence indicating that the Scotch-Irish (he prefers the term *Anglo-Irish*) who settled in the American backcountry brought with them a number of folkways relating to marriage customs, witchcraft beliefs, naming conventions, speechways, music, and so forth that they had inherited from their ancestors in "North Britain" (which for Fischer includes northern Ireland) and which distinguished the Scotch-Irish from the Irish living in the south of Ireland.

Nevertheless, without denying that educated Irish Catholics and/or the Scotch-Irish generally were distinctive in many ways, the evidence gathered by Eid, Doyle, Akenson and others (reviewed above) lends support to what I take to be Michael O'Brien's main point: that we cannot let whatever differences did exist among different groups of Irish obscure the fact that on a number of important dimensions the Irish of all backgrounds in America were quite similar. This is precisely the conclusion that now informs the work of scholars like Kerby Miller. In Miller's (2000, 143) own words:

> It would be inaccurate to conclude that early Irish Protestant and Catholic emigrants or their descendants ever composed a single, homogeneous, or harmonious group. . . . However, much evidence suggests that during this period [the eighteenth and early nineteenth centuries], "Irish" ethnic identity was much more varied, flexible, and inclusive than it would later become, and the social and political issues that engaged the attention of Irish emigrants . . . often transcended the religious divisions that later become so prominent.

And yet, despite the fact that modern scholars are now more likely to emphasize similarity in talking about the pre-Famine Irish—in ways that would do Michael O'Brien proud—there remains one supposed difference between the Scotch-Irish and the Catholic Irish that no one, not even O'Brien himself, thought to challenge in a systematic and sustained way. That one supposed difference is that the Scotch-Irish were generally *staunch* Presbyterians while the pre-Famine Irish Catholics were generally *lax* Catholics. What I want to demonstrate is that this claim is only partly correct and that understanding *why* this claim is only partly correct is the first step in developing a new perspective on Irish American religion in the early Republic.

The Stories Historians Tell

Historians routinely tell two stories about Irish Americans and religion in the pre-Famine period, one having to do with Irish Catholics and the other having to do with Irish Presbyterians (Irish Anglicans seem to have slipped through the cracks). Michael O'Brien himself gave an early version of the now-standard story told about early Irish American Catholics. "The poor Irish Catholics in the Colonies," he said (1919/1971, 266), "finding no church of their own to commune with, in despair abandoned their faith because of their ignorance of its fundamentals" and because of the ridicule that their children faced in schools where "the cry of 'No Popery!' was constantly in their ears." These early Irish Catholics abandoned their faith, in other words, because they were little attached to official Catholicism, because they did not have access to priests and the institutional structures that might have nurtured their faith, and because of others' hostility toward Catholicism. Since O'Brien's time, that story has been repeated, almost word for word, by many other commentators (see, for example, Akenson 1993, 244–246; Byron 1999, 51–52; Doyle 1981, 69–70; Greeley 1988; McCaffrey 1997, 64; McWhiney 1988, 6–7; Miller 1985, 147; K. Miller 2000, 140).

The core elements of this oft-told story are almost certainly correct and, if anything, the story is now more firmly supported by the available evidence than ever before. Following seminal works by Emmet Larkin (1972), Sean Connolly (1982), and others, it is now routine to suggest that Irish Catholics in Ireland experienced a "devotional revolution" following the Famine. The most obvious manifestation of this revolution was that Mass attendance rates, which had traditionally been quite low in most areas, jumped dramatically (D. Miller 2000). Other elements of this devotional revolution included an increased emphasis on the parish as the preferred locus of cultic activities and on the authority of Irish bishops. It is common, in most discussions of the devotional revolution, to contrast the "official Catholicism" that came to predominate in the post-Famine period with the more traditional "folk Catholicism" that had prevailed in Ireland for centuries and that centered on holy well cults. Actually, folk Catholicism had been in decline since the late 1700s. Both Larkin's devotional revolution argument and the decline of holy well cults will be discussed in more detail in the next chapter. For now, the only point I want to make is that most of the Irish Catholics who emigrated to America during the period from 1770 to 1830 were little attached *either* to the Catholicism of the official church *or* to the folk Catholicism that had long prevailed in Ireland. They were truly "lax Catholics" in more ways than one, just as the usual story that historians tell about them claims.

If we now turn to the usual story that historians tell about Irish *Presbyterians* in early America, however, we find that it contrasts sharply with the story told about Irish Catholics. For one thing, this second story is usually far more detailed and focuses on the institutional (Presbyterian) church, which of course was entrenched in the American colonies in a way that the Roman Catholic Church was not. For example, Leonard Trinterud's (1970) classic account of colonial Presbyterianism is concerned with things like: the ways in which early Presbyterian congregations in America were shaped by the Scottish Presbyterian and Irish Presbyterian traditions; the factionalism that developed in the church as a result of the Great Awakening; the rise of the Log Cabin Men; the conflict between the Old Sides and the New Sides; and so on. What is easy to overlook amidst the massive detail on what-leader-said-what-when in historical studies like Trinterud's is that the one question which is *always* front and center in the story told about Irish Catholics is never raised in an explicit and precise way about Irish Presbyterians:

Were the great mass of Irish Presbyterians who came to America strongly attached to their faith and practicing Presbyterians or was this association just part of their background?

For Protestant historians writing about the Scotch-Irish a century ago, during that period of time when glib assertions about the cultural distinctiveness of this group were routine in American historiography, the matter was likely not central because the answer to this question was assumed to be obvious: not only were the vast majority of the Scotch-Irish in early America Presbyterian by background but they were also active participants in the life of the Presbyterian Church. Indeed, their strong involvement with the Presbyterian Church was commonly thought to have given the Scotch-Irish the organizational base that had allowed them to be so influential in promoting support for the Revolution. Addressing the Third Annual Conference of the Scotch-Irish Society of America in 1891, J. H. Bryson succinctly expressed the core ideas of this argument: "As a class, this people [the Scotch-Irish] were largely Presbyterian in their religious opinions; and thereby they became embodied into a compact and powerful Church organization, giving tremendous force and intensity to their influence." Other authors abandoned even the mild hesitancy evident in Bryson's *"largely* Presbyterian" remark. Charles Hanna (1902/1968, 2), in a work that for decades would be cited as a standard reference work on the Scotch-Irish, declared that they, "alone of all the races [in colonial America] had one uniform religion"; he then went on to make clear that this uniformity was both a matter of belief and an active involvement with the Presbyterian Church. Hanna's conclusions would subsequently be echoed in the works of a great many mainstream historians. William Sweet (1930, 172–183) for example, devoted a chapter to the Scotch-Irish in his influential *The Story of Religions in America* and in his opening paragraph left no doubt about the centrality of Presbyterianism in Scotch-Irish culture:

> Political, economic and religious factors all played their part in bringing Scotch-Irish colonists to America. The people who had colonized North Ireland had come largely from the Lowlands of Scotland and had brought to Ireland with them the strenuous Protestant spirit of Scotch Presbyterianism. Since there had been little intermarriage with the native Irish . . . the Presbyterian Church was there well-organized with an able and aggressive ministry.

More recently, Maldwyn Jones (1991, 302), though willing to debunk many of the other claims made about the Scotch-Irish, nevertheless reasserts the claim about their attachment to Presbyterianism:

If Presbyterianism had been the most conspicuous element in Scotch-Irish identity in Ireland, it remained no less so in British America. Zealous in establishing churches and attempting to secure learned clergy, the Scotch-Irish were determined to cling to their religious heritage and to reproduce in the New World the precise religious forms of the Old.

Jones then goes on to discuss the disputes among various factions within the American Presbyterian Church, but in the end he—like Sweet and Hanna before him—presents no real evidence in support of this claim that most of the Scotch-Irish clung tightly to Presbyterianism.

Other modern authors, by contrast, while maintaining a tight focus on the institutional Presbyterian Church in discussing the Scotch-Irish, handle the matter of exactly how many Scotch-Irish were practicing Presbyterians by simply avoiding the issue altogether. What is interesting about these accounts, however, is that here and there these authors invariably remark in passing that the Scotch-Irish may have been as lax in regard to religion as their Irish Catholic contemporaries.

Trinterud (1970, 109), for example, tells us that many of the people brought into the Presbyterian Church by the Great Awakening were "second generation colonists who had little or no religious background." Similarly, he says that "Presbyterianism in Pennsylvania was largely Scotch-Irish" but that the church there was weak because the Scotch-Irish were highly mobile; "there was a great deal of settling and resettling among them, which kept their churches weak and often short-lived" (p. 199). What these brief remarks suggest, of course, is that a large proportion of the Irish in America of Presbyterian background were *not* in fact devout Presbyterians.

More recently, Patrick Griffin (2001, 114ff.) argues that the Presbyterian Church in the American colonies during the first third of the eighteenth century exerted little control over the Ulster Irish because the church had little to offer them. The supposed irrelevance of the Presbyterian Church was compounded, in turn, by a general shortage of clergy and by the difficulty of reaching the frontier settlements where Ulster Protestants lived. In the 1830s, however, the church had made a determined effort to bring order and discipline to Ulster Irish communities in the colonies, by establishing a distinctively Irish presbytery. Unfortunately (Griffin continues) ministers of the new presbytery began to quarrel among themselves and with their Scottish Presbyterian counterparts over a range of confessional issues and civil disputes. The Great Awakening that also began in the 1730s only contributed to the divisions that emerged among Irish

Presbyterian ministers. The net result, Griffin argues, was a weakened and con-
fused church which lost ground to the Baptists, whose consistent emphasis on
mobility, an untrained ministry, local autonomy, and the like was far better suited
to the "culture of movement" (the push for more and more land) that was now
characteristic of the Ulster emigrants. Other commentators (Blethen and Wood
1997; Chepesiuk 2000) pinpoint the same factors—the Great Awakening, internal division, a shortage of ministers—to explain why the Scotch-Irish slipped
away from Presbyterianism and became Baptists and Methodists. Nevertheless,
by suggesting that the Presbyterian Church had little control over the Ulster Irish
throughout the colonial period (which in the end is the claim being made),
Griffin's account could be read as reinforcing the implications of the fragmentary
remarks made by Trinterud about the Scotch-Irish: long before they became Baptists and Methodists, most Scotch-Irish were not members of a Presbyterian
church and not much influenced by the Presbyterian leadership in America.

As far as I know, David Doyle (1981) was the first investigator to call attention—in a clear and explicit way—to the fact that there were fewer practicing
Presbyterians in the United States than might be expected given the strong association in earlier historical accounts between the Ulster Irish and Presbyterianism. Doyle (1981) writes:

> The achievements of Presbyterianism should not be exaggerated. Up to 300,000
> Ulster immigrants went to America by 1766. Given high colonial birth rates, sur-
> vivors and descendants should have numbered more in 1800; yet in that year there
> were reportedly only fifteen thousand members of Presbyterian Churches in the
> United States, and many of them were of English Presbyterian, New England Con-
> gregational and Continental Reformed background. (Pp. 59–60)

For Doyle, the easiest way to explain this is to posit that there were far more Catholics and Anglicans among the Ulster Irish than previously acknowledged. What
he overlooks is the more straightforward possibility suggested by Leroy Eid (1986),
that most of the "Ulster Presbyterians" who came to America were in fact little
attached to their faith and little attached to the Presbyterian Church.

Assessing religiosity in the colonial period is always difficult, and certainly
much depends on what measures of religiosity are used. For example, there is
considerable evidence (reviewed in Carroll 2004) that looking at attendance rates
(what proportion of the local population attended church services on a regular
basis) produces much higher estimates of the "churched population" than looking at formal membership, which is the measure Doyle used in the passage just
cited. On the other hand, given the recurrent suggestions in the early literature

on the Scotch-Irish that they were *staunch* Presbyterians, a focus on formal membership might well be justified. Assuming that to be true, it becomes possible to update Doyle's numerical analysis in light of evidence and arguments that have appeared since the publication of his 1981 book.

First off, Doyle's early estimate of 15,000 Presbyterians in 1800 is likely too low. Although published data on communicants did not become available until 1807, Gaustad and Barlow (2001, 131) estimate that there were already more than 20,000 Presbyterian communicants in 1790 (a decade before the date of Doyle's estimate). That the actual figure in 1790 was probably not much higher than 20,000 seems likely, given that two decades later there were 29,000 communicants in the main body of the Presbyterian Church (Thompson 1895, 77) and that most scholars figure that Presbyterianism experienced a growth in absolute numbers during those two decades (e.g., Finke and Stark 1992, 56; Gaustad and Barlow 2001, 131–132). For the sake of argument, then, let's maximize the number of Presbyterians by estimating that circa 1790 there were something like 24,000 formal communicants. How many of these were of Scotch-Irish extraction? Certainly not all of them, since some would have been, as Doyle suggested, of Scottish and/or New England Congregational background. For the sake of argument, let's assume that three-quarters of those 24,000 Presbyterian communicants, or 18,000, were Scotch-Irish. How does that compare to the overall number of Scotch-Irish living in the United States? Unfortunately, answering *that* question necessitates revisiting one of the hoariest debates connected with the Scotch-Irish in America.

In 1931, a committee of the American Council of Learned Societies (ACLS)— consisting of two historians, two statisticians, and a linguist—published a report that drew upon data on the distribution of surnames in British populations and in the 1790 U.S. census to estimate the proportion of the white population in America in 1790 that came from various "national stocks." In the end, the committee (American Council of Learned Societies 1931, 122) concluded that 6 percent of those household heads had surnames suggesting they were of Ulster Irish descent. Although this conclusion was taken at face value (by most U.S. historians) over the next few decades, it came under strong attack during the 1980s, and these attacks fell into two categories. On the one hand, Don Akenson (1984a; 1984b) argued—with undeniable industry and cleverness—that all attempts to extract national origins information from the surnames in the 1790 Census rested upon implicit assumptions that were almost certainly false. Others, however, particularly Forrest McDonald and Ellen Shapiro McDonald (1980; 1984) and Thomas L. Purvis (1984a; 1984b), argued that by correcting some of the more

TABLE 2

Estimates of Scotch-Irish in United States and in the Presbyterian Church circa 1790

Scotch-Irish as percentage of total white population[1]	Estimated total Scotch-Irish population[2]	Estimated Scotch-Irish communicants of a Presbyterian church	Participation rate (col. 3 as percentage of col. 2)
6%	190,320	18,000[3]	9.5%
10.5%	333,060	18,000	5.4%
15%	475,800	18,000	3.8%

[1]See Doyle (1999, 487) and discussion in text.
[2]Based on a total white population of 3,172,000 in 1790, using percentages in column 1.
[3]See Gaustad and Barlow (2001, 131) and discussion in text.

obvious errors in the procedures used by the ACLS committee it was still possible to extract some useful information, especially if one was willing to settle for ballpark estimates rather than exactitude. By Purvis's (1984b) analysis, the ACLS report seriously undercounted the Scotch-Irish; he found that the proportion of the population who were of Scotch-Irish descent was closer to 10.5 percent. Doyle (1999, 847) summarizes the strains of research in this area by saying that, while the Scotch-Irish in 1790 might have constituted anywhere from 6 percent (i.e., the original ACLS estimate) to 15 percent of the total white population, Purvis's estimate of 10.5 percent is probably closest to the mark.

Given that the total white population in 1790 was roughly 3,172,000 (Mitchell 1998), these figures give us a basis for assessing the degree to which the Scotch-Irish participated—as formal members—in Presbyterianism. The relevant data, presented in Table 2, show that Scotch-Irish participation rates range from a high of 9.5 percent (on the assumption the Scotch-Irish constituted 6 percent of the white population) to a low of 3.8 percent (on the assumption they constituted 15 percent of the white population). That these estimated participation rates seem abysmally low is methodologically comforting. Stark and Finke (1988), using estimation procedures quite different from those used here, suggest that in 1776 only 10 percent of the white population in America were formal members of *any* church. The rate obtained here for the Scotch-Irish participation in Presbyterianism, then, is lower than this national total, but not by an order of magnitude that would cause us to doubt the procedure.

The participation rates shown in Table 2 represent only formal membership, which limits them to adults. In a later work on early American religion (1992), Finke and Stark calculate that if the children in the families of formal members are taken into account, participation rates double. Plus, as already mentioned, using regular attendance rather than formal membership as the gauge increases these rates even further. Nevertheless, the data in Table 2 can still be read as supporting the conclusion derivable from the impressionistic remarks by Trinterud and Griffin: the great mass of the Scotch-Irish did not take an active role in the affairs of the Presbyterian Church.

So what's the point of all this? Very simply the point is this: it is widely accepted that the early Irish, whether of Presbyterian or Catholic in background, got swept up in the rise of the Baptists and Methodists in the early nineteenth century (see, for example, Akenson 1993, 273; Brown and Sorrells 2001, 38). Furthermore, it has long been commonplace to point out that the Scotch-Irish in particular found evangelical Christianity to be especially appealing (Gibson 1860, 338; Thompson 1895, 73). The question is *why* these early Irish Americans became Baptists and Methodists. In the case of Irish Catholics, the usual story, as indicated, is that they were little attached to their faith and lacked institutional support. In the case of Irish Presbyterians, by contrast, the usual story is that although they were strongly attached to their faith and had some institutional support, that support was not sufficient. But if we accept that pre-Famine Irish Americans were more culturally similar than culturally different, and fold in the data that the great bulk of Irish Presbyterians were as little attached to an institutional church as were Irish Catholics, then we need to consider that the stories were the same in both cases. The great advantage of telling the same story for both groups, I suggest, is that it opens up a historiographical possibility that has until now been ignored, namely, that the pre-Famine Irish in America became Baptists and Methodists for reasons having more to do with their *common* experience in America than with their *different* experiences (religious or otherwise) in Ireland. Unfortunately, before we can consider telling this new story, we have to confront a second bias that has warped the study of Irish American religiosity.

Why So Many Studies of Irish American Catholicism?

Studies of Irish American religiosity after the Famine have almost without exception been studies of Irish American Catholicism. Michael Glazier's *The Encyclopedia of the Irish in America* (1999), for example, despite its inclusive title, has a long entry on Irish American Catholicism but no entries, long or short, on Irish American Baptists or Methodists or Presbyterians. Similarly, in *The Churching of America, 1776–1990*, Roger Finke and Rodney Stark (1992) devote an entire chapter to Irish Catholics in the decades following the Famine but say nothing about the Irish when they discuss the rise of the Baptists and Methodists in the early nineteenth century (a discussion which occupies much of their attention). Reginald Byron, in his *Irish America* (1999), does note in passing that most Irish

Americans are Protestant (p. 4), but then, on the same page, calls Albany, New York—"as markedly a Catholic city as Ireland is a markedly Catholic country"— "an ideal laboratory in which to test a number of taken-for-granted ideas about Irish America," and his entire book is then devoted to studying this one particular (Catholic) community.

This pattern of taking "Irishness" into account only when considering Catholicism is also evident when we compare books that focus on the Catholic experience in America with books that focus on the Protestant experience. Books devoted to the history of American Catholicism, like Dolan's (1992) classic account, invariably devote much attention to the Irish, while books concerned with the Protestant tradition in America say little or nothing about the Irish (see, for example, Bonomi 1986). This would explain why Catherine Albanese's (2002) bibliographic essay on American religious history can call attention to several studies that discuss Irish Catholics and the Irish influence on Catholicism in the post-Famine period but mention no studies that discuss the Irish influence on Protantism before or after the Famine. So, why have historians and sociologists paid attention to "Irishness" only when studying Catholicism? Two possibilities come to mind.

The first is the perception that Irish Americans are generally Catholic. As noted at the beginning of this chapter, this perception is factually incorrect: most Irish Americans today are Protestant. Even granting that most Irish Americans are Protestant, the longstanding historiographical emphasis on Irish *Catholics* in the post-Famine period might still make sense if it were true that the Irish have influenced the American Catholic tradition to a degree well beyond their influence on the American Protestant tradition. But here again the data just won't cooperate.

Tables 3 and 4 give the percentages of self-identified Irish Americans in various religious traditions. Table 3 uses traditional denominational categories (e.g., Catholic, Baptist, Methodist, etc.). These data show, for example, that in the South 15 percent of all Baptists and 11 percent of all Methodists are Irish, and outside the South 16 percent of all Catholics are Irish. Looking at the same data slightly differently, Table 4 uses the RELTRAD categorization of Christian denominations suggested by Steensland et al. (2000). One of the advantages of this classification scheme is that it puts black Protestants into a separate category, which is justified, the authors explain (p. 294), by the fact that the cultural impact of black churches has historically been quite different from that of white churches. This analysis reveals, for example, the large presence of Irish in evangelical churches in the South (20%).

The data reported in Tables 3 and 4 suggest that Irish Americans in the South

TABLE 3
*Percentages of Americans in Various Christian Denominations
Who Identify Themselves as Irish, by Region*

Denomination	South	Non-South
Catholic	15	16
Baptist	15	9
Methodist	11	9
Lutheran	10	6
Presbyterian	13	11
Episcopal	12	9
Other	14	10

SOURCE: General Social Survey (1990–2000), National Opinion Research
Center.

TABLE 4
*Percentages of Americans in RELTRAD Religious Affiliation
Categories Who Identify Themselves as Irish, by Region*

Religious Affiliation	South	Non-South
Catholic	15	16
Evangelical Protestant	20	12
Mainline Protestant	12	9
Black Protestant	2	<1
Other	6	4
Unaffiliated	12	12

SOURCE: General Social Survey (1990–2000), National Opinion Research
Center; Steensland et al. (2000)

are present in the Baptist and Methodist traditions to a similar extent, and in the
(white) evangelical Protestant tradition to a greater extent than they are present
in the Catholic tradition outside the South. I concede entirely that these data only
assess *statistical* predominance, and so tell us nothing about the degree to which
the Irish have influenced the institutional structures in the Protestant and Catholic traditions. But in some ways, that is precisely the point: whereas we have lots
of studies that assess the degree to which the Irish have taken on leadership roles
in the Catholic Church in areas outside the South, we have no studies doing something similar in the case of their impact on Protestant churches in the South.

The suggestion that we need to look more carefully at the Irish influence on
American Protestantism is not a new one. Here again Donald Akenson (1993)
has been a voice crying in the wilderness:

> Any serious non-racist history of the Irish in the United States should spend as
> much time upon the Baptists (especially the Southern Baptists), Methodists, Angli-
> cans, and Presbyterians as upon the history of the Catholic Church. The life of

William Bell Riley (the founding father of twentieth-century American fundamen-
talism) should be as well known as, say, that of Cardinal Spellman. . . . Only then
will the historical study in the USA have come of age. (P. 224)

I know of only one body of scholarship whose authors have taken up the challenge that Akenson laid down, and, unfortunately, it does not get us very far in
understanding the dynamics of early Irish American religiosity.

Scotch-Irish Sacramental Traditions

It has become increasingly commonplace in accounts of American religion to
suggest that sacramental traditions originating in Scotland played a central role
in shaping both the revivalism associated with the Great Awakening in the 1700s
and then, later, the camp meeting tradition that became inextricably bound up
with Baptist and Methodist success (see Cohen 1997, 718–719; Fischer 1989, 707–
708; McCauley 1995; Schmidt 2001; Westerkamp 1988). Most of these discussions pay special attention to the Presbyterian "holy fair" tradition that emerged
in Scotland in the early 1600s and quickly spread to Ulster.

Initially, Scottish holy fairs were simply communal rituals at which hundreds,
sometimes thousands, of people received communion while seated at long tables
set up somewhere out of doors. Soon, however, as Leigh Eric Schmidt (2001) has
documented in detail, a number of elements stressing revival and conversion
were added. "What separated [these] festal communions from earlier sacraments
were such characteristics as outdoor preaching, great concourses of people from
an extensive region, long vigils of prayer, powerful experiences of conversion and
confirmation, [and] a number of popular preachers cooperating for extended
services over three days or more" (p. 24). Schmidt goes on to show that these
distinctive elements were also characteristic of similar (though typically smaller)
Presbyterian gatherings that are documented as having been staged in some
Scotch-Irish communities in America during the seventeenth century (see
Schmidt 2001, 59–68).

All in all, then, it does seem reasonable to suggest, just as Schmidt and others do, that a familiarity with the holy fair tradition on the part of some Presbyterians—some Presbyterian ministers in particular—may have shaped many of the
camp meetings associated with the rise of evangelical religion. So, did the Scotch-
Irish in America become Baptists and Methodists because they were "pre-
adapted" to evangelical religion by their familiarity with the Presbyterian holy fair
tradition? McCauley (1995) says that the answer here is yes, and such a message

seems implicit in the analyses by Schmidt and Fischer (1989) as well. The problem with such an interpretation, however, is that it implicitly rests upon precisely the premise that most of the Scotch-Irish in America were strongly attached to the Presbyterian tradition, and that has been put in doubt in the first part of this chapter.

In summary, then, while Schmidt's work establishes that holy fairs (or something similar) were here and there celebrated by *some* Scotch-Irish Presbyterians in America, neither he nor anyone else has presented any evidence suggesting that the *great mass* of the Scotch-Irish in America had any real familiarity with the holy fair tradition. He simply *assumes* that the Scotch-Irish Presbyterians who attended the (relatively small) number of American-style holy fairs he describes would have been typical of the Scotch-Irish population in general. If in fact (as we have seen) there are strong grounds for believing that most Scotch-Irish were not formally affiliated with a Presbyterian church, then what is the basis for believing that most Scotch-Irish participated in anything resembling a holy fair? There isn't any. In short, while the holy fair tradition in Scottish Presbyterianism might well have predisposed a small minority of (practicing) Presbyterians among the Scotch-Irish to embrace the new forms of evangelical Christianity promoted at camp meetings after 1800, it seems insufficient to explain why the Scotch-Irish generally embraced evangelical Christianity.

Starting Fresh: To Be Irish (and Protestant) Is to Be American

So far, I have posited that there are three things we can take to be true of the Irish in early America. First, the various Irish groups found in pre-Famine America were characterized more by cultural similarity than by cultural difference. Second, these early Irish Americans were little attached to either Catholicism *or* Presbyterianism. Third, they—and their immediate descendants—slipped easily into the Methodist and Baptist traditions during the late eighteenth and early nineteenth centuries. In addition, we can posit with reasonable certainty that the Irish in America strongly supported the Revolution.

Although there were Irish on both sides of the revolutionary struggle, most commentators who have assessed the available evidence have found that at least in the Middle Colonies and in the South, the bulk of the Irish (whether of Presbyterian, Catholic, or Anglican background) supported the Revolution (Doyle 1981, 109–151; Ickringill 1999; Mitchell 1999). The issue of why the Irish in these regions supported the Revolution, however, is open to interpretation. For Michael O'Brien himself (see, in particular, O'Brien 1919/1971) it was obvious: having suffered under British rule in Ireland, the Irish were predisposed against British rule in America. Irish historians, such as W. E. H. Lecky and J. A. Woodburn (1898), have also stressed anti-British feeling when explaining Irish American support for the Revolution. This sort of argument is still very popular. Arthur Mitchell (1999), for example, points out that neither class nor emigrant status can explain Irish support for the Revolution, given that, generally, lower-class groups in the colonies were split in their allegiances and that both revolutionaries and loyalists drew heavily from recent immigrants. For Mitchell, the only thing left is the classic position, namely, that the Irish supported the Revolution because they had "suffered under English rule at home." David Doyle (1981, 109–151), on the other hand, argues that, while memories of suffering under English rule *were* likely the reason that relatively recent Irish immigrants supported the Revolution, older Irish immigrants' revolutionary support was borne of their experiences in America. Although Doyle's argument is nuanced, the basic idea is that the older Irish—both the Scotch-Irish and the Catholic Irish—supported the Revolution because its emphasis on local autonomy and democracy promised them a society in which they could better secure the rights, positions, and power previously reserved for Anglo-American elites.

I will leave it to others to sort out the reasons *why* Irish Americans embraced the American Revolution with considerable fervor. That they did so, however, provides us with a basis for explaining the two patterns noted earlier: (1) why the pre-Famine Irish abandoned the pattern of relative indifference that was characteristic of both the Catholic Irish and the Scotch-Irish and became practicing Methodists and Baptists, and (2) why so many American Protestants, especially in the South, have maintained their Irish identity for more than two centuries.

The Rise of the Baptists and the Methodists

One of the great religious evolutions in America in the wake of the Revolution was a rise in the popularity of evangelical sects, mainly among the Methodists and the Baptists. This is hardly surprising. On the contrary, as any number of commentators have pointed out, many of the values central to the rhetoric of the Revolution coincide with the values that defined the Methodist and Baptist experiences in early America. Just as the rhetoric of the Revolution exhibited both an antiaristocratic bias and a strong emphasis on individualism, the Methodists and Baptists stressed the importance of a lay (and untrained) ministry and the centrality of the individual conversion experience. Some commentators, like Lipset (1990), say merely that the values associated with evangelical Protestantism reinforced the values of the Revolution. For some time now, however, a number of historians (Hatch 1989; Mathews 1969; Schneider 1991) have advanced a much stronger argument, that the success of the Revolution created in the new Republic a cultural climate in which people were encouraged to incorporate the values associated with the Revolution into their religious thought. Nathan O. Hatch's version of this argument has been particularly influential. His argument, in a nutshell, is that the tremendous success of the Revolution eroded traditional authority, empowered ordinary people to think for themselves independently of established doctrine, and generated a passion for equality. Carried into the religious realm, Hatch argues, this led people to reject the traditional distinction that set clergy apart from others, to take their "deepest emotional impulses" at face value, and to believe that they could create a quite different and much better world in which to live.

The tremendous success of the Methodists and Baptists (both among whites, and, in the case of the Baptists, among blacks as well) reflects the fact that these groups embraced and incorporated these same impulses and values. Methodist and Baptist success generally, in other words, derives from the fact that these groups were the embodiment of the Revolution in the religious sphere. Given that Irish Americans embraced the values of the Revolution so strongly, it hardly seems surprising that they would be attracted to religious groups that incorporated these values. Irish Americans were pre-adapted to become Methodists and Baptists, in other words, because of their commitment to the Revolution.

Why Have So Many Southern Protestants Retained an Irish Identity for So Long?

Kerby Miller (2000) points out that, according to the results of the 1990 census, fully 20 percent of all white southerners described themselves as Irish. Miller argues (p. 141) that, since only 2 percent of all white southerners in the 1860 census were Irish *born,* and given the paucity of Famine emigrants in the Old South, these Irish southerners must be the descendants of the pre-Famine Irish who settled in the South:

[I]t would appear that by 1990 a surprisingly large number of the remote descendants of the South's early Irish Protestant settlers—those who had emigrated prior to the American Revolution, or at the latest, prior to the 1830s—were . . . willing to identify themselves with the birthplace of their ancestors who had left Ireland 200 or even 250 years earlier.

Michael Hout and Joshua Goldstein (1994) sought to answer a similar question, wondering how 4.5 million Irish immigrants (their estimate of how many Irish had come to the United States by 1920) could have become the 40 million Irish Americans recorded in the 1980 census (the first U.S. census that included a question about ethnicity). Hout and Goldstein's analysis, which looked at data not just on the Irish Americans but also on British Americans, German Americans, and Italian Americans, revealed that the number of Irish Americans was far in excess of what natural increase or intermarriage would account for. Their research suggests that this is because of an especially strong subjective factor that they describe as an "unexplained closeness to Ireland" (p. 79) that has persisted over time. In his own discussion of the Hout/Goldstein study, Andrew Greeley (1999) identifies the microprocess that is the proximate cause of the disproportionately large number of Americans who self-identify as Irish: "Intermarriage certainly played a part . . . , creating a large population of part-Irish, part-something-else Americans. When the census asked about their ethnicity, a very high proportion of the part-something-else said 'Irish' . . . [suggesting that] it is fashionable to be Irish." Greeley, unfortunately, does not address *why* so many Americans would find an Irish identity to be the fashionable choice given the other choices open to them.

In the case of American Catholics, the reason for emphasizing one's Irish heritage would seem not difficult to discern. For more than a century and a half now there has been a strong tie in the popular imagination between being Irish and being Catholic and a general belief that the Irish are especially *devout* Catholics (i.e., attend Mass regularly, support the church, etc.). Certainly, any number of commentators have suggested that in the post-Famine period Irish American Catholics have been the mainstay of the American Catholic Church and the standard against which other Catholics were judged. This phenomenon is more complex than it seems (as will be discussed in the next chapter), but it is true that, for *Catholic* Americans, claiming an Irish identity can function as a way of presenting themselves to others as *good* Catholics, and that helps to explain why so many Catholics who are "part-Irish/part-something-else" (to use Greeley's phrase) would identify as Irish.

By contrast, why so many *Protestant* Americans would continue to claim an Irish identity is more problematic. The puzzle can be resolved, however, by recognizing that Protestant Americans who claim an Irish identity are likely associating themselves with the character traits stereotypically associated with the Scotch-Irish. I suggest that, however much modern scholars have demolished the "Scotch-Irish" category and moved away from analyses that assign character traits to the Scotch-Irish (or to any ethnic group, for that matter), this category and this way of thinking remain alive and well in the popular imagination. Simply, in American popular culture, the pre-Famine Protestant Irish continue to be seen in exactly the same way that so infuriated Michael O'Brien a century ago: as a people who are determined, independent, individualistic, committed to liberty, self-sufficient, open to change, and so forth, and who thereby embody the ideals of the American Revolution and the nation born of it.

In *The Mind of the South* (1941), a book that remains enormously popular in the South despite its historical flaws (see Eagles 1992), W. F. Cash describes intense individualism as a central element in southern culture and claims that it derived partly from the frontier conditions of the Old South and partly because many southerners were "of the blood of the Scotch and the Irish." This same emphasis on the cultural distinctiveness of the Scotch-Irish, and in particular, on their inherent individualism, continues to pervade fictional accounts of the Scotch-Irish. The book jacket for Thomas A. Lewis's *West from Shenandoah* (2003), for instance, tells us that the novel recounts "the powerful and inspiring story of America's first westerners, the fiercely independent Scotch-Irish immigrants who flocked to America in the early eighteenth century . . . and reveals why the American Revolution could not have been won without the indispensable contribution of these Scotch-Irish pioneers."

This same emphasis on the intense individualism of the Scotch-Irish and their association with American democracy is also a stock element in popular nonfiction histories of this group, such as those written by Rory Fitzpatrick (1989) and Billy Kennedy (1995; 1997; 1998). The books by Fitzpatrick and Kennedy, to be sure, might need to be taken with a grain of salt, since both authors seem concerned with promoting a more positive view of Ulster Protestants. But consider how James Webb (2004)—Naval Academy graduate, Vietnam veteran, assistant secretary of defense in the Reagan administration—introduces his own history of the Scotch-Irish to an implicitly American audience:

> The Scots-Irish (sometimes also called the Scotch-Irish) are all around you, even though you probably don't know it. They are a force that shapes our culture, more in the abstract power of emotion than through the argumentative force of law. In their insistent individualism they are not likely to put an ethnic label on themselves when they debate societal issues. . . . Two hundred years ago the mountains built a fierce and uncomplaining self-reliance into an already hardened people. To them, joining a group and putting themselves at the mercy of someone else's collectivist

judgment makes about as much sense as letting the government take their guns. And nobody is going to get their guns.

A page later, he tells us that "the Scotch-Irish did not merely come to America, they became America [even though] modern America has forgotten who they were (and are)." The argument Webb states, that there is a fit between traditional Scotch-Irish values and modern mainstream American culture, has been favorably received by reputable scholars (see, for example, Reed 2005).

Given the continuing resilience of these old stereotypes about the Scotch-Irish personality and about the centrality of the Scotch-Irish to the rise of America as a nation, it isn't surprising that the classic works of Scotch-Irish historiography are still being marketed as authoritative and are still selling well, with the general public if not with academics. Many genealogical websites continue to recommend Charles A. Hanna's *The Scotch-Irish* (originally published 1902, reprinted 1968) and Henry Jones Ford's *The Scotch-Irish in America* (originally published 1915, reprinted 2004) as basic reference sources to people wishing to research their Scotch-Irish ancestry.

Clearly, the character traits associated with "being Irish," in the minds of *Protestant* Americans, continue to resonate with the rhetoric of the American Revolution and with the emphases of evangelical Christianity. In all three contexts— Scotch-Irishness, the American Revolution, and evangelical Christianity—there is an emphasis on rugged individualism and autonomy, on having the courage to stand up for what you believe, and on opposition to hierarchical authority. The result is that, just as "being Baptist" or "being Methodist" in the early Republic was a way of acting out the ideals of the Revolution in the religious realm (which explains the dramatic rise of these sects in the wake of the Revolution), so claiming an Irish identity is a way for contemporary Protestant Americans to associate themselves with the values of the American Revolution, or, if you will, a way of using ethnicity to "be American."

I hasten to add that it matters not at all if Protestant Irish Americans really are more independent, more courageous, and more antihierarchical than other Americans. What does matter is that, given the stereotypes about the Scotch-Irish that continue to exist in American popular culture, claiming an Irish identity allows Protestant Americans to associate themselves with these quintessentially American values.

My assertion is that the strong persistence of an Irish identity among so many American Protestants, especially in the South, is *not*, as Hout and Goldstein would have it, reflective of an "unexplained closeness to Ireland." What it reflects, rather, is a strong tie to *America* in the present. For American Protestants, in other words, "to be Irish" is to present yourself as someone who embodies the continuing spirit of the American Revolution.

CHAPTER TWO

Why the Famine Irish Became Catholic in America

The story of the Great Famine, which devastated Ireland in the late 1840s, is a story that has been told many times. While scholarly views of what caused the Famine, and who was or was not responsible, have shifted back and forth over time, what has remained constant—at least for anyone who reads the record with even minimal care—is a chilling sense of the death and devastation that swept over the Irish people. Although some scholars, like Donald Akenson (1993), rightly point out that other famines in other countries have killed larger numbers of people and that the Famine in Ireland only accelerated existing patterns of Irish emigration, there seems no denying the centrality of the Famine to modern Irish history and the ways we think about that history.

Between 1841 and 1851 Ireland's population declined by at least one-fifth (and possibly a bit more, depending on how you regard the official statistics). Most commentaries suggest that about a million Irish died outright from the effects of the Famine and that more than half a million emigrated. Emigration did not necessarily mean survival, of course. Already weakened by the Famine, a great many emigrants fell prey to the typhoid fever and dysentery that spread easily in the crowded quarters of the ships that carried them across the ocean. To take the best-documented case: evidence suggests that in 1847 about 20,000 Irish men, women, and children died on the ships bringing them to the Canadian receiving station at Grosse Île (Quebec) or in the poorly equipped camp set up there to receive them (Quigley 1997). Fortunately for me, one of the people who survived both the Famine and the process of emigration was Margaret Fogarty (1812–1896), who would become my great-great-great-grandmother.

Margaret's husband, John Larkin, was one of the casualties of the Famine, and in 1849 Margaret and her four young children left Ireland for America. After crossing the Atlantic, she made straight for Cincinnati. As unlikely as it may seem, I know something about Margaret's very first day in Cincinnati, and it is something that is directly relevant to the concern of this chapter, namely, the relationship between the Famine Irish and Catholicism. My knowledge of that first day comes from a typewritten letter sent to my paternal grandmother, Mae Worthington, in January 1925 by one of her aunts, just after the death of Mae's father. The purpose of the letter, as the writer explained, was to show that "God never gives heavier crosses than we could bear." Mae had written them about her father's death.

> Kate read your letter to mother [Margaret Larkin, one of Margaret Fogarty's four children]. Her eyesight is so dim now she can't read. Poor thing she cried so hard. She then began to tell us how our Grandmother came to this country with four little children, the oldest nine years old, and how she managed. You know Mother is always witty. She told us about them coming up the Ohio, landing in Cincinnati on Sunday. Grandmother and another lady, they met on the journey, left the children on the steamer, and went up in the city to find a church, that they might hear Mass. Grandmother met one of the Fogarty's, a cousin. He recognized her and asked for her husband. She told him he was dead. He then told her to get the children and he would take all of them to his home. He had only been married a very short time. Wasn't that some bride who took in this gang of strangers to her? Well, the funny part of it was, they made some toddy for them. Mother says, she guesses they did not expect to give her any, as she was very young. But she got some anyway, and not knowing, she drank it all, and in few minutes, she fell off the chair "dead drunk." This is how she spent her first day in Cincinnati. You see they got along alright.

Since Margaret Larkin, the woman who told this story to the writer of the letter, would only have been about nine at the time of the event, it's entirely possible that her memory had been shaped and filtered by what others—her own mother in particular—had told her, and so by what these others had wanted to remember and what they had wanted to forget. Still, the one detail that rings true is this: one of the first things that Margaret Fogarty did upon arriving in the area where she wanted to settle in the United States was to search out a local Catholic church. The critical question is *why?* When I first read this story years ago, the answer seemed obvious: like most Irish Catholics, Margaret had been "a good Catholic" and so did the things, like going to Mass on Sunday, that good Catholics did. Now, however, I'm less certain.

Although my goal in this chapter is to suggest that the existing scholarly understanding of the Famine Irish and American Catholicism needs to be revised, the chapter will also explain why I have changed my thinking on the subject.

The Irish as the Gold Standard for American Catholicism

An account of Irish American Catholicism is almost always central to any discussion of American Catholicism generally. Part of the reason for this is purely demographic: Irish Americans, as compared to other national groups, have historically accounted for a disproportionate share of both the laity and the hierarchy in the American Catholic Church. Estimates indicate, for example, that in 1860 more than a third of the total Catholic population in the United States was Irish born (Taves 1986, 7); almost two-thirds were of Irish descent (Carey 2004, 30). Over the next few decades, Catholic immigration from continental Europe (mainly from German-speaking regions and Italy) would dilute Irish predominance among the laity a bit, but it would still remain considerable. David Doyle (1980, 178) estimated that by 1900 Irish Americans (both the Irish born and those of Irish descent) accounted for "close to half" of all American Catholics. More recent commentators (see, for example, Dolan 1992, 143; McCaffrey 1999, 138) consider Doyle's "close to half" estimate too high, but everyone agrees that around the turn of the twentieth century Irish Americans were at the very least a plurality within the American Catholic Church.

That the Irish dominated the clergy and hierarchy of the American Church is more certain. In 1880, the percentages of the clergy who were Irish American was 69 percent in Boston, 60 percent in Baltimore; 47 percent in St. Louis; and 44 percent in Chicago (Doorley 1987, 72–77). Moreover, in 1886 thirty-five (51%) of the sixty-eight Catholic bishops in America were Irish born or of Irish descent (Doorley 2001, 37). In 1920, it was still the case that two-thirds of Catholic bishops were Irish American, and in New England that proportion was three-fourths (Barrett and Roediger 2005, 18). Of the twenty-six archdioceses in existence by the late 1950s, at least seventeen were headed by archbishops of Irish descent (Shannon 1960, 209); and as late as 1972, nearly half (48%) of American Catholic bishops were Irish American (Dolan 1992, 143–144). Furthermore, in some jurisdictions Irish dominance of the Catholic hierarchy has long been nearly absolute. Over the period 1808–2002, eleven bishops and archbishops oversaw the Diocese of New York (which became an archdiocese in 1851), and all but one have been Irish or of Irish descent (Shelley 2001, 2).

The disproportionate representation of Irish Americans among the laity and clergy of the American Catholic Church insured that the *type* of Catholicism favored by the Irish in America became normative. "Although the American Catholic Church," wrote Roger Finke and Rodney Stark (1992, 136), "was an amazing mosaic, the fundamental characteristics of American Catholicism, as it was taught, preached and practiced, were Irish." Lawrence McCaffrey (1999, 129) makes much the same point: while the Irish have influenced American life in many ways, "their most important impact was on the character and personality of American Catholicism." The traits that have long distinguished Irish American Catholicism—the most important of which, as Michael Doorley (2001) notes, are "regular religious observance, unquestioning faith, respect for clerical authority, and support for parish schools"—became the standard by which the American church judged *all* Catholics. Italian American Catholics, in particular, were singled out for special condemnation by church authorities (especially those who were themselves Irish) for failing to meet the Irish standard (Orsi 1985, 55–56).

The Irish standard for judging Catholics generally was not used by church officials only; it also pervades the scholarly literature on American Catholicism. During the 1970s and 1980s, when studies of "white ethnics" came into fashion, the question whether other Catholics were or were not becoming more like the Irish was routinely raised. Rudolph Vecoli (1977, 37–38), for example, toward the end of what is still a widely cited article on Italian American Catholicism, concluded that

> in terms of certain religious practices, the second- and even more the third-generation Italians do seem to be approaching the Irish Catholic norm (for instance, supporting the church financially, sending children to Catholic schools. . . . However, on the sacramental index, attendance at Mass, reception of Holy Communion, and confession, the significant discrepancy between Irish and Italian behavior is not only maintained in the second and third generations, but even increases.

Others writing in the same period reached the same conclusions (among them, Abrahamson 1975). More recently, Louis Gesualdi (2004) determined—contra Vecoli—that Italian American Catholics in white-collar occupations (but not those in blue-collar occupations) are quite similar to Irish Catholics with regard to religious participation and belief. The important point, however, is that, even now, scholars take the Irish as the gold standard against which other American Catholics are judged.

The Puzzle

But *why* did the Irish in America flock to the Catholic Church and become such good Catholics? For commentators writing prior to 1970, the answer seemed obvious: the Irish in Ireland had for centuries been strongly attached to the Catholic tradition and the Catholic Church. Some scholars were positively lyrical in making this claim. Carl Wittke (1956, 89), for example, described how "in times that were dark, priests and laymen had shared the miseries of their unhappy island . . . the attachment of the Irish people to their persecuted Church was never shaken." Similarly, Thomas McAvoy, in his widely read *A History of the Catholic Church in the United States* (1969, 245), argued that dominance of American Catholicism by the Irish "was not exactly new because, wherever Roman Catholicism has flourished in the English-speaking world since the Reformation, the most faithful group had been the Irish." McAvoy wrote that the deep attachment of the Famine Irish to Catholicism was "their chief consolation in their desperate condition" (p. 3) and that it was one of the very few Irish cultural traditions which survived the voyage across the Atlantic. Scholars like Wittke and McAvoy felt no obligation to present any *evidence* in support of their contentions, and they were always a little vague about what constituted attachment to Catholic traditions and to the Catholic Church, mainly because they regarded this as just something that everyone *knew* to be true.

It seems clear in retrospect that these claims by Wittke and McAvoy (a priest and chair of the history department at the University of Notre Dame from 1939–1960) were accepted at face value because they were so consistent with what leaders (especially Irish American leaders) of the American Catholic Church had been saying for quite some time. During the church's Third Plenary Council, held in Baltimore in 1884, Bernard J. McQuaid, Bishop of Rochester (and the son of Irish emigrants from County Tyrone) declared:

> The first immigrants coming in large numbers were from Ireland. Of all the people of Europe they were the best fitted for religion in a new country. Brave by nature, inured to poverty and hardship, just released from a struggle unto death for the faith, accustomed to the practice of religion in its simplest forms, cherishing dearly their priests whom they learned to support directly, actively engaged in building humble chapels on the sites of ruined churches and in replacing altars, they were not appalled by the wretchedness of religious equipments and surrounding in their new homes on this side of the Atlantic. (cited in Liptak 1989, 78)

A bit later, in 1907, the Irish-born John Cardinal Farley, Archbishop of New York, said that the Catholic Church in New York had "only one class of people to draw upon for the support of [its] churches and schools" and that Irish Americans were that class (cited in Shelley 2001, 1–2). A few years later, W. H. Agnew (1913, 258–259), a Jesuit priest, said of the earliest Irish immigrants:

[They] came to America heroically attached to their religion, well instructed in it, faithful in the use of its Sacraments, and ready to die for it. . . . The Church was the center of their infant world. . . . The priest of God was pointed out to them as the visible embodiment of God's power and goodness [and] to think evil of God's priest was for them an iniquity.

This very same view of the Famine Irish was shared by Protestant commentators in the nineteenth century, though they obviously gave it a different valuation.

As Robert Dunne (2002) has demonstrated, the complaint most characteristic of nativist Protestant tirades against the Famine Irish, at their worst in the 1840s and early 1850s, was that these immigrants were under the influence and control of Catholic priests, who owed their political allegiance to Rome. Such a view presupposes exactly what the church's own view presupposes: that the Famine Irish embraced the church, in the person on their local Catholic priest, as soon as they stepped off the boats. Unfortunately, as most readers will already know, the claim that these Irish had been strongly attached to Catholicism and/or the Catholic Church in Ireland is more problematic than the remarks by scholars like Wittke and McAvoy, by church leaders, and by Protestant critics would suggest.

Some time ago, Emmet Larkin (1972) argued that, during the middle of the nineteenth century, Catholic leaders in Ireland, most notably Paul Cardinal Cullen, successfully promoted a "devotional revolution" that dramatically changed the texture of Catholic practice in Ireland. Several scholars have taken issue with Larkin's use of the word *revolution* here, arguing either that Larkin's "revolution" was just the final phase in a process of a Tridentine reform that had begun much earlier (McGrath 1991) or that participation in official Catholic rituals like the Mass had declined during the century before the Famine and so Larkin's "revolution" was to some extent a return to earlier participation levels (D. Miller 2005). Still, no one writing after Larkin has challenged his basic point, that Catholic practice in Ireland in the decades immediately following the Famine was dramatically different from what it had been in the decades immediately preceding the Famime. Mass attendance rates, in particular, which had been high in some areas of Ireland but extremely low in others during the early 1800s, were high in *all* areas of Ireland after the devotional revolution (D. Miller 1975; 2000; 2005).

Although Larkin's work produced a gestalt shift in scholarly thinking about Irish Catholicism in Ireland, its effect on the study of Irish American Catholicism has been minimal. Indeed, most American scholars have used Larkin's argument to *reinforce* the traditional position, namely, that the Famine immigrants were devout Catholics when they stepped off the boat. Patricia Good (1975, 9), for example, in her case study of an Irish American parish in nineteenth-century Pittsburgh, concluded that the Irish driven by the Famine to emigrate had "gained comfort from the devotional revolution initiated by Cardinal Cullen [because it] provided the suffering Catholic masses with at least some sense of meaning and spiritual consolation to their dreary lives." Jay Dolan (1975, 45–58) made the same claim, though perhaps more modestly: he estimated that about half (only half) of the Irish emigrants who arrived in New York after the Famine brought with them a commitment to Catholicism that had been shaped by the devotional revolution and for that reason took an active role in the affairs of their local parish. Dolan, however, is really in a minority. Most American scholars, like Good, make no attempt to qualify the suggestion that Irish Catholic immigrants to the United States had been shaped by the devotional revolution and so were "good Catholics" when they arrived in America. Roger Finke and Rodney Stark (1992, 136–138) make no bones about their uncritical acceptance of the claim: "Without pausing to explore the causes of the Irish devotional revolution here, we may note that this revolution spread to America with successive waves of immigrants (Larkin 1972). And in combination with the immense predominance of Irish clergy, the sect-like qualities of Irish Catholicism predominated as well." And Finke and Stark's conclusion here continues to be taken at face value in scholarly discussions of Irish American religion (for example, Quinlan 2005, 147–148). What is at least mildly puzzling about all versions of this commonly made argument—locating the source of Irish American Catholic piety in Ireland's devotional revolution—is that they run directly counter to what Larkin himself said about the Famine emigrants.

In both his original (1972) article and in later work (e.g., 1984), Larkin is very clear in arguing that the devotional revolution in Ireland was associated most of all with the "respectable" (= well-off) farmer class among the Catholic population and *not* with the Catholic majority, which consisted of laborers, cottiers, and paupers. What happened during the Famine and ensured that the devotional revolution would affect Irish Catholicism in general *in Ireland* was that laborers, cottiers, and paupers were either killed off or driven to emigrate but the well-off farmer class was little affected by the Famine. For Larkin, these two intertwined demographic processes ensured that the variant of Catholicism associated with the well-off farmer class came to predominate in Ireland. A logical consequence of this argument, which Larkin notes explicitly, is that the vast majority of Irish Catholics who emigrated in the immediate wake of the Famine *would have been little committed to the sort of Catholicism that Cardinal Cullen was promoting.*

Last but not least . . . what was significant in the devotional revolution is its importance for understanding the Great Diaspora of the Irish in the nineteenth century.
. . . *Most of the two million Irish who emigrated between 1847 and 1860 were part of the
pre-Famine generation of non-practicing Catholics.* . . . What the famine Irish actually
represented, therefore, was a culture of poverty that had been in the making in Ireland since the late eighteenth century. . . . The crucial point is that after the famine
that culture of poverty was broken up in Ireland by emigration and the new circumstances created by that breakup allowed for the emergence of other values. (Larkin
1972, 651, emphasis added)

This part of Larkin's argument is simply ignored by commentators like Finke and
Stark and Dolan.

In other cases, commentators seem aware of Larkin's argument but nevertheless continue to suggest that post-Famine Irish American religiosity was rooted
in Ireland's devotional revolution. For example, in an essay on the Irish in New
York, Lawrence McCaffrey (1996, 218–219) notes—correctly, given the Larkin
argument—that the devotional revolution can only reasonably be seen as having
affected post-1877 Irish immigrants to that city. In a subsequent essay, however,
McCaffrey (1997, 81) writes, "Post-Famine Irish emigrants, priests, nuns, and
laity brought what Emmett Larkin has described as a Devotional Revolution with
them to the New World." McCaffrey thus associates the devotional revolution
with *all* post-Famine immigrants, including that mass of Irish emigrants who
settled in the U.S. in the immediate wake of the Famine.

David Gleeson (2001, 85), in his study of Irish Catholics in the American
South, takes note of Larkin's contention that Famine emigrants were not devotional revolution Catholics but dismisses it, saying, "The Irish in the South
brought their devotion with them and sought the comfort of the church parish
life. Even when they had not experienced Cullen's reforms in Ireland, they provided similar raw material for zealous clerics in America." His evidence for this,
however, consists entirely in a number of anecdotal references to particular Irish
Catholics in the South who contributed to the support of a local Catholic church.
Even putting aside the fact that most of the people whom Gleeson mentions were
well-off (and so not representative of the Famine Irish generally), the logical flaw
in his argument seems evident. Thus, Gleeson *starts* with evidence of Irish
Catholic religiosity in the United States (they supported their local church),
assumes that this was caused by their deep attachment to the devotional life of the
Catholic Church in Ireland, and then uses this (their deep attachment to Catholi-

cism in Ireland) to *explain* his initial finding. The argument succeeds only by assuming what it sets out to prove.

In summary, then, investigators (at least American investigators) who cite Larkin's work on the devotional revolution in Ireland as the source of Irish American Catholic piety either ignore entirely Larkin's contention that the immigrants who came to the United States in the immediate wake of the Famine were *not* affected by that devotional revolution or they acknowledge Larkin's argument but simply assert or imply the reverse. What thus becomes common to the work of all these commentators is the suggestion that the roots of the deep attachment of Irish Americans to the variant of Catholicism that shaped the American Church are to be found *in Ireland*. Ignored entirely is the possibility, suggested by Larkin's work, that if Famine immigrants were not affected by the devotional revolution, their attachment to the variant of Catholicism they embraced in America was likely the result of their experiences in *America*. Indeed, if we accept Larkin's argument about Famine emigrants, the question we really need to ask is "How and why did the Famine Irish *become* 'good' Catholics in America."

How the Irish Became Catholic in America

Although the Irish in pre-Famine Ireland may not have been especially observant Catholics, using measures like mass attendance and the reception of the sacraments, a thriving tradition of popular Catholicism did exist at least from the time of the Counter Reformation. This form of popular Catholicism was centered on holy well cults, rounding rituals (the practice of walking around a well or stone cairn a precise number of times—usually three, seven, nine, or fifteen—in a clockwise direction) and patterns. Patterns (also called patrons) were communal events that drew people from all levels of Irish society, both males and females, both rural and urban. Patterns included a mix of religious and secular and religious activities. Rounding rituals were central to the religious experience at a pattern. Local priests attended these events and did say mass and preach the occasional sermon, but such activities were "add-ons." Secular activities, usually held at the end of the day, after the religious activities, typically included drinking, dancing, and faction fights between rival groups of males.

Most commentators who discuss the Famine Irish in America, if they mention this form of popular Catholicism at all, say simply that it failed to cross the Atlantic with the emigrants because it was too closely tied to the conditions of life in Ireland and/or to particular sites there (see, for example, Clarke 1993, 46–47;

Mannion 1991, 90–91). What these writers overlook, however, is the evidence that, in Ireland, attachment to these communal forms of popular Catholicism Ireland had been on the decline since the late 1700s, long before the increase in Irish migration to North America in the 1830s and (even more dramatically) the 1840s. Eugene Hynes (1978, 141–142) pointed out that evidence of a decades-old *pre*-Famine decline in the popularity of this form of Catholicism could be found in the written recollections of authors like William Wilde (1815–1876). The best evidence for a pre-Famine decline in the popularity of holy well cults and the associated rituals and celebrations, however, is to be found in the Ordnance Survey letters.

During the 1830s, John O'Donovan and other Ordnance Survey investigators (but mainly O'Donovan) scoured the Irish countryside asking questions about local holy wells, patterns, and other sites of "antiquarian" interest. Their reports (which are available in typescript at the Royal Irish Academy, Dublin, and elsewhere) are pervaded with informant comments about once-popular holy wells that had fallen into disuse and about once-popular patterns at some particular site that had not been celebrated for years. (For a discussion of the Ordnance Survey letters and their value in assessing holy well cults, as well as a discussion of the changing social conditions in pre-Famine Ireland that likely undermined the appeal of holy well cults and patterns, see Carroll 1999, 151–158.)

What all this means—to repeat the point that was made in passing in Chapter 1—is that the mass of Irish Catholic immigrants who swept across the Atlantic in the years immediately following the Famine to settle in the United States would have been little attached *either* to the official Catholic tradition (again, assuming for the moment that Larkin was right) *or* to the form of popular Catholicism that had previously prevailed in Ireland. They would, in other words, have been indifferent to the practice of Catholicism in any form, and it is against this baseline that we must explain their transformation into the mainstay of the American Catholic Church.

Kerby Miller (1985) is one of the few scholars who has discussed the religious transformation of the Famine Irish in America in a precise and extended manner. First, he takes explicit note of this tenuous attachment of most Famine Irish to official Catholicism, something commentators like Finke, Stark, Dolan, and others ignore. Miller writes (p. 327):

[N]on-practicing or "anonymous" Catholics from southern and western Ireland probably dominated the peasant exodus of 1845–55, and large numbers rarely or never observed formal religious obligations in the New World. Thus, during the

1850s and 1860s at least half the Irish in New York City's Sixth Ward, including a great majority of the unskilled laborers, hardly ever attended mass; in Ohio, one priest lamented "scarcely one of ten of our Irish on the railroad goes to his duty, one half are grown up to 20–25 years and never made their first communion [and] know nothing of their catechism."

Miller then goes on to argue that these religiously indifferent Irish were quickly pushed into the arms of the official church, most of all by *nativist hostility.* The appeal of the church, in other words, was that it was an institution which—along with the Democratic Party—"served to insulate emigrants and traditional Irish values from nativist hostility" (328).

While Miller's argument might at first sight seem to fit the facts of the situation in cities like New York and Boston (i.e., anti-Catholic hostility *was* intense in those cities and the Irish there *did* become good Catholics), there are at least two problems with his argument.

First, there is the matter of what options were available to Irish Americans. Because the Famine Irish *did* become "good Catholics," there has always been a historiographical predisposition to take that behavior as a given and so not to delve deeply into its explanation. Dolan and Stark/Finke explain it away by reference to Ireland's devotional revolution, while others, like Miller, explain it away by reference to nativist hostility. Such explanations fail to consider the other logical possibility and to ask, Why didn't large numbers of the Famine Irish slip easily into Protestantism of one sort or another? After all, that is precisely what large numbers of pre-Famine Irish of Catholic background did. This omission seems critical in the case of Miller's argument, since becoming Protestant (*conversion* would be too strong a word here, assuming that the Famine Irish were religiously indifferent) would be an obvious way of blunting anti-Catholic hostility.

Only Donald Akenson (1993, 244–252), as far as I know, has addressed this question in an explicit way. His answer starts with two characteristics that distinguish the experience of the Famine Irish immigrants from those of the pre-Famine period: (1) whereas the Irish who immigrated in the pre-Famine period were overwhelmingly male, Famine immigrants were more evenly divided between males and females; and (2) as an institution, the American Catholic Church was far more accessible to Irish immigrants in the post-Famine period than it had been in the pre-Famine period. Consequently, Akenson argues, in the pre-Famine period the absence of Irish Catholic females forced Irish Catholic males to marry into Protestant families and so likely to be "pulled into" Protestantism by their wives and in-laws. Also, that there was typically no Catholic church in their local community made this more likely. But Famine and post-Famine immigrants were in a different situation. The gender ratio was more balanced among later immigrants, so they could more easily find an Irish mate with a Catholic background. The Catholic Church being more developed in America by then, they also were more likely to have a Catholic church in their local community. Marrying a Catholic spouse in a Catholic church, concludes Akenson, reinforced their Catholic identity.

For Akenson, this argument explains why the Irish became devout Catholics, but of course it doesn't. After all, even taking his argument at face value, it would only explain why Famine immigrants would have maintained a Catholic *identity*, but we know that a Catholic identity did not always bring along with it a desire to participate in the sacramental life of the church. Similarly, later in the nineteenth century, most Italian immigrants *thought of* themselves as Catholic (that is, they had a Catholic identity), and yet the "Italian problem" that generated so much debate within the American Catholic Church (and which will be discussed in the next chapter) was precisely that in their religious practice Italian Americans came nowhere close to meeting the standards that by then had been set by the Irish.

Still, assuming that post-Famine marriage patterns indeed functioned to reinforce a Catholic identity among Famine immigrants gives us a basis for understanding why "converting to Protestantism" would not have been a viable response to anti-Catholic hostility for Famine immigrants. After all, during the last two-thirds of the nineteenth century, there was an increasing interconnection between "being Irish" and "being Catholic," and so converting to Protestantism would have been a move away from one's Irish identity—something that would not have been true for Irish immigrants in the pre-Famine period. So, if anti-Catholic hostility had an effect at all, it would have been more likely to drive Famine and post-Famine immigrants toward the Catholic Church than toward any form of Protestantism. Does that mean that, in the end, Kerby Miller is correct in seeing "nativist hostility" as most responsible for making Famine immigrants practicing Catholics? I still don't think so, because there is another problem with Miller's argument.

As Edward O'Donnell (1997) has pointed out, the Irish experience in cities on the Eastern Seaboard, like New York and Boston, was often quite different from the Irish experience in cities like Albany, Detroit, Cleveland, St. Louis, New Orleans, Denver, and San Francisco. Part of this difference, it happens, has to do with nativist hostility: in these other areas, Famine immigrants encountered far less hostility than was the case in cities like Boston and New York, and yet they still became "good Catholics." Take the specific case of San Francisco, which at least one commentator has called "one of the most hospitable places on earth" for Famine immigrants (Meagher 2005, 85).

The San Francisco Irish

A great many Irish immigrants made their way to northern California during the 1850s and 1860s. Typically, as Malcolm Campbell (2002) points out, they were Famine emigrants who had first settled in either eastern U.S. cities or in Australia or New Zealand. It was almost certainly the discovery of gold at Sutter's Mill in 1848 which first made California an attractive destination to Famine emigrants, but more Irish quickly settled and made a life for themselves in San Francisco and the San Francisco Bay area. By 1852 there were already 4,200 Irish-born individuals in San Francisco. By 1870, Irish immigrants were the largest foreign-born population in the state and accounted for almost 10 percent of its total population; 48 percent of the state's Irish-born population lived in San Francisco itself and 14 percent lived in one of the five surrounding counties (Campbell 2002, 67–69). By 1880, 37 percent of the city's white population was Irish by birth or descent and these were overwhelmingly Catholic (Burchell 1979, 3–4). By this time, the Irish community in San Francisco had become (in absolute numbers) the sixth largest Irish community in the United States, after New York, Philadelphia, Boston, Chicago, and St. Louis (Walsh 1978, 12).

Although there is no denying that the San Francisco Irish encountered some nativist hostility (especially during the 1850s, when they were targeted by the Committee of Vigilance and by Know-Nothing politicians), the hostility they encountered was far less intense than that faced by the Irish in the East—something that Catholic commentators of the period were quick to point out. (For some of the comments made by contemporary observers in this regard, see Burchell 1979, 6–7.) Both Rischin (1978) and Walsh (1976) suggest that the lessened hostility faced by the Irish in San Francisco resulted from: the absence of a long-established Yankee elite, an established tradition of Catholicism inherited from the recent Spanish past, and the fact (itself a function of these first two things) that the Famine Irish and their children in San Francisco were able to move more quickly into positions of authority in local politics and the local police force than was true in eastern cities. And yet, despite the relative absence of hostility toward them in San Francisco, the Irish there very quickly became faithful Catholics, just like the Famine Irish elsewhere.

The best evidence of how quickly the San Francisco Irish became practicing Catholics is the number of churches built to serve congregations that were pre-

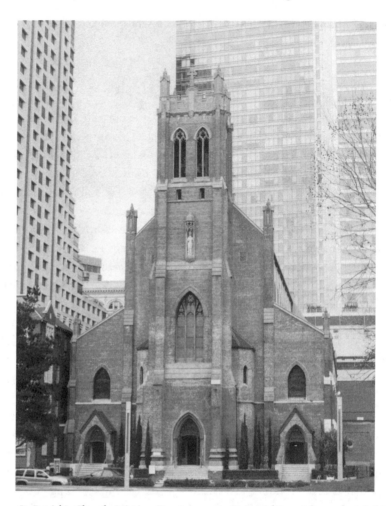

Fig. 2. St. Patrick's Church, Mission Street, in 2005. St. Patrick's parish was founded in 1851 to serve San Francisco's Irish community. The church building was largely destroyed in the 1906 earthquake; its replacement, pictured here, was designed to resemble the original structure.

dominantly Irish. The very first parish church established by Bishop Joseph Sadoc Alemany after his arrival in late 1850, for example, was St. Patrick's on Market Street (later relocated to Mission Street, see Figure 2), and it was established specifically for the benefit of the growing Irish population (McGloin 1978, 40). Almost immediately, however, it became apparent that St. Patrick's was too small. Even as early as 1853, only two years after St. Patrick's had been been built, contemporary observers noted that the congregation was increasing so rapidly that a new building was being planned (Soulé, Gihon, and Nisbet 1855, 697). Among the other churches built in San Francisco in this early period to serve mainly or entirely Irish congregations were St. Mary's in 1854, St. Joseph's in 1861, St. Brigid's in 1863, and St. Peter's in 1867 (Avella 2000, 263).

One of the things that made this spate of church building possible, and that is further evidence that the San Francisco Irish had embraced the church, is that much of the money that financed the construction of these new churches came from the Irish community. Moreover, as Burchell's (1979, 87–92) careful study shows, this support came not simply from a few elites (though Irish elites did contribute handsomely to these projects) but rather from the broad spectrum of the Irish community in San Francisco. Given all this, it hardly seems surprising that by the 1860s church leaders, including Bishop Alemany, and leaders in the Irish community, were boasting about the flourishing state of Catholicism in the city and in particular about the high rates of church attendance (for some of the remarks, see Burchell 1979, 4–5; McGloin 1978, 31–41).

But, for a clearer picture, we need to look at Irish emigrants outside the United States. After all, as Donald Akenson has been telling us for years, although the Famine Irish likely encountered a certain amount of hostility in all contexts where they faced an English-speaking Protestant majority, the nativist hostility the Famine Irish encountered in the United States was far more intense than that which they encountered in places like Canada, Australia, and New Zealand. That is precisely why, as Akenson has also been telling us for years, we need to study the Irish outside the United States if we want to control for the effects of this intense nativist hostility as we think about the links between being Irish and behaviors like choice of occupation, settlement in a rural versus urban area, and upward mobility. When we do look at the Famine Irish who settled outside the United States, we find that they too became "good Catholics."

The Irish in Toronto

The Irish Catholic community in Toronto, in particular, has been the subject of several excellent studies (Clarke 1988; 1993; McGowan 1999; Nicolson 1983; 1985), and collectively these studies establish three things. First, the Catholic community in nineteenth-century Toronto was overwhelmingly Irish. Nicolson's estimate is that the Irish accounted for 90 percent of the Catholic population of the city in 1851 and 85 percent in 1880. Second, Larkin was quite correct in his assessment of Famine immigrants: upon their arrival in Canada, they did not attend mass, did not participate in the sacramental life of the church, and were generally ignorant of the Lord's Prayer, the Apostle's Creed, and the like (on this issue, see Clarke 1993, 48–50). But a third fact is most important, that the Famine Irish in Toronto very quickly—more or less between 1850 and 1880—became "good" practicing Catholics.

As in Ireland itself and in the United States during this same period, mass attendance jumped dramatically. An 1882 survey conducted by a Toronto newspaper found that 70 percent of the city's Irish Catholics attended Sunday Mass (Clarke 1993, 61). As well, Irish Catholics in Toronto—like their counterparts in Ireland and America—increasingly embraced a range of extraliturgical devotions that included devotion to the Sacred Heart of Jesus, devotion to the Immaculate Conception of Mary, dedication of the month of May to Mary, a variety of devotions centered on the Eucharist, and the increased use of scapulars and rosaries (Clarke 1993, 58–61; McGowan 1999, 92–93). There was also a rapid increase in the number of churches, convents, and aid societies associated with the Catholic community during the 1850s and 1860s (Nicolson 1985, 62–63).

The net result of what can only be called Toronto's own devotional revolution is that, by the end of the century, the Irish in Toronto—who had arrived as lax Catholics in the aftermath of the Famine—were almost as devout as Catholics in Ireland and easily *more* devout than their Protestant neighbors. In 1901, the Canadian government collected data from various Christian denominations on a variety of issues, including the number of their members who were regular communicants or who attended Sunday school. That data (reported in McGowan 1999, 94) indicated that 86 percent of Toronto's Catholics (who were still mainly Irish) were communicants or Sunday school attendees. The comparable figures reported for other denominations were: Anglicans, 37 percent; Presbyterians, 42 percent; Methodists, 57 percent; and Baptists, 66 percent.

Explaining Devotional Revolutions

At this point, four things should be reasonably clear. First, that the Famine Irish who settled in the United States were initially religiously indifferent; second, that over the course of a generation or two, they experienced what might be called an American devotional revolution, which transformed them into the mainstay of the American Catholic Church; third, that this transformation is somehow rooted in their experience in America, not in Ireland; fourth, that while nativist anti-Catholic hostility may have contributed to this transformation, there was something else going on as well.

And yet, although it seems likely that the devotional revolution among the

Irish in America must be explained in terms of their experience in America, there is no denying that the type of Catholicism Irish American immigrants and their immediate descendants embraced was very similar to the type of Catholicism that the strong-farmer class in Ireland adopted (these were tenant farmers with large enough holdings to live comfortably). For this reason, I think, it will be useful to take a second and more detailed look at how Larkin and others have explained the appeal of that form of Catholicism.

In his original article Larkin (1972) suggested that the devotional revolution in Ireland had four causes: (1) Catholicism provided the Irish with a national identity during a period when their culture was being Anglicized. (2) Particular members of the hierarchy, notably Paul Cardinal Cullen, promoted increased adherence to Tridentine norms (like the need to attend mass regularly). (3) The population decline caused by the Famine substantially improved the ratio of priests to people (and so the degree to which the clergy could themselves encourage adherence to those norms). (4) While the Famine killed off or drove away those groups who were least committed to Tridentine Catholicism, it little affected the Catholic strong-farmer class, which was the one group that had embraced Tridentine Catholicism in the pre-Famine period. In his later work, Larkin, explaining *why* the strong-farmer class in Ireland had embraced Tridentine Catholicism in the pre-Famine period, made use of the national identity argument in point 1 above. Basically, what he suggested (1984, 8) was that "this farmer elite" was "the nation-forming class" and so they had turned to Catholicism as a way of building a distinct national identity.

Eugene Hynes pointed out that Larkin's argument did not really explain why Irish Catholics adopted the *particular* sort of Catholicism being promoted by Cullen. In other words, even granting that "being Catholic" became increasingly central to the nationalist vision of "being Irish," this doesn't really explain why Irish Catholics embraced the particular values and devotions that constituted the devotional revolution. Hynes (1978; 1988; 1990) developed his own explanation of the devotional revolution, and Larkin (1984, 6) suggested that Hynes's argument could easily be taken as supplementing his own.

Hynes argues that the living standards of the Catholic strong farmers in Ireland improved dramatically during the late eighteenth century as a result of the relaxation of the Penal Laws, the commercialization of Irish agriculture, and the increased demand for Irish foodstuffs in Britain. These changes, along with the rising expectations they engendered in the strong-farmer class, led members of that class to develop new means of maintaining control over their capital, and in particular, over the land and livestock they possessed. One outcome of this process, Hynes argues, was an increasing preference among strong farmers for the stem family. Under this family system, there was only one heir, almost always a son, and this son was typically married off to the daughter of a family of similar status. Land was thus kept under the family's control through the practice of impartible inheritance and a family's capital was augmented by the dowry that the son's wife brought to the marriage. One consequence of the stem family system was that, in most cases, only one son and one daughter within each family married, which meant that there were many sons and daughters who never married.

Hynes suggests that increasing use of the stem family system by the strong-farmer class created two problems and that understanding these problems helps us understand why that class found the sort of Catholicism being promoted by the nineteenth-century church appealing. The first of these problems he calls "personnel management" (1988, 166), that is, getting everyone in the family to subordinate their personal interests to the goals of the family even though this often meant great personal sacrifice (especially for the non-marrying sons and daughters). This problem could only be solved by getting all family members to accept the authority of the father. The stem family, in other words, required a strong emphasis on paternal authority. The second problem faced by the stem family followed from the fact that most sons and daughters were required to forgo marriage. In this situation, sexual activity on the part of these sons and daughters would have resulted in illegitimate births that potentially could have resulted in a serious drain on a family's wealth. As a result, it was very much in the interest of the strong-farmer class to promote an emphasis on sexual restraint.

It happens, Hynes argues, that the same two cultural emphases that worked to strengthen the stem family—an emphasis on paternal authority and an emphasis on sexual restraint—were central to the sort of Romanized Catholicism being promoted by the nineteenth-century church. An emphasis on paternal authority was evident in the church's campaign to strengthen the authority of the pope, while an emphasis on sexual restraint was implicit in the church's campaign to promote the Mary cult and its strong insistence on Mary's virginity. For Hynes, in other words, the strong-farmer class in Ireland embraced the Catholicism promoted by Cardinal Cullen because it fit well with the cultural emphases necessary for the maintenance of the stem family.

Obviously the *specifics* of the argument advanced by Hynes to explain the devotional revolution in Ireland are of little or no use in explaining why the Famine Irish in America became good Catholics. The Famine Irish in the United States, after all, did not possess land that needed to be conserved; they were not characterized by the stem family and its cultural needs. But what is more promising, I suggest, is the *type* of argument that Hynes advances, namely, that a particular social group embraces a particular form of institutional religion because there is an affinity between the *cultural* values embraced by the group (for reasons that may have nothing to do with religion) and the *religious* values being promulgated by the religious institution. While this sort of affinity argument has typically not been applied to the study of Catholicism—Hynes being the notable exception— it has long been used quite successfully by scholars studying the Protestant tradition, and in particular, the American Protestant tradition.

Max Weber (1946), for example, used an affinity argument to explain the immense popularity of the Protestant sects (mainly Methodist and Baptist) that he encountered during his 1904 visit to the United States. Basically, Weber argued that these sects were popular with local businessmen because the traits needed both to get into these sects *and* to remain a member in good standing—traits like honesty, trustworthiness, an aversion to gambling—were the same traits that members of a community wanted in the people they did business with. Becoming a member in good standing of a Baptist or Methodist church, in other words, was a way that a local businessman could certify to the community that he was honest, could be trusted to pay his debts, and so on—which is precisely why, Weber argued, businessmen in the United States joined these particular churches in such large numbers.

A similar affinity argument has been used to explain why the Methodists and Baptists held a special appeal for white women in the early Republic. The argument in this case is that many of the qualities of ideal Christians in these evangelical sects were qualities stereotypically associated with women. Evangelical thought privileged orality over the written word, emotion and corporeal experience (as jointly evident most of all in the conversion experience) over formal doctrine and rational thought, and the need for an ordered and disciplined life that involved submissiveness to Christ (Leonard 2003, 161–162; Lindman 2000; Lobody 1993; Lyerly 1998, 94–118). This affinity did not translate into power sharing—men still retained most of the control in local congregations—but the fit between stereotypical female qualities and the qualities expected of the "ideal Christian" in these evangelical sects helps explain why these sects initially held a special appeal to women.

Rosemary Hopcroft (1997) is yet another investigator who has used an affinity argument to explain Protestant success, though her concern is with Protestant success in the rural areas of sixteenth-century Europe. Hopcroft's central claim— which is supported by the historical data she presents—is that the best predictor of Protestant success in these rural areas was the presence of a local tradition of individualized property rights. She asserts that a tradition of individualized property rights (and a correspondingly low degree of communal control over property) promoted a generalized "spirit of individualism" (p. 172), which made the communities involved more receptive to religious sects that were, like most variants of Protestantism, pervaded with a strongly individualistic emphasis.

Although affinity arguments have often been used by scholars studying Protestantism, American Protestantism in particular, Hynes's argument is the only example I can think of of their use in connection with the study of European Catholicism, and I know of no one who has developed an affinity argument to explain why certain groups in the United States embraced Catholicism. This is what I want to do in the remainder of this chapter. What I will be arguing is that the Famine Irish (or at least a subset of them), who arrived in the United States indifferent to the practice of Catholicism, very quickly became ardent Catholics because of a fit between the particular variant of Catholicism being promoted by the American Catholic Church and interests that emerged among these immigrants as a result of their experience in America. In developing this argument, it will be useful to proceed in steps, the first of which involves taking a closer look at the Catholicism being promoted by the American Catholic Church in the nineteenth century.

Romanized Catholicism in the Nineteenth Century

During the middle third of the nineteenth century, the Roman hierarchy of the Catholic Church engaged in a campaign to change the nature and texture of Catholic practice throughout the world. One of the primary goals of this campaign was to centralize authority within the church. Central to this campaign was what would come to be called the "ultramontanist" emphasis on the papacy and on the need for clerics and laity alike to obey papal directives unquestioningly. Generally, ultramontanists aimed at establishing a top-down chain of command in which the laity obeyed their local priests, priests obeyed their bishop, and bishops fell in line behind the pope. Tied to this emphasis on papal supremacy and on obedience to clerical superiors was the view that the church should be free to make decisions on matters of importance to Catholics (notably educational matters) with little or no interference from the state. This drive to centralize authority within the church was led by energetic church leaders—often cardinals with strong ties to the Roman Curia, almost always bishops—operating in a variety of national contexts. In Europe, these included Cardinal Wiseman in England; Cardinal von Geissel, Archbishop of Cologne; Cardinal Pie, Bishop of Poitiers; and, of course, Cardinal Cullen in Ireland, who figures so prominently in Larkin's account of Ireland's devotional revolution. (On all of these men as ultramontanists, see the various essays in von Arx 1998.) In North America, these leaders included Bishop Kendrick of Philadelphia (discussed in Light 1988), Archbishop Hughes of New York (Kenny 2000, 112–116), Bishop Charbonnel of Toronto (Clarke 1993, 62–96), and Bishop Bourget of Montreal (Cimechella 1986). The decision of the First Vatican Council (1869–1870) to affirm the doctrine of papal infallibility shortly after Garibaldi's invasion of the Papal States in 1867 and only a few months before the fall of Rome to the forces of the new Italian government (in September 1870) can be seen as encapsulating both what these nineteenth-century ultramontanists wanted to *achieve* and what they wanted to *avoid*.

In selling an increased emphasis on obedience to ordinary Catholics, the ultramontanists did not depict it as something new. Quite the contrary, they sought legitimacy for this emphasis by suggesting that it had long been a part of the Catholic tradition—even if that meant tweaking the historical record here and there. A good example of how this was done, at least in regard to Irish Americans, involves the Profession of Faith, which was regularly included in the devotional guides, like *St. Vincent's Manual* (1859, 44–48) and *St. John's Manual* (1856, 22–25), that were marketed to Irish American Catholics in the mid-nineteenth century. In these two guides, the Profession of Faith starts with the following heading and introductory sentence:

> A Profession of Catholic Faith
> Extracted from the Council of Trent
> By His Holiness, Pope Pius IV
>
> I [Name], Believe and profess with a firm faith, all and every one of those things, which are contained in the Symbol of Faith used in the Holy Catholic (Roman) Church, viz . . .

The profession goes on to enunciate a number of Catholic beliefs relating to Christ, sacred scripture, the sacraments, the mass, the veneration of Mary and the saints, and so on. And, toward the end of the list, lies this statement about obedience:

> I Acknowledge the Holy Catholic Apostolic Roman Church to be the Mother and Mistress of all Churches; and *I promise true obedience to the Bishop of Rome* [emphasis added], the Successor of St. Peter, Prince of the Apostles, Vicar of Jesus Christ on earth.

By saying (in the heading) that this "Profession of Faith" had been "extracted from the Council of Trent by Pius IV," these guides were implying that lay Catholics' pledging obedience to the pope had been a central part of the Catholic tradition for centuries. What was not acknowledged was that the Council of Trent did not intend this profession of faith for the laity at all.

It is true that the profession of faith reproduced in these nineteenth-century devotional guides was developed by Pius IV (elected pope in 1560 and so the pope who oversaw the final years of the Council of Trent), and the profession was largely derived from the doctrines and decrees passed at Trent. Pius IV, however, meant it only as an oath to be taken by anyone holding an ecclesiastical office (Loughlin 1913), and the intent was clearly to insure that office holders fell into line with the pope in promoting the Tridentine reforms. That the original profession of faith was intended for office holders is made clear by the wording of the decree passed at Trent that mandated this oath. That decree (in Chapter 2 of the "Decree concerning reform") states that in light of "the distress of the times and the malice of increasing heresies" all clerics eligible to attend a provincial synod must publicly embrace all the doctrines and decrees passed at Trent and "profess true obedience to the supreme Roman pontiff" (see Schroeder 1950, 233–234). This mandate that *clerics* "profess true obedience" to the pope is the *only* decree passed at Trent that explicitly mentions obedience to the pope. There is nothing in any of the decrees passed at Trent that requires the *laity* to profess obedience to the pope. It seems that ultramontanists in the nineteenth century turned an oath that had been designed centuries earlier to insure the loyalty of bishops and other church officials into an oath that obligated ordinary lay Catholics to obey the pope.

As mentioned, it was the ultramontane emphasis on obedience that, according to Hynes, made ultramontane Catholicism appealing to a strong-farmer class in Ireland, because these same emphases were so crucial to the maintenance of the stem family system and thus to the preservation of the family's land. Did this emphasis on obedience and discipline *also* have some appeal to Famine immigrants to the United States (who did not have land to preserve and who were not characterized by the stem family)? Answering that question requires that we shift from religion to demography.

The Demographic Distinctiveness of the Famine Irish

When they first arrived in the United States, the Famine Irish were different in at least two significant ways from other European immigrant streams. The first difference has to do with gender: while males predominated in most other European immigrant groups, the Irish were almost equally divided between males and females. Over the period 1852–1860, for example, 51 percent of immigrants from Ireland were male and 49 percent were female (Akenson 1993, 44; Fitzpatrick 1984, 7; Meagher 2005, 174). Moreover, in certain locales, females sometimes constituted the majority. For example, of the 204,000 Irish-born individuals living in New York at the time of the 1860 census, 117,000 (57%) were female (Steinberg 1989, 162). The second distinction of the Irish was their marital status. Most European immigrant streams were composed mainly of family groups and unmarried males, but Irish immigrants included many unmarried males *and* unmarried females. Nor was the presence of so many unmarried men and women in the Irish Catholic population a transitory experience; on the contrary, Famine immigrants who were unmarried when they arrived were less likely than other immigrants to *ever* marry and, if they did marry, more likely to delay marriage until a relatively late age (Diner 1983, 43–53).

This is not to say that kinship ties were unimportant to Irish immigrants. One need only look at the remittances that Famine immigrants sent back to Ireland to know that such ties did matter—greatly. Between 1846 and 1855, Irish immigrants in North America sent approximately £8,753,000 back to Ireland (Blessing 1977, 130). Given the poverty of the Famine immigrants in America—something much emphasized in contemporary accounts—this is a truly prodigious sum. And much of this money, it would appear, was intended to help relatives—siblings in particular—emigrate. One study showed that in 1848 more than three-quarters of those emigrating from Ireland paid their fares with remittance money (Blessing 1977, 135). Obviously, the reluctance of the Famine Irish to marry was not the result of a devaluation of family. But there's more. Even once married, the high rates of unemployment among Irish males worked to destabilize Irish family life, mainly by promoting paternal absence (often simply because the fathers were away seeking work) or by weakening the father's authority within the home, something that in itself likely promoted his absence (Diner 1983, 43–69).

Theoretically, these demographic patterns are important for at least two reasons. First, the high proportion of unmarried males and females and the frequent weakness of the paternal role in families indicate that the appeal of Romanized Catholicism to the Famine Irish was likely not family based, that is, did not result from a fit between the needs of the Irish American family and this variant of Catholicism, which, according to Hynes, explained the appeal of Romanized Catholicism in Ireland. A good explanation of why the Famine Irish became good Catholics must explain why Romanized Catholicism appealed to unmarried Irish Americans and Irish Americans living in families where fathers were weak or absent. Second, the ratio between males and females raises a cautionary flag. It suggests that we need to make gender a central element in our explanation of why the Famine Irish became Catholic. In fact, when we scan the literature on Irish American Catholicism during the decades immediately following the Famine through a gendered lens, an obvious pattern leaps to the eye.

Gender, Nationalism, and Catholicism

In the two decades or so following the Famine, male Irish American Catholics were very much involved in Irish nationalist associations but little involved with religion, while for female Irish American Catholics this pattern was reversed (see Braude 1997, 106; Diner 1983, 120–138; McCaffrey 1999, 130–131; Meagher 2005, 177–178; Taves 1986, 18–19). The same pattern was evident among the Irish Catholics in Canada (Clarke 1993, 62–96; Trigger 1997, 83–105). One interesting thing about this gendered behavior—but something that has been ignored by all earlier commentators—is that it provides support for Hynes's critique of Larkin.

Larkin, remember, argued that the appeal of Romanized Catholicism to the strong-farmer class in Ireland derived from the fact that they were the "nation-building" class and because there was an increasing interconnection between "being Irish" and "being Catholic." Hynes's critique was that, while this argument might well explain why the strong-farmer class retained a Catholic *identity*, it did not explain why they embraced the particular variant of Catholicism then being promoted by Rome. The behavior of Famine Irish males in the U.S. bears out the point Hynes made. Irish American males in the two decades or so following the Famine *were* Irish nationalists, something that might reasonably have ensured (given the interconnection between Catholicism and nationalism at this point) that they would retain a Catholic identity and would explain why they didn't embrace Protestantism. But this did *not* cause them to become *good* Catholics, that is, to participate actively in the life of the church.

The finding that Irish American Catholicism was initially gendered and that the women were more religious than the men is also important because it is a *familiar* pattern. It is now fairly conventional in studies of Western religion to talk about a "feminization of religion" which occurred in the nineteenth century. It is interesting, however, that in this case the usual explanations offered for the "feminization of religion" during the nineteenth century do not apply.

Accounting for the Feminization of Religion in the Nineteenth Century

Barbara Pope (1988, 52) points out that the phrase "feminization of religion" was first popularized by historians studying New England Protestant groups, and it refered to three things: an increase in the number and proportion of women participating in church life; their increasing influence as a result; and various changes in doctrine and symbolism that reflected women's needs and experiences. Subsequent investigators went on to document a similar feminization of piety outside of New England in both the Protestant and Catholic traditions. A feminization of piety during the nineteenth century has now been documented in the Anglican high church tradition (Reed 1988), the British evangelical tradition (Brown 2001), Catholicism in France (Harris 1999; Pope 1988), and American Catholicism generally (Dolan 1992, 230–233). It has also been found among Cajun Catholics in Louisiana, a case that will be discussed at length in Chapter 4. In explaining why this feminization of piety occurred, investigators have generally advanced two separate hypotheses, and there seems to be a rough correlation between which of these two hypotheses a researcher prefers and whether the researcher's focus is on Protestants or Catholics.

Scholars concerned with the feminization of piety in the Protestant tradition have tended to emphasize the "male flight" hypothesis, that is, that religion became increasingly feminized because male participation in formal religious activities diminished (Bonomi 1986, 111–115; Westerkamp 1999, 79–81). Generally, these investigators see this withdrawal as having been provoked mainly by the erosion of male lay authority as authority in local congregations came increasingly to be exercised solely by a professional ministry. There is a substantial amount of historical evidence to support the male flight interpretation. For example, feminization of piety was least pronounced in those Protestant groups where lay males retained a substantial amount of control; also, even within a single denomination, feminization was most likely in congregations with settled ministers and least likely in congregations without settled ministers (see Bonomi 1986, 111–115, for a review of the evidence).

Scholars studying the feminization of Catholicism, by contrast, have tended to advance what might be called a "female sociability" hypothesis. The general idea here is that during the nineteenth century the church was one of the few institutional settings where women could socialize with non-family members and engage in the honest exchange of ideas on issues of mutual concern. Ruth Harris

(1999, 234–235), for example, suggests that a large part of the appeal of Catholicism to middle-class women in France was that the church provided them with "a unique opportunity to talk about religious preoccupations and to confront issues of identity and selfhood, to share with intelligent educated men [i.e., their confessors and spiritual directors] problems close to their hearts."

The male flight and female sociability hypotheses are of course not mutually exclusive. Ralph Gibson (1989), unlike Harris, uses both arguments simultaneously to account for the feminization of piety in the French Catholic tradition. Then, too, it seems clear that the male flight hypothesis, though developed mainly by scholars studying the Protestant tradition, fits the history of European Catholicism quite well. In the early modern period, for example, the rituals and celebrations most central to the lived experience of Catholicism in many Catholic societies were the rituals and celebrations organized by lay confraternities—and this confraternal religion was overwhelmingly masculine. True, some female confraternities did exist, but in areas like Spain, the Spanish Americas, and Italy the most important celebrations were those organized and enacted by confraternities whose leadership was exclusively male and whose membership was either predominantly or exclusively male (for a sampling of the literature on this subject, see Donnelly and Maher 1999; Meyers and Hopkins 1988). Even where female confraternities did exist, they were often under lay male control, and more specifically under the control of male kin. During the eighteenth century, however, the autonomy of Catholic confraternities increasingly came under attack from both church and state. As lay (male) control eroded, Catholic men—just as the male flight hypothesis predicts—increasingly abandoned religion, with the result that Catholic practice became increasingly feminized.

Can either the male flight or the female sociability argument help us understand why Irish American Catholicism was initially "feminized"? As to the first hypothesis, the answer is clearly no. Male flight cannot explain the early feminization of Irish American Catholicism for the simple reason—*pace* Larkin—that Irish male immigrants were not active participants in the sacramental life of the church to begin with. The female sociability argument, by contrast, seems more promising. True, it would likely be too much of a stretch to suggest that Irish American women, who were overwhelmingly working class, flocked to the church so that they could enjoy the sort of intellectual discussion which, Harris tells us, was so appealing to middle-class female Catholics in France. On the other hand, Robert Orsi has explained the appeal of Italian American festas around the turn of the century (Orsi 1985) and the appeal of devotion to St. Jude (Orsi 1996) in the 1940s and 1950s by arguing that these devotions provided immigrant women and their daughters with opportunities to discuss—with women similar to themselves—a variety of personal problems associated with marriage and family life. At one level, then, it would certainly be plausible to suggest that Irish American women in the mid-nineteenth century participated in church because it provided a "safe" institutional context in which they could raise issues and problems they shared in common with each other. Nevertheless, even though plausible, such an interpretation is flawed in the same way that Larkin's national identity argument is flawed: while it might explain why Irish American women participated in some church activities, it does not really explain why they embraced and internalized (as they apparently did) the particular variant of Catholicism being promoted by ultramontanist leaders.

Why might the ultramontane emphasis on obedience have fit well the needs and concerns of Irish Catholic women in the United States as, following Hynes, it did with the needs and concerns of the stem family in Ireland? Asking this particular question leads us directly into two distinct bodies of scholarly literature that, when combined, provide us with an answer.

Domestic Service and the Need for Discipline

One of the best-established facts about Irish American life during the nineteenth century is that the occupational niche most associated with Irish American women was domestic service (Meagher 2005, 175–176). Already in 1855, for instance, nearly three-quarters of all domestics in New York City were Irish and nearly half of all Irish-born women under the age of 50 worked as domestics (Kenny 2000, 110). Kelleher (2003, 196–197) reports that in 1880 nearly half of all Irish-born women in Chicago aged 15 to 24 worked as domestic servants in private households and that if the designation "domestic service" is expanded to include both household servants and "hotel help," that proportion jumps to over 80 percent. In 1900 it was still the case that more than 70 percent of employed Irish-born women in the United States were in domestic service (Miller, Doyle, and Kelleher 1995, 54) and that the Irish-born constituted 41 percent of all foreign-born servants (Katzman 1978, 66).

I might add that the United States was by no means the only outpost of the Irish diaspora where Irish Catholic females entered domestic service in large numbers. During the nineteenth and early twentieth centuries, domestic service was the single most common occupation for Irish females in all the urban centers where the Irish settled (Akenson 1993). In his study of Hamilton, Ontario, for example, Michael Katz (1975) found that in the 1851 census 61 percent of Irish

Catholic females aged 17–19 were domestic servants; in the 1861 census this percentage (for the same group) was 58 percent. Overall, Katz suggests (p. 289), such data make it highly likely that "almost every Irish Catholic young woman who came to Canada spent part of her life as a resident domestic servant."

Although there were many things about domestic service that would have been unappealing to Irish women (not the least of which was the condescending attitude that many employers had toward all things Irish), it did offer a number of advantages. Most obviously, domestic service paid well, at least compared to the sort of jobs that Irish males could get (if they were lucky enough to get a job) and employment was relatively steady. All this, plus the fact that room and board were often provided, meant that Irish American women were typically able to build up savings in a way that was not possible for their male counterparts (on this point, see Diner 1983, 70–105; Miller, Doyle, and Kelleher 1995).

Purely financial considerations aside, domestic service provided Irish women with another important advantage: it brought them into daily contact with the culture of middle-class Anglo-Americans and so aided in the their acculturation and upward mobility. Hasia Diner (1999, 964) provides a succinct account of this process:

> Domestic servants . . . gained an exposure to American culture [and] learned how middle-class Americans lived. In their employers' homes they developed standards of American consumption, in terms of language, food, furnishings, dress, and gender roles. Irish women who labored as domestic servants in these middle-class homes and then married seem to have modeled their consumption patterns in part on what they had seen on the job.

Yet, even granting that a great many Irish women did come to adopt middle-class values as the result of domestic service, there is still a theoretical issue that needs to be resolved: what was the *mechanism* that caused this to occur? What Diner seems to be suggesting, in the passage just cited, is that Irish American domestics embraced middle-class values and practices simply by virtue of having observed them—what we might call "cultural transformation by osmosis." Kerby Miller and his colleagues (1995, 55) have suggested that Irish domestics internalized middle-class Victorian values because this was what they had to do to keep their jobs. Diane Hotten-Somers (2003), however, has recently suggested that something more complex was going on.

Middle-class wives, Hotten-Somers reminds us, were charged with the ultimate responsibility of ensuring that their households met certain (middle-class) cultural standards. Some of these standards involved the expectation—central to the cult of domesticity that emerged in the nineteenth century—that the middle-class home "should be a haven in a heartless world for their husband and children" (2003, p. 230); but other standards involved more practical matters, like an emphasis on cleanliness and orderliness. But to ensure that these standards were met, middle-class women had to depend on their servants—especially if they wanted to free themselves (as they apparently did) from many of the most onerous household tasks. The result, Hotten-Somers argues, is that mistresses actively involved themselves in the process of transmitting middle-class values to their Irish domestic servants—and if an inexperienced mistress might not know how to do this, there were any number of books and articles to which she could turn for advice.

One such advisor, Mary Allen West, in a journal that catered to a Protestant audience, provided this advice to inexperienced mistresses (1889, 406):

> Systematize work; let each day have its appropriate labor, with margins for the unexpected that always happens, so that when Nora wakes up in the morning she loses no time in wondering what is to be done that day. Having established your system, abide by it, even at the expense of some inconvenience to yourself. Routine work soon becomes second nature, and is performed automatically, thus preventing jars.

Given the emphasis on planfulness and discipline here, such a passage—with only a few minor modifications—could easily be mistaken for the sort of advice presented in *Poor Richard's Almanac,* the source from which Weber would later take so many of the aphorisms that summed up the Protestant work ethic.

A similar emphasis on the need for domestic servants to acquire middle-class values and habits appears in the published advice given to domestic servants themselves. *Advice to Irish Girls in America* (1872), by Margaret Anne Cusack,[1] was addressed explicitly to female domestics who were both Irish and Catholic, and much of her advice was presented using a religious idiom. Cusack, for example, suggests (pp. 87–88) that Irish servants start off the day by saying morning prayers in their room before going down to their work, and then she tells them what to pray for:

— If you are passionate, say "My God help me to keep my temper to-day, however I may be provoked."

— If you are proud, say: "My God help me to be humble to-day, however, I may be tempted to be proud."

— If you are slothful, say "My God, help me to work well and faithfully to-day, and to overcome my natural indolence."

— If you are fond of eating and drinking, say "My God, help me to overcome my love of eating and drinking to-day."

Implicit in this advice is the suggestion that a good domestic needs to acquire a strong sense of self-control. Cusack later spends an entire chapter (pp. 94–102) explaining why honesty and frugality are necessary traits in a domestic. She also advises her readers to adjust to being the object of surveillance:

> Masters and mistresses naturally watch their servants. They cannot help doing so, for so much depends on what they do, and say, and act. They will soon see if a servant does her duty honestly, and they will make their own remarks, though perhaps the girl may never hear them.

Though Cusack writes from a thoroughly Catholic perspective (in later chapters, for example, she explains Catholic doctrine, the differences between Catholicism and Protestantism, and how servants should respond to anti-Catholic bias), the list of attributes she sees as necessary in a good domestic—self-control, honesty and frugality, a willingness to accept scrutiny by others—are, again, the same sorts of middle-class values that Weber saw as central to the Protestant ethic and the same values that would have been of central importance in middle-class American homes generally during the late nineteenth century.

In the end, then, everyone agrees that Irish domestics needed to acquire middle-class values and habits. Diner suggests that the learning process was accomplished by simple observation; Hotten-Somers suggests that middle-class wives played a critical role in the process; and the existence of books like Cusack's suggests that many domestics might have followed the published advice they were given. But I propose that there was something else that worked to equip Irish maids with the middle-class attitudes and habits they needed if they were to properly discharge their duties as maids, and it is something that has been hiding in plain sight for some time: the process of becoming a good Catholic.

Catholicism and Social Discipline

For some time now, a number of scholars, mainly working in Italy and Germany, have called attention to the critical role played by religion in the rise of the modern state in Europe (Gorski 2003a; see especially Prodi 1989; the various essays in Prodi 1994; Reinhard 1989). Their core argument, which builds upon earlier arguments developed by Max Weber, Norbert Elias, and Michel Foucault, is that the new forms of religion that emerged in the wake of the Reformation, in both the Protestant and the Catholic traditions, had the effect (however unintended) of creating the sort of populations on which the modern state depends.

Wolfgang Reinhard (1989), in particular, argues that during the sixteenth century the Catholic Church and the various Protestant churches did the same thing: they transformed themselves into stable groups with well-defined boundaries, a process that he calls "confessionalization." For each group, this was accomplished by (1) settling on a clear statement of doctrine (as occurred for Lutherans with the Augsburg Confession of 1530 and for Catholics at the Council of Trent a few decades later), and (2) eliminating elements in their rituals that might lead to confusion (i.e., elements that might make Catholic rituals seem Protestant or Protestant rituals Catholic). Catholic and Protestant authorities then mounted concerted campaigns to ensure that these newly formulated doctrines and rituals were made central to the religious life of their respective constituencies. This was done in part by using older methods (like preaching) and newer technologies (like printing) to present the doctrines and rituals to these constituencies. But partly, too, churches sought to promote devotional homogeneity through what Paolo Prodi and his students have called *"disciplinamento sociale,"* social disciplining. Partly, this meant simply an increased emphasis on obedience to those in authority. More importantly, however, it involved promoting noncoercive methods of social control. Two methods were especially important: getting people to submit voluntarily to increased surveillance by church authorities (epitomized, at least in the Catholic case, by an increased emphasis on the confessional) and by ensuring that the laity internalized the new norms and values and so self-monitored their own behavior accordingly. Precisely because these ecclesiastical campaigns were so effective in shaping the personality of church members, they created precisely the sort of populations on which the modern state depends, which are—as Reinhard (1989, 397) points out—populations willing to embrace discipline and to be the object of bureaucratic administration.

So what has any of this to do with Irish American Catholicism? I am not aware of anyone working in the social disciplining tradition who has shown an interest in Irish Catholicism, let alone Irish American Catholicism. Nevertheless, the literature just reviewed is relevant to the concerns of this chapter, because the Romanization campaign mounted by the church in the nineteenth century (and which proved so successful in the case of the Famine Irish in America) mimics all the emphases that marked the social disciplining campaign that had been mounted by the post-Reformation church centuries earlier.

The Romanizers sought to *confessionalize* Catholicism by promoting a distinctive set of devotions throughout the Catholic world that very clearly distinguished

Catholics from other Christians. After all, there was nothing in any Protestant tradition (or, for that matter, in any Orthodox Christian tradition) that resembled the devotions most favored by the Romanizers, like devotions to Sacred Heart of Jesus, the Forty Hours, the Immaculate Conception, and so on. Also central to the Romanization campaign, as mentioned several times now, was a strong emphasis on the need for the laity to be obedient—to the pope, to their bishop, and to their local priest. Then, too, it is not difficult to see the attempts by church authorities to secure control over the education of Catholics as an effort to ensure that Catholic laity would internalize Catholic norms and values at an early age and so be able to monitor their own behavior.

Scholars like Reinhard and Prodi, of course, are concerned with great and grand issues like the rise of the modern state and the way in which the social disciplining of European populations contributed to the rise of the state. My argument here is far more prosaic: Irish American women embraced Romanized Catholicism (in ways that Irish American men did not) because—at least at a general level—there was an affinity between the values and behaviors being promoted by the Romanizers and the cultural standards these women were expected to meet by the middle-class families who employed them as domestics. By becoming "good" Catholics they acquired in a fairly obvious way a number of traits desired in a "good" domestic: a willingness to accept authority and discipline, to monitor their own activities, to accept intense surveillance, to be reliable and diligent in their duties, and so forth. The requirement to attend mass on Sundays and holy days of obligation (a "precept of the Church" and one mentioned in all devotional manuals of the period) presupposes an ability to meet deadlines, just as the requirement to fast (take only one meal) or to abstain from meat on certain days during the year presupposes the ability to defer immediate gratification—again, qualities desirable in a domestic. The requirement that Catholics contribute to the support of their local church (another precept of the Church given prominence in devotional manuals of the period) necessitates frugality and a commitment to saving money—both of which, again, were virtues favored in middle-class Protestants households.

Loose Ends

Two problems remain to be resolved. The first is similar to the problem encountered in connection with Miller's nativist hostility hypothesis: even granting that Irish domestics were under strong pressure to reshape their personalities to their employers' expectations, why didn't Irish American Catholics combat hostility toward them by simply becoming Protestant? Would Protestantism have served them as well as Catholicism? Some American historians studying Protestantism (see, for example, Mathews 1969) have advanced an argument similar to the social disciplining theorists', namely, that during the early nineteenth century evangelical Christianity "disciplined" individuals in ways that fit well with the requirements of the emerging national state. Becoming Protestant would have blunted the anti-Catholic bias of Anglo-American employers. So, why wasn't that option taken? The second problem is, of course, explaining why Irish American males—who were certainly not employed as domestics—also (eventually) became good Catholics. In fact, both problems can be resolved by going back, again, to the fact that "being Catholic" and "being Irish" became increasingly intertwined as the nineteenth century progressed. Given that "being Catholic" was increasingly central to an Irish identity, at least for post-Famine emigrants, an Irish domestic who became Protestant would be giving up part of her identity as Irish, something that would mean disassociating herself not only from Ireland but also from family and friends who wished to retain their Irishness. The cost of doing this, I suggest, was just too great. The need to maintain an Irish identity ensured that, for example, Irish domestics would turn to Catholicism, not Protestantism, for the social disciplining that their jobs required.

Male Famine emigrants, as already mentioned, were predisposed to maintain an Irish—and, so, simultaneously, a Catholic—identity because of the intense nationalism that characterized this group at mid-century. Maintaining a Catholic/Irish identity should have inclined them toward religious/ethnic endogamy, that is, toward marrying an Irish Catholic wife, and that is precisely what they did. More than 80 percent of the Irish men who came to the United States in the mid-1800s married Irish Catholic women, a percentage that didn't begin to decline until the 1880s. Husbands and sons were therefore drawn into becoming practicing Catholics by virtue of their association with Irish American women.

Conclusion

So, do I really mean to suggest that it was Irish American women's status as domestics which created in them a predisposition to become good Catholics? Yes, I do. If the affinity between the values required to maintain the stem family and Romanized Catholicism could lead the strong-farmer class in Ireland to embrace Tridentine Catholicism (Hynes), and if the affinity between the values required in business and those central to evangelical Christianity could ensure the success of evangelical Christianity in small town America at the turn of the twentieth century (Weber), then it strikes me as entirely plausible that because Irish American women were under strong pressure from their employers to demonstrate middle-class values they would have been predisposed to undergo the social disciplining that was part and parcel of becoming a good Catholic in nineteenth century America.

None of this is to deny that other factors also contributed to the transformation of Irish immigrants into the gold standard of the American Catholicism. Indeed, I have already identified factors which would have predisposed Irish immigrants to think of themselves as Catholics and to attend a local Catholic church:

- the increasing interconnection between "being Irish" and "being Catholic"
- nativist anti-Irish hostility where it existed
- a desire, especially among women, to gather in a safe institutional context outside the home to discuss issues of concern to immigrants

There were certainly other, eminently practical, considerations that would have brought newly arrived immigrants to the Catholic church. And the effect was cumulative; the more Irish who participated in the local Catholic church, the more it became a gathering place where immigrants new to the area could make contact with relatives, find out what employment opportunities existed in the area, and so on. The fact that many Irish immigrants likely did attend church mostly for practical reasons like these, rather than out of a sense of piety, probably explains why so many pastors in the Midwest and the far West during the period when these areas were first being settled by Famine immigrants (1850–1880) complained that their Irish parishioners were Catholic in name only (Blessing 1977, 245). Indeed, I now suspect that when my ancestor Margaret Fogarty, whose story I told at the beginning of this chapter, got off the boat that first Sunday in Cincinnati to locate a Catholic church, she likely did it more because she was concerned with finding lodging for her and her children than because of a deep attachment to the mass. That she *did* secure shelter for herself and her children because of someone she met at that church only lends plausibility to this interpretation.

Nevertheless, all of these incentives for the Famine Irish to retain a Catholic identity or loosely associate themselves with their local Catholic church do not explain why they and their children became such good Catholics *so quickly*, why they so readily internalized the norms being promoted by the American Catholic Church and regulated their behavior accordingly. To explain *that* we need to examine something that has been overlooked in all existing discussions of Irish American Catholicism: the fact that Irish females in America moved overwhelmingly into domestic service, where success depended upon subjecting themselves to a process of social disciplining, which the ultramontanists then controlling the church were only too willing to provide.

CHAPTER THREE

Italian American Catholicism

The Standard Story and Its Problems

The period from the mid-1960s to the mid-1980s was something of a golden age for the academic study of Italian American Catholicism. Scholarly monographs on particular Italian American communities proliferated, and these monographs inevitably included a chapter on religion. Some of the publications (notably Vecoli 1969; 1977) continue to be cited as authoritative characterizations of Italian American Catholicism. This period also saw the establishment of programs that made it easier for scholars to share and accumulate materials relating to Italian Americans. For example, the American-Italian Historical Association was established in 1966; the stated goal of the association's annual conferences (still continuing) was to promote an understanding of the Italian experience in America by bringing together scholars from a variety of disciplines. Similarly, the Center for Migration Studies (founded in 1966) built up a wide-ranging collection of material relating to Italian American Catholicism and published a number of monographs that were rooted in those materials.

That the study of Italian Americans should have become fashionable during the 1960s and 1970s is not surprising. During this period, social scientists became fascinated with the study of "white ethnics," a label that dumped Italian Americans into the same category as Polish Americans, German Americans, Irish Americans, and so forth (see, for example, Glazer and Moynihan 1970; Greeley 1971; Novak 1972). In retrospect, it seems clear that this scholarly fascination was in large part a response to the demands for social change being made by black and Hispanic Americans. This linkage, however, operated on two levels, both of which we now see to be problematic.

First, as Micaela di Leonardo (1991; 1998, 82–98) has suggested, the "white ethnic" literature was pervaded by a number of empirical claims borrowed directly from the work of authors writing in the black nationalist and Chicano nationalist traditions. These included the claim that the groups involved (whether white or non-white) were associated with ethnically homogeneous inner-city neighborhoods and with cultural traits that had persisted over time despite the group's immersion in a WASP-dominated culture. Unfortunately, as di Leonardo also suggests, there is now much evidence that white European immigrants, Italian Americans in particular, were characterized by far more cultural diversity, and were far less tied to neighborhood, than these early studies suggested (di Leonardo 1984; see also Steinberg 1989).

The literature on these groups was also linked to the demands for change being made at the time because that literature suggested that the experience of nineteenth- and early-twentieth-century immigrants could provide useful lessons about how to bring blacks and Hispanics into the American mainstream. These studies did this, di Leonardo suggested, by positing that certain cultural institutions, especially the family, had been of central importance in securing upward mobility for white immigrants and that problems with these same institutions (e.g., paternal absence, the inability of mothers to control their children, etc.) were what was largely responsible for the fact that non-whites, blacks in particular, were not yet as successful. Such a model was (and is) problematic, di Leonardo continued, because it diverts attention from those structural conditions (like institutional racism, ethnic/racial migration, union seniority systems, and so on) that were of most concern to the groups pressing for social change. The white ethnic literature, in other words, provided scholars (themselves usually white) with a way of solving the "problem" of black and Hispanic disenfranchisement in ways that did not involve challenging white privilege.

Although the study of white European immigrants still has its champions (see for example Vecoli 1996), it is no longer the academic fashion that it once was. Nevertheless, in the specific case of Italian American Catholicism, academics continue to tell what might be called the Standard Story that was popularized (though not invented) during the golden age of white ethnic studies. Furthermore, unlike the emphasis on neighborhood and family in those early studies of white ethnics, the problems of which have now been revealed by scholars like Micaela di Leonardo and Stephen Steinberg, no one has disputed the Standard Story that scholars tell about Italian American Catholicism. Finding the problems in that Standard Story is what this chapter is all about.

My claim is not so much that the Standard Story is wrong (although in some of its details it clearly is wrong) as that it has caused scholars—most of whom are, strangely enough, Italian Americans themselves—to overlook historical patterns that might otherwise provide new insight into the Italian American experience.

Examining these patterns in turn leads to a consideration of *why* the Standard Story—for all its flaws—has retained such a hold over the scholarly imagination. But I'm getting ahead of things. First, what is the Standard Story that scholars tell about Italian American Catholicism?

Pagan Catholicism Crosses the Ocean in the Hearts and Steamer Trunks of Italian Immigrants

In what I am here calling the Standard Story (versions of which can be found in Barrett and Roediger 2005; Bona 2004; DiGiovani 2003; Gambino 1974; Iorizzo and Mondello 1980; Nelli 1980; Pozzetta 1995; Starr 1994; Varacalli 1986; Vecoli 1964; 1969; and Williams 1938), the Italian immigrants who came to the U.S. in the late nineteenth and early twentieth centuries were characterized by *campanilismo*, that is, by a strong attachment to the culture they had known in their natal villages and, in particular, to the sort of Catholicism that had prevailed in those villages. This Catholicism was centered on the patron saints and madonnas who had protected their home villages and was associated with many ritual practices (outdoor processions, appeals for special favors, etc.) characterized by emotional exuberance and ostentatious display. Typically, the Standard Story continues, the folk Catholicism of these Italian immigrants had been formed centuries earlier from the fusion of Christian and pre-Christian elements and reflected the fact that Italy—Southern Italy in particular—had come under the influence of various Mediterranean cultures over the centuries. Rudolph Vecoli (1969, 228) expresses this element of the Standard Story in this way: "In their religion, [Italian] peasants were intensely parochial and traditional. While nominally Roman Catholics, theirs was a folk religion, a fusion of Christian and pre-Christian elements, of animism, polytheism and sorcery with the sacraments of the Church." Some later commentators have repeated Vecoli's characterization verbatim (see for example Mangione and Morreale 1992, 326). Others have said the same thing using only slightly different words. Richard Gambino (1974, 194), for examples, tells us: "Italian-American religious attitudes are unique. They are rooted in a fantastic amalgam of pagan customs, magical beliefs, Mohammedan practices, Christian doctrines, and, most of all, contadino pragmaticism. . . . The special isolating conditions of the Mezzogiorno preserved [these] old customs intact until the period of mass immigration to the United States." What is always missing from these accounts, I must add, is any *evidence* to support the claim being made. In the literature on Italian American Catholicism, the "pagan origins" of the Catholicism presumably brought to the United States by Italian immigrants is always taken to be one of those self-evident truths—comparable to the claim that "the Irish have always been devout" which so often appeared in pre-1970 commentaries on Irish Catholicism—that simply does not need to be documented.

Given the deep attachment of these early immigrants to this variant of Catholicism, the Standard Story continues, it is hardly surprising that it survived the voyage across the Atlantic. In Williams's (1938, 146) words, Italian immigrants "usually had to leave household goods behind for want of transportation money, but their saints and madonnas could be borne over the thousands of miles of ocean, locked in their hearts, and, where possible, also securely packed in their bundles." In turn, this old religion provided immigrants with a way of easing the transition to a new country, because they staged festivals modeled on *feste* in honor of the saints or madonnas who had protected their villages in Italy. Thus, says Vecoli (1969, 231–232):

> The mutual aid societies formed by South Italians bore the names of the patron saints of their respective villages [and] the primary function of these societies was to sponsor the festa of the saint or madonna as the religious confraternity had in the village. The festa was the most authentic expression of South Italian culture transplanted to the New World. . . . Everything was contrived to create the illusion of being once more in the Old Country.

Vecoli's point here has been echoed by many subsequent commentators. Writing more than a decade later, for example, Patrick Gallo (1981, 189) tells us:

> Most of the *feste* were local affairs in honor of the patron saint of a city. These feast days were not only an expression of devotion, they also reflected the nostalgia for the life they have left behind. The procession, the street fair, the crowds of *paesani* created the illusion of being once more back home.

But if the Standard Story tells us something about the sort of religion to which Italian immigrants were attached, it also tells us something about the sort of religion to which they were not attached: they were not attached to the variant of Catholicism favored by the Irish-dominated American Church (discussed in the previous chapter). In particular, Italian Americans were little motivated to do the things at which Irish American Catholics excelled: contribute to the support of their local church, attend Mass on Sundays and holy days of obligation, and obey their priests.

Within the logic of the Standard Story, then, Italian immigrants to the United States were deeply religious but were committed to a type of folk Catholicism that shared little with the Catholicism of the American church. For many commentators (see Barrett and Roediger 2005, 21; DiCarlo 1994, 202–203; Iorizzo and Mondello 1980, 220–221; Lopreato 1970, 87–93), this explains why Irish American clerics (and Irish American Catholics generally) were so hostile to their Italian co-religionists: not only did Italian Catholics fail to meet Irish standards in regard to Catholic practice, but Irish Americans found the pagan nature of Italian Catholicism repugnant. Joseph Varacalli (2006, 77) captures this element in the Standard Story succinctly: "Southern Italian religiosity, however, was both village-centered and heavily infused with folk elements and, as such, was scorned by the more official interpreters of that Catholic faith, which, practically, meant the Irish bishops and priests." Something else implied by this part of the Standard Story is the claim that the allegiance of Italian Americans to the type of Catholicism they had known in Italy impeded their "conversion" to the sort of Catholicism favored by the American church (see for example Varacalli 1986).

Interestingly, most of the articles and monographs that tell the Standard Story have relatively little to say about Italian American Catholicism during the interwar years except to comment briefly on the debate within the church on whether providing Italian Americans with Italian-speaking priests would help or hinder the Americanization process. This omission is important—as we shall see below—because close attention to the religious behavior of Italian Americans in the period between the two World Wars forces a major revision of the Standard Story.

In any event, the Standard Story typically jumps from the pre–World War I period, when Italian Americans were staging their many colorful outdoor festas in the streets of their ethnically homogeneous neighborhoods, to the period after World War II, when a great many Italian Americans were leaving the inner cities for the suburbs. By then, we are told, *campanilismo* had been replaced in the minds of most Italian Americans either by a general "Italian American" identity or, more simply, by an "American" identity—with a corresponding decline in their attachment to the saints and madonnas that had been so important to the first generation of immigrants. "As late as the 1940s," write Iorizzo and Mondello (1980, 226), "street neighborhoods of Italian-Americans in East Harlem still held festivals in honor of patron saints [but subsequently] as village loyalties gave way to a universal Italian-American identity, only the largest observance [in honor of Our Lady of Mt. Carmel] remained."

Still, just as nineteenth-century social evolutionists allowed for cultural survivals (practices from an early stage of social evolution that persisted into later stages even though they no longer served their original function), academics telling the Standard Story allow for something similar. Vecoli (1977, 38), for example, tells us that, after visiting Italian churches throughout the United States in the early 1970s, he can attest that the statues of those early patron saints, "brought with such love and sacrifice from Italy," can still be found somewhere in most of the churches and that efforts to remove them continue to provoke strong protest. Some early festas continued to survive, but without the religious significance they once had. Thus, suggest Iorizzo and Mondello (1980, 227), "over the years the feasts of the paesani made way for the festivals of the Italian-Americans, which in turn have become American celebrations [as] Italian merchants have marketed their saints' day festivals as skillfully as Chinese Americans have marketed their food."

But, suppose we ask a question that is never asked: Is the Standard Story true? It turns out that the answer to this question is not straightforward. Certainly, there are some elements in the Standard Story that need to be revised. As a start, the Standard Story presents a view of Italian Catholicism in *Italy* that has increasingly gone out of fashion among European scholars. Quite some time ago, for example, Jean Delumeau (1977, 166–170) attacked what he called the "seductive but facile" (p. 166) idea that many of the elements found in European folk religion were pagan survivals. In fact, he argued, many of the elements typically seen to be of pagan origin emerged only in the early modern period as Counter Reformation ideas penetrated the countryside and came to be "folklorized," that is, shaped and modified in light of the mode of thinking which prevailed in the countryside. Although Delumeau examined mainly French materials, scholars working with materials from Italy have reached similar conclusions. Gabriele De Rosa (1983), for instance, points out that during the 1960s scholars studying folk religion in Italy increasingly set aside an emphasis on pagan-Christian syncretism in favor of dialectical models that see religious rituals and beliefs as emerging from the interactions between distinct social groups, each pursuing its own political, economic, or spiritual goals. And, certainly, there is much historical evidence indicating that many Catholic cults in Italy which might strike modern audiences as having pagan roots in fact emerged during the early modern period (for examples, see Carroll 1992; 1996).

On the other hand, the Standard Story could easily be modified to take account of this recent deemphasis of the pagan origins of Italian Catholicism by European scholars. After all, within the logic of the Standard Story, it does not really matter if Italian Americans were committed to a type of religion that was several millennia old or only several centuries old; what matters is that it was a type of Catholicism very much at odds with the Catholicism favored by the American church. Even in this modified form, however, the Standard Story would still be problematic, for two reasons, one having to do with *campanilismo* and the other having to do with what Italian Americans were doing in the period between the two world wars.

Reconsidering *Campanilismo*

Did early Italian immigrants to the United States in fact stage colorful outdoor festas in honor of particular saints and madonnas? Yes, they did. Speaking of the Italians in New York, Cantelmo (1906, 161) provides a good contemporary account of such festivals:

> The religious festas that attract public attention if only because they are so frequent . . . are the exact reproductions of the informal celebrations characteristic of particular villages in the Mezzogiorno. Elizabeth [Street] . . . is especially famous for festas of this sort. The Sicilians that live there don't let a week go by without honoring one saint or the other. On these occasions, the streets are adorned, from one end to the other, by a thick array of tricolor lanterns. An altar is erected on the sidewalk and the saint is located there under a canopy with candles all around. The faithful come to pray in front of the altar [and] to leave their offering. All the while a musical band goes up and down the street throughout the day and, in which must be called a test of endurance, blow with determination into their brass instruments. . . . The festa of our Lady of Mt. Carmel that takes place in Little Italy, the Italian quarter of the upper city, includes all the hubbub and all the theatricality of the smaller festas [but on a larger scale]. . . . From twenty to thirty thousand Italians attend this festa, which lasts two or three days, with grand processions, firecrackers, music of all sorts, and a grand fireworks display at the end.

Other accounts published in this same period (see the examples cited in DiCarlo 1990, 85–160) describe Italian American festas in the same way. So, doesn't this mean that the Standard Story is correct? Not quite.

According to the Standard Story, Italians brought with them a folk Catholicism pervaded by *campanilismo,* that is, a Catholicism centered on the patron saints and madonnas associated with their home villages. The first warning flag that something is amiss with this assertion is that many of the festas most popular with Italians living in the United States during the very earliest years of Italian immigration were *not* associated with those localized saints and madonnas.

For example, modern accounts of the well-known festa in honor of Our Lady

of Mt. Carmel in East Harlem routinely mention that this festa was first established in 1881 by Italians from the town of Polla (Province of Salerno) who had
celebrated this festa in Polla itself (see DiCarlo 1990, 103; Orsi 1985, 51; Pistella
1954, 41). This recurrent emphasis on the Polla origins of this well-known festa
creates the impression that it was very much a festa that appealed mainly to Italians from Polla. The problem with this sort of interpretation is that while immigrants from Polla may have established this festa, the very popularity of the festa
is itself evidence that the festa had an appeal that transcended *campanilismo.*
While Cantelmo records that twenty to thirty thousand Italians attended the Madonna del Carmine festa, another account from the same period (Lynch 1901, 118)
puts the figure at closer to forty to fifty thousand Italians. Given these numbers,
it hardly seems likely that attendees were all, or even mainly, from the town of
Polla and the surrounding area. In other words, this festa had a *pan-Italian* appeal
even in the early years of Italian settlement in the United States. Recognizing that
this festa had a pan-Italian appeal helps explain why a festa organized around this
particular madonna became so popular and why churches dedicated to the Madonna del Carmine were common in Italian American communities throughout
the United States, regardless of the specific regional origins of the local Italians
(Primeggia 2004, 30).

Interestingly, I think, an early Italian-language account of the Church of Madonna del Carmine on 115th Street (Ferrante 1906, 91) fails to mention the Polla
origins of this madonna but says instead that this particular church became "the
Italian church" mainly "because of the intense filial devotion toward the Virgin
that lies buried deep inside the people of Southern Italy." The implication here,
in other words, unlike the implication in modern scholarly accounts telling the
Standard Story, is that the "Madonna of 115th St." (to quote from the title of Robert
Orsi's well-known book) was the focus of a popular festa because she was popular with all Southern Italians, not just with those from Polla.

Other festas that became especially popular in the New York area during this
early period, and which were also associated with cults that had a broad (not a
localized) appeal in Italy include

- the festa in honor of San Rocco, established in 1888 at the Church of St.
  Joachim on Roosevelt Street in New York (DiCarlo 1990, 85–86);
- the festa in honor of St. Anthony of Padua, celebrated at the church of the
  same name on Sullivan Street in the late 1800s (DiCarlo 1990, 171–185);
  and

- the festa in honor of the Assumption, established in 1910 on Long Island and the oldest continuing festa in the New York metropolitan area (LaGumina 1987, 8).

I do not deny that many Italian American festas were modeled on the festas held in particular villages in Italy and did appeal mainly to people from those villages. The point is simply that several of the most popular festas from those early years were *not* associated with cults tied to a specific location in Italy and did have a relatively broad appeal within the Italian American community. In other words, the commitment of these early immigrants to festas in honor of local patrons did not prevent them from participating also in festas that had a pan-Italian appeal. I am saying that *campanilismo* has been overemphasized in describing the Catholicism favored by early Italian immigrants to the United States. Such a claim is not entirely new.

Some time ago, John Briggs (1978) sought to gauge the extent of *campanilismo* by using church registers to examine Italian American marriage patterns in various American cities. He found that only a minority of immigrants chose to marry someone from their ancestral commune in Italy. Briggs took this data as suggesting that *campanilismo* was nowhere near as strong as commentators like Vecoli (see in particular Vecoli 1964) had made it out to be. The data from other analyses reinforce Briggs's conclusion here, though commentators often struggle hard to ignore that. For example, as evidence that during the early years of settlement Italian immigrants in Chicago *were* characterized by *campanilismo,* Nelli (1970, 195) points out that, of the 103 marriages at Holy Guardian Angel Church in 1906 involving a bride and groom from the same province, the vast majority (78 of 103, or 76%) involved couples from the same village. Nelli ignores a larger pattern evident in his own data (see his Table 11): looking at *all* the marriages of Italian Americans at this church in this same year, 1906, including interprovincial marriages, less than half (78 of 200, or 39%) involved couples from the same village.

Other investigators have undermined the historiographical emphasis on *campanilismo* by looking at the economic organization of Italian American communities in the early decades of Italian immigration. Sebastian Fichera (2003), for example, points out that while many of the businesses and mutual aid societies in the San Francisco Italian community were indeed linked to social networks rooted in some particular region of Italy, these businesses and societies had always coexisted with others that flourished precisely because they served, and drew support from, *all* segments of the local Italian American community. Fichera points to the Societá Italiana di Mutua Beneficenza (founded in 1858); the Fontana cannery (established in the 1890s), and the Bank of Italy (founded in 1904).

Finally, quite some time ago Silvano Tomasi (1975, 117–175) made the same point about early Italian American religiosity that I am making here: the festas most popular with early immigrants were ones with a pan-Italian, not a localized, appeal. Tomasi's explanation for this is that the earliest immigrants really shared little in common except their commitment to a religion built around festas and public processions. They were not Italian nationalists, since most of them had either opposed Unification or been indifferent to the matter. True, they all spoke Italian but often in mutually unintelligible dialects. The immigrants did have in common that they were generally unskilled and poorly paid laborers working in urban environments, but he argues that the work they did in America was far too disconnected from the work they had done in Italy (and from the traditional ways of thinking about that work) for it to be an effective basis for social solidarity. But their shared religious practices could be used as the basis for social solidarity. They therefore turned to this sort of religion, Tomasi argues, as a way of *eroding campanilismo* and so building a sense of themselves as "Italian" that could provide them with the "security, identity and appropriate environment they needed to move from one civilization to another" (p. 126). Although Tomasi's argument is usually overlooked in discussions of Italian American Catholicism (see Starr 1985, 34 for an exception), it is, I think, entirely consistent with the material reviewed above: the most popular early festas were those organized around madonnas and saints (like the Madonna del Carmine, San Rocco, St. Anthony) who were broadly popular in Italy.

The Italians of San Francisco

The second pattern that seems inconsistent with the Standard Story—and even more damaging—is this: a great many of the festas that were associated with saints and madonnas tied to a specific location in Italy emerged not in the early years of Italian settlement in the United States, 1880–1910, but rather in the aftermath of World War I, when the great age of Italian immigration was coming to an end. Because this upsurge in "localized" festas following World War I is a pattern that has been ignored by previous commentators, it will be useful to begin the discussion by looking carefully at a particularly instructive case, one that (as I mentioned in the Introduction) in some ways gave rise to this book.

During the mid-nineteenth century, the discovery of gold in Northern California attracted a few Italian immigrants to that state, and some of these eventually settled in San Francisco. Italians were not really very numerous in the area during this period, however, especially relative to, say, the Irish. In 1860, for example, there were only 2,805 Italian-born individuals (mainly male) living in the entire state (Nelli 1980), and by 1870 there were only about 1,600 Italians living in San Francisco itself, as compared to 20,000 Irish (Cinel 1982, 18). Only during the 1880s—which is when the most intense phase of Italian immigration to the U.S. began—did Italians begin arriving in San Francisco in relatively large numbers, and most of these settled in the North Beach area of the city. By the time the Immigration Act of 1924 slowed immigration from Italy to a trickle, the San Francisco Italian community had become the sixth largest in the country in absolute numbers and was second only to New York in the proportion of the local foreign-born population who were Italian (Cinel 1982, 19).

As was true in many other Italian communities in the United States, the earliest Italian immigrants to San Francisco were mainly from Northern Italy. What made the San Francisco case a bit different, however, is that this northern predominance continued even after 1880, unlike Italian American communities on the East Coast. Cinel's (1982, 19–34) analysis of marriage and naturalization records indicates that in the late nineteenth and early twentieth centuries, Italians from Northern Italy—most of whom were from Liguria, the region that includes Genoa—accounted for about two-thirds of the San Francisco Italian community. This differs from the pattern associated with most cities on the Eastern Seaboard, where Italians from Southern Italy—especially Campania (the region that includes Naples) and Sicily—came to predominate by the late 1800s.[1]

Almost as soon as Italians began arriving in San Francisco in appreciable numbers, church authorities established a few churches to serve this new constituency. In 1875, Our Lady of Guadalupe Church (whose modern incarnation still stands just above the entrance to the Stockton Street Tunnel) was established to serve the "Latin" community, a category that was meant to include both Spanish speakers and Italians. During the early 1880s, presumably as a result of the increased immigration during this period, it was decided that Italians needed their own church. As a result, the Church of San Pietro was built in North Beach in 1884 specifically for Italians. This church, renamed Santi Pietro e Paolo (hereafter SSPP) in 1888, was formally designated an Italian national church in 1897. This meant that it had no precise parish boundaries and could draw (or attempt to draw) Italian American Catholics from the entire San Francisco Bay area. In 1898, the pastor at SSPP established Corpus Christi as a satellite church in the outer Mission District to serve the large number of Italians, mainly truck farmers, who had settled in that area (Baccari, Scarpaci, and Zavattaro 1985, 38). In 1912, diocesan authorities established Immaculate Conception on Folsom Street as another Italian national church (Frangini 1914).

SSPP, always the main Italian church in San Francisco, was destroyed in the 1906 earthquake but a substitute structure was built within the year. In 1908 a fund-raising campaign was begun to build a larger and more permanent SSPP, and by 1914, the spacious crypt of the new church had been completed and served as a place to celebrate mass. The new—and architecturally quite impressive— SSPP was completed in 1924, and this is the church that still stands just opposite Washington Square in North Beach.

The best way to understand the significance of SSPP to the Standard Story told about Italian American Catholicism is to visit the three chapels at the back of the church. Because San Francisco is a popular tourist destination and a favored location for academic conferences, and since SSPP is a comfortable 10–15 minute walk from either Chinatown or Fisherman's Wharf, I suspect that a great many readers of this book will have the opportunity to do just that. What still remains in those back chapels, even though the congregation at SSPP long ago became predominantly Chinese American, are a number of images depicting madonnas associated with a specific village or region in Italy.

The most prominent of these localized madonnas is the Madonna della Guardia, whose statue is set above her own altar in the chapel immediately to the right as you enter (see Figure 3). The Italian sanctuary of the Madonna della Guardia in Italy is on Monte Figogna, just outside Genoa, and she has for centuries been the single most popular madonna in Liguria (Carroll 1992, 64–71). Other localized madonnas still represented in one or the other of these back chapels include:

- The Madonna dei Miracoli di Cicagna, whose sanctuary is in the town of Cicagna in the Val Fontanabuona (Liguria), and so close to the village of Lorsica, from which so many of San Francisco's Italians emigrated;
- The Madonna del Lume, Patron of the village of Porticello (Sicily)
- The Madonna del Pettoruto, whose sanctuary is near the community of San Sosti in Calabria

The temptation is to see these back chapel madonnas as the ones who figure so prominently in the first part of the Standard Story, the madonnas to whom early immigrants clung so tightly—both figuratively and literally—as they crossed the ocean. Under this interpretation, the statues and other images found in the three back chapels at SSPP would seem an example Vecoli's observation that most of the churches which once served Italian immigrants still have rooms containing

Fig. 3. Altar dedicated to the Madonna della Guardia in one of the three chapels at the back of Saints Peter and Paul Church in the North Beach area of San Francisco.

the images of saints and madonnas "brought with such love and sacrifice from Italy." Indeed, some accounts of the San Francisco Italian community have interpreted the back chapel madonnas at SSPP in just this way. Deana Gumina (1978, 47), for example, in a section of her book *The Italians of San Francisco*, in discussing life in North Beach during the late 1800s, tells us:

> No matter how long ago these Italian immigrants had migrated, they never failed to hold a fair or festival in honor of the patron saint of their birthplace. This too proves the importance of "campanilismo." The most popular of these regional feasts was the blessing of the fishing fleet in October [in honor of] "La Madonna del Lume di

Porticello." . . . There were numerous devotions to the Blessed Mother, such as the Madonna della Guardia and the Madonna della Grazia.

For Gumina, in other words, the back chapel madonnas still resident at SSPP are indeed—just as the Standard Story suggests—the madonnas to whom early Italian immigrants clung so tightly as part of their *campanilismo*.

However, if we do what commentators like Gumina do not do and pay careful attention to just *when* the back chapel madonnas at SSPP made their first appearance there, what we find is something quite different from what the Standard Story leads us to expect. There is nothing in the documentary record to suggest that prior to World War I the Italian Americans associated with SSPP had any interest whatsoever in cults organized around localized saints or madonnas. The fact is that every one of the cults organized around the "localized" madonnas now resident in the back chapels of SSPP appears in the documentary record in the aftermath of the First World War.

Madonna della Guardia was the first to arrive. Sometime circa 1918, an informal society dedicated to this madonna was formed by a group of parishioners at SSPP (one of them my great-grandaunt, Maria Demartini).[2] It is noteworthy that most of these parishioners were Northern Italians. In those early years, Society members met for a community dinner on the occasion of this madonna's feast day (August 29th) and fostered devotion to her by purchasing and distributing holy cards and other sacramental objects. It seems to have taken a few years for this devotion to be legitimated by the clergy, but in the September 1922 issue of *Il messagiero di Don Bosco*, SSPP's parish bulletin, it was announced (p. 7) that, at the request of "a group of devoted Genovesi," that is, people from the Genoa region, the festa of this madonna would for the first time be solemnly celebrated on her feast day. In August 1925 a call went out for donations to be used to purchase a statue of this madonna and an associated altar to go in the new church building, and by October of the same year the parish bulletin could report that $1,800.00 had already been raised. The statue and altar subsequently purchased are the ones currently in place at SSPP. From this point forward, descriptions of this madonna's festa in both the parish bulletin and local Italian-language newspapers (see for example, *L'Italia*, 28 August 1926) make it clear that the annual festa involved moving the statue to one of the side altars at the front of the church, celebrating a High Mass on the morning of the feast day and holding a ceremony in the evening that included prayers and preaching, processing with the statue inside the church and serving a community dinner.

Almost immediately a second localized madonna made her appearance at

SSPP: the parish bulletin for September 1925 announced (p. 3), "A group of fine *connazionali* from Cicagna and the surrounding area have called upon us to solemnize their regional festa in honor of the Madonnna dei Miracoli—and we are only too glad to do so" and her festa was celebrated for the first time that month. Cicagna, being in the Val Fontanabuona, is near the village of Lorsica, where so many San Francisco Italians were from. The Madonna dei Miracoli, then, was another localized madonna whose cult was being promoted by Northern Italians. In that same bulletin, the pastor at SSPP set out an official policy (p. 4) on the celebration of these regional festas which (1) established certain limits but also (2) explained why they were valuable:

> In all cases, these regional festas revitalize one's faith and provide an incentive to receive the Blessed Sacrament. So long as they are stripped of the theatricality and exterioriality that we unfortunately see elsewhere, such festas are good both for those who take an active role in the celebration and for those who watch—and it is something that also benefits the Church itself. Of course it goes without saying that these festas must be organized under the supervision of our parish priests.

Left unexplained, of course, is why, if such festas were indeed so useful to Italian Catholics, they had not been celebrated at SSPP during the preceding forty years.

As far as I can ascertain from the parish bulletin, the Madonna della Guardia and the Madonna dei Miracoli di Cicagna were the only localized madonnas installed at SSPP during the 1920s. Another cluster of localized madonnas, however, emerged during the 1930s, only this time they were (with one exception) madonnas tied to communities locations in Southern Italy. Table 5 lists all the localized madonnas associated with cults at SSPP, starting with the Madonna della Guardia, and the year when each madonna's festa was first celebrated in the parish (based on information from the parish bulletin).

The case of the Madonna del Lume (whose festa was first celebrated in 1938) is especially interesting, since she was the first madonna at SSPP to be honored with an outdoor procession. In August 1938 a number of fishermen whose ancestral home was Porticello, Sicily, with the approval of the pastor at SSPP, submitted a petition to Archbishop Mitty (on file in the archdiocesan archives) asking for permission to stage a procession from SSPP to their fishing boats at Fisherman's Wharf. They noted that such a procession would be similar not simply to the processions staged in Porticello but also to the processions staged by fellow fishermen in eastern U.S. cities.

On the face of it, then, the development of Italian American Catholicism in San Francisco seems to turn the Standard Story on its head. During the first four

TABLE 5
*Localized Madonnas at Saints Peter and Paul Church, San Francisco,
by Date of First Appearance in the Parish Bulletin*

Year First Mentioned	Name	Associated Location in Italy
1922	Madonna della Guardia	Primary sanctuary is on Monte Figogna, near Genoa (Liguria)
1925	Madonna dei Miracoli	Patron of Cicagna, in the Val Fontanabuona (Liguria)
1937	Madonna della Misericordia	Patron of the city of Savona and communities in Val Letimbro (Liguria)
1938	Madonna del Lume	Patron of Porticello (Sicily)
1939	Madonna delle Grazie	Patron of Verbicaro (Calabria)
1940	Madonna di Trapani	Sanctuary is near Trapani (Sicily)
1940	Madonna del Pettoruto	Sanctuary is in San Sosti (Calabria)

decades of Italian settlement (1880–1920) there was nothing particularly distinctive about the Catholicism of the San Francisco Italian community. Then, starting in the early 1920s, we see the emergence of cults organized about madonnas tied to specific villages and regions in Italy, a process that continues in the late 1930s and which only then comes to involve the sort of outdoor procession that is supposedly characteristic of folk religion in Southern Italy.

The *absence* of local and regional festas in the San Francisco Italian American community over the period from 1880–1915 is not especially problematic. By the late nineteenth century, it was commonplace for Italians from Northern Italy to think of themselves as more civilized and less emotional than Italians from Southern Italy. It seems plausible to suggest, then, that this sort of thinking predisposed Italian Americans in North Beach—who were predominantly from the North—to disassociate themselves from the sort of ostentatious festas more commonly found in eastern U.S. cities (where Southern Italians predominated). But what obviously *is* problematic in the case of San Francisco—at least against the backdrop of the Standard Story—is the proliferation of festas organized around localized madonnas after World War I, especially given that Northerners were at the forefront in promoting this type of festa.

The Rise of "Localized" Cults Elsewhere following World War I

Because religious devotions organized around localized madonnas and saints were generally absent in San Francisco during the first few decades of Italian settlement there, the emergence of such devotions in the post–World War I period is relatively easy to detect in the documentary record (at least once we set the

Standard Story aside and read that record in a way that allows for this possibility). By the same token, of course, what happened in other Italian American communities is more difficult to determine, because the Standard Story seems to have more credibility. In these other cases, we know that some festas in honor of localized saints and madonnas *were* staged in the earliest years of Italian settlement in the United States. Something else that might cloud our vision in examining what happened in other areas is the claim, made by scholars like Stefano Luconi (2001, 39–55), that U.S. participation in the First World War as an ally of Italy fostered an Italian national identity among Italian Americans and that this national identity as "Italians" eroded the regional identities to which they had previously been committed. Under this view, we would expect less of an emphasis on regional diversity among Italian Americans in the period immediately following World War I. Nevertheless, once we allow the San Francisco case to sensitize us to the importance of determining just when a festa was first celebrated, a careful reading of existing studies brings to light evidence that localized festas were also established in other Italian American communities just as the great age of Italian immigration was coming to a close. Consider first what is unquestionably the most important example here: the festa of San Gennaro in Manhattan.

The San Gennaro festa has long been among the most popular, if not *the* most popular, Italian festa in the United States. Estimates by the New York City Police Department during the mid-1980s (cited in DiCarlo 1990, 198) indicate that between one and a half to two million people attended this particular festa annually at that time. The festa has also figured in a great many movies (like *Godfather II*), books, and television shows (a *CSI: New York* episode in 2005, for example, featured the festival as a backdrop). This very popular festa is centered on a figure who is strongly localized: for several centuries San Gennaro has been the primary patron of the city of Naples, and the festa in his honor at Naples (which involves the liquefaction of his blood) has long been one of the best-known festas in Italy itself. And yet, despite the fact that New York's San Gennaro festa might seem to be the prototype of all localized festas, and despite the fact that Neapolitans settled in New York beginning in the 1880s, this festa was not established there until 1928 (DiCarlo 1990, 189–202). The San Gennaro festa, therefore, emerged in Manhattan's Little Italy at almost exactly the same time that Italian Americans in San Francisco decided to celebrate festas in honor of the Madonna della Guardia and the Madonna dei Miracoli di Cicagna.

Another important festa in the New York area that continues to be celebrated, and which rivals the San Gennaro festa in popularity, is also centered on a strongly localized saint. This is Brooklyn's festa in honor of St. Paulinus, patron of Nola (a city near Naples). Although the St. Paulinus festa is celebrated over a period that can last for two weeks or more, during which time attendees devote themselves to a mix of religious and secular activities, the high point—as Salvatore Primeggia and Joseph Varacalli (1996) point out—is "Giglio Sunday." On this day, more than a hundred men carry the Giglio, a tower that is about 65 feet high and that weighs about 4 tons, in procession to the local church; there they are met by a second group of men carrying a huge boat. The Brooklyn festa is modeled on a similar (but even more elaborate) festa that has been staged in Nola itself for centuries. And yet, despite the fact that Nolani had settled in the Brooklyn area well before the turn of the century, the available documentary evidence suggests that the Brooklyn festa in honor of St. Paulinus only emerged in the 1920s (Posen and Sciorra 1983, 32).

Additional examples of especially popular Italian American festas that (1) honored localized saints or madonnas and (2) made their American appearance only in the 1920s and 1930s include: the festa in honor of Santa Rosalia (Patron saint of Palermo) at Monterey, California, established in 1934 (Speroni 1955); the festa in honor of the Madonna della Rocca, patron of Alesandria della Rocca, Sicily, established in Tampa, Florida, in the early 1930s (Mormino and Pozzetta 1987, 223); the festa in honor of San Benedetto, patron of San Fratello, Sicily, established in Manhattan during the mid-1920s (D'Angelo 1994); and the festa in honor of San Rocco, patron of Patrica, near Rome, established in Aliquippa, Pennsylvania, in 1925 (Urick 1969).

Although it would certainly be useful to root through the archives of Italian churches throughout the United States to determine if there were other festas in honor of localized saints and madonnas which emerged in the 1920s and 1930s, the examples mentioned in the preceding paragraphs—especially given that they involve two of the most popular Italian American festas—seem (to me, at least) sufficient to establish that the San Francisco case was not unique. Simply put, contrary to what the Standard Story leads us to expect, a number of very popular festas organized around saintly patrons tied to a specific community in Italy came into existence in the United States only in the aftermath of World War I, as the age of Italian immigration was coming to a close.

As an aside, I should note that, in discussing these post–First World War festas, many commentators have done what Gumina did in the San Francisco case: assimilate the history of these festas in terms of the Standard Story by implying—without ever saying it directly—that they emerged in the earliest years of Italian settlement. Jerre Mangione and Ben Morreale (1992, 169), for example, begin their discussion of Italian feast days by suggesting that they were common in Italian communities around "the turn of the century"; then they quickly move to a paragraph (p. 170) stating that the San Gennaro festival was among the most popular of these festivals. Similarly, Luciano Iorizzo and Salvatore Mondello (1980) discuss the Manhattan festa in honor of San Benedetto in a section of their book where they are describing churches established for Italian immigrants in the late 1800s. The strong implication in both cases is that the festa being described first emerged in the late nineteenth century when in fact, as noted above, both festas were established in the 1920s.

What still needs to be explained, of course, is *why* Italian Americans would have developed a renewed interest in localized festas in the years following World War I. While the Standard Story's assertion that Italian immigrants staged festas centered on localized saints and madonnas to recreate something familiar in an otherwise new and strange location might indeed explain why festas of this type were established in the late 1800s (as some were), it hardly seems adequate to explain why so many such festas emerged in the 1920s and '30s. But, if we set the Standard Story aside and look to the Italian experience in America—not Italy—for the cause of this upsurge, then something quite obvious leaps to mind.

The Nativist Revival and Its Effect on Italian American Culture

The last two decades of the nineteenth century and the first two decades of the twentieth saw rising nativist sentiment among middle-class white Protestants in the United States, and this group used its considerable power to attack groups and practices seen to be a threat to their vision of what America should be (Dolan 2002, 127–189 provides an especially succinct account of this movement). Although Italian immigrants were not the only group targeted in this nativist campaign, several things made them a preferred target. First, by the turn of the century, Italians were the largest of the immigrant groups entering the United States and so were especially indicative of the immigration "problem." The Dillingham Commission (Dillingham 1911, I:97), for example, reported that more than two million Italian immigrants had entered the United States from 1899 to 1910, which was more than twice the number in each of the next two largest groups ("Hebrews" and Poles). Second, as Joseph Cosco (2003) points out, American popular thinking in this period was strongly racialized, and although many immigrant groups were considered "less than white," Italians were especially likely to be seen as "colored" by virtue of their complexion and their greater willingness to associate with blacks. For Cosco, the best single indicator of Italian racial status around the turn of the twentieth century is the fact that Italians were the only immigrants who were lynched in any significant number. Third, Italians were at least nominally Catholic and so were targets of the anti-Catholicism that had been a part of all American nativist movements since the arrival of the Famine Irish in the mid-nineteenth century. And finally, as if all this were not bad enough, Italians—more so than most other immigrant groups—were linked to criminal activity.

By the turn of the century, "the image of a mysterious, blood-thirsty Black Hand society" (Cosco 2003, 38) had become a stock element in newspaper and magazine stories about Italian immigrants. But, just as importantly, this popular stereotype was often legitimized by U.S. political leaders. The 1911 Report of the Dillingham Commission, for example, although it otherwise sought to debunk the notion that immigrants were predisposed to crime, was quite clear in suggesting that in the case of Italian immigrants the popular stereotype was correct. The commission (Dillingham 1911, I:33) said that, while it was true that immigrants in general were more likely to commit crimes, this was due mainly to two things: immigrants often violated minor local ordinances (for example, prohibiting noncitizens from peddling) and immigrants were disproportionately young males, the group most prone to crime even among the native-born. But against this backdrop of apparent even-handedness, the commission nevertheless singled out Italians as being especially prone to violent crime and gave two reasons for this. The first was that Southern Italians were by nature "excitable, impulsive, highly imaginative, [and] impractical" (I:33). The second was that criminal organizations were a fact of life in Southern Italy. The report specifically mentioned "the secret organizations of the Mafia and Comorra [sic], institutions of great influence among the people, which take the law into their hands and are responsible for much of the crime, flourish throughout southern Italy" (I:251). Not surprisingly, then, the commission went on to conclude (II:164):

> The increase in offenses of personal violence in this country is largely traceable to immigration from southern Europe and especially from Italy. This is most marked in connection with the crime of homicide: of all the various races and nationality groups appearing in the data collected the Italian stands out prominently as having the largest percentage of cases of homicide among its crimes.

In retrospect, it is easy to find flaws in the reasoning that led to this conclusion. In the commission's assessment of the link between Italian immigrants and violent crime, no attempt was made to control for recency of immigration or income levels, even though both things might plausibly have correlated with the likelihood of committing violent crime. But more importantly, the commission never really got around to presenting data which established either that rates of violent crime had indeed increased with increased immigration or that Italians were overrepresented among those convicted of violent crime as compared to the general population. In an era when social scientific reasoning was at best embryonic, such flaws were overlooked. What counted was only that an authoritative Senate committee was telling the American people that Italian immigrants were a source of danger to law-abiding citizens.

The building nativist backlash against immigrants generally, and against Italian Americans in particular, reached a peak around the First World War. The two most visible consequences of this backlash, and certainly the two that fell most heavily on Italian Americans, were a revised immigration policy and Prohibition. Although the Dillingham Commission, with one lone dissenter, had endorsed a literacy test as the best way to restrict and control immigration, it was one of the six other recommendations they listed that ultimately proved to be more important. The commission proposed that there be "a limitation of the number of each race arriving each year to a certain percentage of the average of that race arriving during a given period of years" (Dillingham 1911, I:47–48). It was this proposal by the Dillingham Commission that led directly to a critical turning point in U.S. immigration history, the establishment of immigration quotas based on national origins.

In 1921 Congress passed the Emergency Quota Act. This act did two things: first, it put a cap on the overall number of immigrants that would be admitted; and second, it allocated to each national group from Europe, Italians included, a quota equivalent to 3 percent of the total number of foreign-born persons from that group living in the United States at the time of the 1910 census. A second and even more restrictive immigration bill was passed in 1924. In this new bill, the percentage used in calculating national quotas was reduced from 3 percent to 2 percent and the baseline for calculating quotes became the 1890 census. Italians were especially hard-hit by pushing the baseline back from 1910 to 1890, because Italian immigration had increased dramatically over precisely those two intervening decades.

Some idea of the impact of these rules on Italian immigration can be found in the remarks made by Representative Albert Johnson (cited in Daniels 1997, 135), a strong supporter of the 1924 bill, who pointed out that a 2 percent quota using the results of the 1920 census (which was by then available) would create a quota of 42,000 Italian immigrants, while applying a 2 percent quota to the results of the 1890 census would generate only 4,000 slots for Italian immigrants, a reduction of more than 90 percent. Although the 1924 law was not as effective in capping immigration in general as it was meant to be, it did have the effect of ensuring that most European immigrants after 1924 were from Britain, Ireland, or Germany rather than from Southern and Central Europe (Daniels 1997, 140–141). Regarding Italian immigration specifically, the new law was if anything more effective than supporters like Albert Johnson had predicted. Thus, while 285,731 Italian immigrants had entered the United States in 1907, in 1922 only 42,057 had arrived and by 1925, the first year after the passage of the new act, the number had declined further, to 3,845 (Shanks 2001, 93), for an overall reduction of more than 98 percent.[3]

A second, though perhaps slightly less obvious, consequence of the rising nativist campaign against immigrants was Prohibition. Although a few American Catholic leaders supported Prohibition, most were against it; Prohibition drew its support mainly from the same segment of the population (white middle-class Protestants) who most supported restrictions on immigration. Indeed, to the American Protestant groups promoting Prohibition, there was a clear connection between alcohol consumption, immigrants, and the threat to American culture. James Timberlake (1963, 117) provides a succinct account of the links perceived to exist here: "To old stock Americans, liquor demoralized the immigrant, kept him in poverty, intensified his discontent, unfitted him to exercise the duties of responsible citizenship and prevented him from becoming Americanized." Implicit in this sort of thinking is the claim that "old stock Americans" (the standard code word for native-born Protestants) possessed an inborn capacity for self-discipline that had contributed to the American way of life; indeed, those supporting Prohibition were often quite willing to say this explicitly. For example, in explaining who did and did not support Prohibition, Harry S. Warner (1928, 42) declared:

> It was among those that have been most influenced by ideals of liberty and religious freedom . . . who have shown the ability to organize and unite for the accomplishment of desired results, that the revolt against drink was most extensive and severe.
> . . . The sort of people who organized the new form of government—a republic organized the social adventure that was marked, in 1920, by the going into effect of an Eighteenth Amendment to the Constitution of their forefathers.

On balance, the message here seems clear: Prohibition is supported by the same sort of people who made the American Revolution a success, and it is also something that over time will improve the moral fiber of those immigrant groups who presently threaten the democratic ideals that have been central to the Revolution.

From the perspective of Italian Americans, by contrast, it was not Prohibition's effect on drinking behavior per se that made it so problematic. Italians, after all, were a wine-drinking culture, well-accustomed to making wine at home, and the original legislation enacting Prohibition did permit a certain amount of wine to be made and consumed in the privacy of a person's home. Nevertheless, while it might still be legal for Italian Americans to consume wine at home, they understood all too well the symbolic importance of Prohibition: it suggested that cultures like theirs, in which the consumption of alcohol (in whatever quantities) was an essential part of the social rituals associated with births, weddings, daily meals, and so forth, were inferior to and morally suspect according to an implicit American Protestant norm.

The devaluation of Italian culture implicit in the logic of Prohibition almost certainly explains why Italian Americans were in the forefront of violating the law. The involvement of Italian Americans in organized bootlegging activities—epitomized by the likes of Johnny Torrio, Al Capone, Frank Nitti, Tony Accardo, and Joe Masseria—is a familiar story that need not be repeated here. Less appreciated, perhaps, is the degree to which ordinary Italian Americans violated Prohibition laws. In 1929, 27 percent of those arrested in San Francisco for violating Prohibition laws were Italian Americans born in Italy (Giovinco 1968, 21), and the percentage would obviously be higher if it also included Italian Americans born in the United States.[4]

Italian Americans employed several strategies in responding to the nativist assault epitomized by the new immigration policy and by Prohibition. One such strategy was simply to return to Italy, and indeed return migration increased dramatically in this period. American immigration reports indicate that in 1890 the number of people returning to Italy was only 10 percent of the number arriving from there; this statistic increased to 34 percent for the period 1891–1900, to 57 percent for the period 1901–1910, and to a fairly dramatic 82 percent for the period 1911–1920 (Tomasi 1975, 18–19). But what of the Italian Americans who chose to remain in the United States? How did they respond to the nativist assault? Likely there were many ways of responding, but a significant number, I suggest, responded by valorizing their *Italianità* using a religious idiom, by taking a renewed pride in the very things—like festas—that most distinguished them from their fellow Catholics and that most attracted disparaging remarks from their nativist critics.

I believe that the upsurge in new Italian festas in the 1920s—events whose focus on saints and madonnas and whose outdoor exuberance and emotionalism were a direct repudiation of the white middle-class Protestant vision of religion—was a creative response on the part of Italian Americans to the nativist campaign being waged against them and that had caused two sets of hurtful laws to be passed by the federal government. These new festas, in other words, were a way of affirming the value of "being Italian" in the face of federal laws and popular attitudes which devalued Italian culture. Still, while this might explain why Italian Americans were predisposed to embrace the festa experience, it does not quite explain why so many of the festas they created were centered on strongly localized saints and madonnas. After all, new (or renewed) festas centering on "generically Italian" saints and madonnas, like San Rocco and the Madonna del Carmine, could also have functioned as affirmations of *Italianità*.

The key to understanding the special appeal of festas centering on localized saints and madonnas, I think, lies in recognizing that a great many Italian Americans held the same view of Italy and Italian Catholicism as the academics telling the Standard Story: the Italy of their ancestors was a strongly regionalized society in which different local communities were each strongly attached to their own special saintly patron. But whereas academics telling the Standard Story see in this an Italy pervaded by *campanilismo* and parochialism, Italian Americans, I believe, saw something else: a society that was tolerant of local diversity in a way that American society was not. Establishing and promoting new festas organized around saints and madonnas that were explicitly tied to some particular community in Italy was a way for Italian Americans to affirm the value of local diversity and so to protest the emphasis on cultural homogeneity that was implicit in the nativist campaign being waged against them.

The underlying contention here, namely, that an emphasis on Italy's local diversity was an act of resistance to an emphasis on cultural homogeneity, is not itself new. In commenting on Italian American community life during the early 1990s, for example, Rudolph Vecoli (1996, 10–11) tells us:

> [Italian American] interest in Italy . . . increasingly takes the form of a reaffirmation of specific regional or local origins. Associations based on such ties are burgeoning: Figli di Calabria, Piemontesi nel Mondo, Trentini nel Mondo, Cuore Napoletano, Lucchesi nel Mondo, etc. . . . For myself, I derive a greater satisfaction from my Lucchese-American identity based on specific cultural traditions than the more abstract idea of being Italian American. *Since I abhor the idea of all melting pots, I applaud this revival of localized dialects and traditions.* (Emphasis added.)

For Vecoli, in other words, an emphasis on Italy's cultural diversity at the local level is a way of resisting the melting pot ideology. I am suggesting only that a great many Italian Americans in the 1920s and 1930s held this same attitude, which is precisely why they responded to the nativist campaign being waged against them by establishing and promoting new Catholic festas (like those honoring the Madonna della Guardia, the Madonna del Lume, San Gennaro, San Paulinus, etc.) organized around saints and madonnas tied to very specific local communities in Italy.

Taking Stock

Thus far I have suggested that there are two patterns associated with Italian American Catholicism which are not consistent with the Standard Story. The first is that the Catholicism of the first Italian immigrants was less pervaded by *campanilismo* than generally thought, and the second is that many of the most popular cults organized around localized saints and madonnas emerged not in the early years of Italian settlement but rather in the wake of the First World War. The first pattern demonstrates that Italian Americans were easily able to overcome *campanilismo* even in the earliest years of Italian settlement, while the second pattern can be seen as a creative response to the nativist campaign that reached a peak around the First World War. In contrast to the Standard Story, which constructs Italian immigrants as an intensively parochial people clinging passively to age-old traditions learned in their home villages, what emerges from this analysis is a characterization of Italian Americans that not only frees them from the "prisoner of tradition" imagery implicit in the Standard Story but also interprets the rise of localized festas in the aftermath of World War I as a self-assertive reaction to the changing social circumstances.

But all of this raises a new question, one that has more to do with historiography than history. If the Standard Story has caused us to ignore a number of historical patterns and theoretical possibilities that are consistent with those patterns, why has it retained such a hold over the scholarly imagination for so long?

The Origins of the Standard Story

As we saw in the previous chapter, it has long been common for scholars to state that the Famine Irish were good Catholics as soon as they arrived in the United States. This claim rests squarely on what church leaders themselves were saying in the late nineteenth and early twentieth centuries. Is the same thing true in this case, that is, in telling the Standard Story about Italian American Catholicism, are scholars simply repeating what leaders of the American Catholic Church were saying about Italian immigrants? The answer depends on what part of the Standard Story we are talking about.

Certainly, it is easy to locate statements by leaders of the American church suggesting that Italian immigrants came nowhere close to being "good" Catholics in the way that the Irish were good Catholics (for examples here, see Tomasi 1975, 43–60). But did leaders of the American church believe that Italian immigrants were committed to a Catholicism pervaded by pagan elements and that their commitment to this pagan Catholicism impeded their "conversion" to the sort of Catholicism favored in America? Scholars telling the Standard Story often imply that the answer here is yes on both counts.

Rudolph Vecoli, for example, tells us that "Americans, Catholics and Protestants alike, came to regard the Italian immigrants as little better than pagans and idolaters" (1969, 233) and that "with few exceptions, American Protestants *and* [Vecoli's emphasis] Catholics agreed that the Italian immigrants were characterized by ignorance of Christian doctrine, image worship, superstitious emotionalism; in short, they were not true Christians" (1977, 25). Vecoli's claim that *Protestant* commentators leveled charges of idolatry and paganism at Italian Americans is, of course, something easy to document; and, indeed, a review of these Protestant claims will be critical to the argument that I will be developing about Protestant influence and the study of Catholicism in the final section of this chapter. But, is Vecoli right in suggesting that *Catholic* leaders (generally) held the same attitude? Here we need to look carefully at the evidence that Vecoli brings forward in support of this contention. Vecoli (1969, 234) tells us:

> The indictment of the religious culture of the Italians [by Catholic leaders] was summed up in the Jesuit journal, *America:* "Piety does not consist in processions or carrying candles, in prostrations before a statue of the Madonna, in processions in honor of patron saints of villages, but true piety consists in the daily fulfillment of the religious duties exacted of us by God Almighty and His Church and it consists in a love for the Church and her ministers. In these points, no matter how numerous be the Italian processions, no matter how heavy the candles, no matter how many lights they carry, the Italian immigrant seems very deficient." (See Figure 4.)

The passage that Vecoli is quoting appeared in the October 1914 issue of *America* and was written by a "Mr. Herbert Hadley." Hadley's letter was only one of twenty-nine letters on the "Italian problem" published in that journal between October and December of that year (when the editor brought the discussion to a close).

Are the views that Hadley expresses in the passage quoted above representative of what was said in all the letters published, and are they representative of the views held by the leadership of the American church generally (which Vecoli

Fig. 4. Men and boys outside a store in New York's Little Italy, 1908. Note the three immense, heavily ornamented candles and the pile of slightly smaller ones; such candles were votive offerings carried in procession during a festa. Courtesy of Library of Congress, Prints and Photographs Division, LC-USZ62-114764.

implies)? The answer in both cases is no. While some of the writers who took part in the *America* debate did indeed share Hadley's evident disdain for Italian and Italian American religious practices, many others did not. But what is even more important, I suggest, is that a correlation emerges when we consider the relationship between *who* was writing each particular letter and *what* was being said. Generally, letters written by clerics who had worked closely with Italian Americans were relatively tolerant of Italian religious practices while letters written by laymen (like Hadley) or by clerics who had had little or no direct experience with Italian Americans were not tolerant. Writing in direct response to Hadley, for example, Joseph M. Sorrentino, S.J. (1914, 194) said:

> As to statues, processions, heavy candles, emotionalism, etc., let me remind my opponents that as a Catholic priest, I know as well as they do that religion does not consist in such exterior practices; often, however, they are a sign of the Faith abiding in the heart and, moreover, are a real help in drawing people nearer to God. The Catholic Church approves of them.

Like Sorrentino, many of the clerics who were sympathetic to Italian Catholicism had Italian names, something that might be taken as compromising their objectivity, but others did not. Edmund M. Dunne (1914a), Bishop of Peoria, for instance, also contributed to the *America* debate. Dunne had been pastor at Guardian Angel parish in Chicago (which he describes as "the largest Italian parish in America") and in light of that experience had this to say about Italian American religiosity:

> My experience has been to see the church crowded on the feasts of SS. Peter and Paul, Nativity of John the Baptist, SS. Vitus, Roch, Lucy, Sebastian and the feasts of the Blessed Virgin just the same as on Sunday. As to approaching the sacraments, I have been kept hearing the confessions of Italian men until after two o'clock Holy Thursday morning. Poor Sicilians have come fasting twenty-one miles on the train in order to fulfill their Easter Duty.

The important thing to note here is what is missing: there is nothing whatsoever in Dunne's account (either in this passage or in the entire letter) to suggest that he saw anything pagan about Italian Catholic practice nor anything in distinctively Italian religious practices that was a bar to Italians becoming good Catholics.

Dunne's *America* letter, I grant, needed to be concise, but Bishop Dunne also made no mention of pagan elements when he discussed Italian American Catholicism at greater length, even when directing criticisms at this variant of Catholicism. In one of the essays in his *Memoirs of Zi Pre'* (Dunne 1914b, 13–27), for example, he noted that there were over forty different pious societies in Guardian Angel parish, each dedicated to a particular saint or madonna, and that each society held an annual festa in honor of its patron that included a public parade, with brass band and fireworks, and a High Mass. The *only* critical remark that he makes in discussing these societies is that the money they spend to hire a brass band at a member's funeral might be better spent paying off the debts inherited by the member's family. This aside, however, there is nothing in his discussion to suggest that he saw the devotional activities associated with these annual festas as problematic and certainly not as pagan in any sense.

Although Dunne was the only bishop to participate in the *America* debate, his views—Vecoli notwithstanding—seem consistent with the views held by other American bishops. Some time ago, Henry Browne (1946) provided a comprehensive overview of the American hierarchy's view of the "Italian problem" in the last two decades of the nineteenth century. Browne's study is significant for at least two reasons. First, the Standard Story implies that the immigrants who arrived during this particular period (1880–1900) were especially committed to a pagan Catholicism they had known in Italy; second, Browne relied heavily on unpublished and otherwise difficult-to-get materials that he found in various diocesan and archdiocesan archives. What emerges from Browne's analysis is that, in both their public and private statements, American prelates leveled the same two criticisms against Italian immigrants over and over again: that they had been poorly instructed in the faith while in Italy, and that once in the United States they did not go to church or receive the sacraments often enough and were disinclined to support their local church. Browne's analysis also suggests that American prelates were in agreement on the general outlines of what needed to be done about these problems. As a start, they wanted the clergy in Italy to do a much better job of instructing the immigrants before they left home; the American bishops were more than willing to say this openly, even though it meant criticizing the clergy in the pope's homeland. A letter sent to Rome in the name of the American hierarchy following the Plenary Council held at Baltimore in 1884 declares, "The pastoral solicitude of the Bishops of the provinces of Italy ought to be aroused again and again [that] they might enrich these poor and unlearned peasants with religious instruction" (cited in Browne 1946, 60). American bishops were also in general agreement in believing that Italian immigrants would become better Catholics if they could be provided with priests who spoke Italian. The only major disagreement among American bishops, Browne found, had to do with the institutional structure that would bring together Italian American Catholics and Italian-speaking priests. Some bishops wanted such priests to be assigned to regular parishes; others wanted to establish "duplex parishes," that is, two parallel parish structures, one for Italians and one for non-Italians, at the same church—which usually meant, as Browne notes, that Italians would meet in the basement; and still others favored the establishment of Italian national parishes, of the sort that would in time be established at SSPP in San Francisco. Here again, though, what is most important in Browne's review of the attitudes of American prelates on the Italian problem is what is missing: there is nothing in the materials that Browne reviews to suggest that American prelates saw Italian religious practices as pagan—in origin or character—or saw them as a barrier to making Italians better Catholics.

That American prelates were quite willing to tolerate the supposedly pagan practices identified by Vecoli and others can also be established by looking closely at what these prelates did when confronted with these practices. For example, the very first church to be organized as an Italian national parish was Santa Maria Maddalena de Pazzi in Philadelphia, established in 1852 to serve the mainly Northern Italians who had settled in that city. During the 1880s, under the impact of

increased Italian immigration, construction was begun on a new church, conse-
crated in 1907. An official account of the consecration ceremonies was written by
Father Antonio Isoleri (1911), who had been pastor at this church since 1870. Isoleri's account makes it clear that these ceremonies were attended by a number of
important church leaders. These included Patrick John Ryan, Archbishop of Philadelphia; Bishop Edmund Prendergast, Ryan's auxiliary; Father Luke McCabe,
Professor of Dogmatic Theology at St. Charles Borromeo Seminary; Father John
F. McQuade, Rector of the Cathedral of SS. Peter and Paul in Philadelphia, as well
as a number of pastors from other churches in Philadelphia or nearby areas. While
many of the pastors in attendance did have Italian names, others had names like
Ludwig, Ward, Donovan, Korves, Trainor, Gough, and Moles. The fact that so many
non-Italian prelates and pastors attended the consecration ceremonies of this Italian national church is significant, because it means that they were implicitly legitimizing the sort of religious practices that took place at Santa Maria Maddalena
de Pazzi.

Those practices were on display at the event itself. At the end of the consecration ceremonies came an elaborate outdoor procession involving seven musical
bands and more than a dozen pious societies, each carrying a statue of its patron
saint. As these statues passed through the streets, devotees attached a variety of
gold rings and bracelets as votive offerings—especially, Isoleri (1911, 19) tells us,
to the statues of the Madonna del Carmine, San Rocco, and Santa Maria Maddelena de Pazzi herself. This, of course, is precisely the sort of procession and devotional behavior which, according to Vecoli and others, caused leaders of the American church to look upon Italian American religious practices with disdain; and
yet the simple fact that Archbishop Ryan and so many others were willing to attend
the consecration ceremonies would seem to suggest that leaders of the American
church were at the very least willing to tolerate such practices.

But, in attending the 1907 consecration ceremonies, Archbishop Ryan and
others were giving legitimacy to more than just the parade described above. They
were also giving implicit legitimacy to a range of other practices known to be
associated with this particular church. In one section of his book (pp. 77–84), Isoleri describes the "special graces and favors" that had been granted to individuals
in Philadelphia after they had appealed to Santa Maria Maddelena de Pazzi for
help. Most of the cases described in this section involve people who received a
miraculous cure after making a vow, for instance, after promising a gold ring or
some other votive offering if the saint would grant their wish. Although the practice of praying to a saint for favors is not distinctively Italian (given that the official church has long said that saints can act as intercessors), the emphasis on *quid*

pro quo (you give me favor, I will give you a gift) *is* very much part of the Italian Catholic experience yet not normally associated with the sort of Catholicism favored by the American church.

Other devotional practices, even *more* distinctly Italian and further from the ways of the official church, are evident in cases like these:

> On the solemn feast of St. Mary Maddelena de Pazzi, Sunday, May 30th, 1897, a woman in tears dragged herself, publicly, on her knees, with tongue to the ground, from the door to the sanctuary rail, to fulfill a vow for grace received through the intercession of [the saint]. (Isoleri 1911, 82–83)

> After having been set free [from prison], Alfonso G. was fired at five times, but escaped unhurt. On the 29th of May, 1898, at 9 o'clock Mass, barefooted, on his knees, with tongue on the floor, he dragged himself up from the main church door to the sanctuary railing, in fulfillment of a vow [to Santa Maria Maddelena de Pazzi] for deliverance, acquittal and escape. (Ibid., 83)

The tongue-dragging mentioned in these two accounts is a devotional practice that was widespread in Southern Italy (Carroll 1992, 132–135) and is precisely the sort of practice that supposedly brought Italian Catholics into disrepute with the American church. Yet, here again, the fact that parishioners at Santa Maddelena de Pazzi engaged in practices of this sort did not prevent church leaders from attending the 1907 consecration ceremonies. That diocesan authorities were aware of these practices, I should note, is evident from the fact that Isoleri's book carries a *nihil obstat* granted by a church censor and the *imprimatur* of Archbishop Prendergast (who had succeeded Archbishop Ryan in 1911). While a *nihil obstat* and an *imprimatur* do not mean that archdiocesan authorities endorsed everything said in the book, it does mean that they had read the book and were willing to say publicly that they saw nothing in it—including the section on tongue dragging—that represented a threat to Catholic doctrine, Catholic dogma, or the unanimous teaching of Catholic theologians.

On balance, then, there seems little evidence for the claim, made by Vecoli and others telling the Standard Story, that most American church leaders in the pre–World War I period saw distinctively Italian religious practices as pagan and/or a bar to Italian Americans becoming truly Catholic. On the contrary, it would appear that church leaders either paid very little attention to these practices or (more usually) saw them in exactly the same way that the pastor at SSPP in San Francisco saw them in the 1920s: as practices that bound Italian Catholics to the church and so as something that could prove useful in the long-term campaign to raise Italian Americans to the Irish standard.

But this still leaves us with a puzzle: if church leaders prior to the First World War did not see the supposedly pagan nature of Italian Catholics as problematic or—in particular—as a barrier to making Italian Americans better Catholics, how and why did both of these claims become so central to the Standard Story? While a full answer to this question will be given in the Conclusion, as part of a larger argument that addresses several of the histioriographical patterns identified in this book, a first approximation to that answer can usefully be given here.

Protestant Apologetics and the Academic Study of Religion

It is now commonplace to state that during the nineteenth century, the academic study of religion in Britain and North America was shaped by a number of master narratives that were ultimately Protestant in origin. One of these master narratives, the only one I want to consider here, might be called the degradation narrative. The degradation narrative originated in the distinctively Protestant view that Christianity had originally been a pristine religion, very much centered on an interiorized concern with otherworldly salvation, but that over time it had become encrusted with a number of sacramental and/or magical practices. Within the logic of the degradation narrative, the end result of this process of encrustation was the Roman Catholic Church. In the nineteenth century, Charles A. Goodrich, a Protestant minister from Connecticut, provided a succinct statement of the degradation narrative in his book *A Pictorial and Descriptive View of All Religions* (1851). In his opening paragraph on Roman Catholicism (p. 247), Goodrich wrote:

> The Roman Catholics hold all the fundamental tenets of the Christian religion. They worship one God in three persons [and] receive with the same certainty all the other articles of the Apostles' creed. The Protestants do not differ with them in relation to the fundamentals of this belief; but affirm that the Catholics have made a number of additions, some of which are repugnant to the Apostles' creed, and tend to weaken the fundamental tenets. They further affirm that the Roman Catholics are too indulgent in their toleration of an infinite number of customs which deviate from the spirit of Christianity.

Under this view of things, the great value of the Reformation (in Protestant eyes) was that it had restored Christianity to its original form.

While the degradation narrative was at first only a Protestant view of Christian history, it eventually became a template that implicitly structured the study of non-Christian religions. Norman Girardot (2002, 86–89, 318–319, 590–591), for example, has demonstrated how this narrative shaped the study of Chinese religion during the nineteenth century. Under the influence of the degradation narrative, Girardot argues, scholars came to see Daoism as having been originally a philosophy concerned with the highest and purest aspects of human nature but which over the centuries had come to be diluted by superstitions and magical practices. Similarly, Philip Almond (1988) has shown how the degradation narrative shaped the academic perception of Buddhism in Victorian England. On the one hand, Almond notes, Protestant intellectuals were relatively sympathetic to the figure of Buddha himself, given that he was often constructed as a Luther-like character who had sought to reform a sacramental Brahmanist religion; on the other, they were relatively critical of Buddhist practice, especially Buddhist monasticism, because of its many resemblances to Roman Catholic practice. Finally, in what is perhaps the best-known argument in this vein, Jonathan Smith (1990) stated that the degradation narrative has warped—and continues to warp—the study of the pagan religions of late antiquity. Basically, Smith's argument is that, in their drive to construct Christianity as a pristine religion that had become encrusted with magical practices, scholars were predisposed to see Christianity as essentially different from the mystery cults of the Roman world. As a result, they constructed the religions of late antiquity as surrogates for Roman Catholicism by focusing attention on the things in these cults that seemed similar to Roman Catholicism and which made Roman Catholicism objectionable in the Protestant vision. The larger point that Smith wants to make is that, if we set aside the degradation narrative that has structured scholarship on the religions of late antiquity, then a new and more nuanced appreciation of the similarities between early Christianity and Roman mystery cults is possible.

What is the relevance of all this to the study of Italian American Catholicism? Very simply this: the Standard Story, I suggest, is the result of using the degradation narrative as a template for studying Italian Catholicism just as it has been used a template for studying Chinese religion, Buddhism, and the religions of late antiquity. After all, to say that Italian Catholicism came to be fused with pagan elements (a central element in the Standard Story) implies that it was originally something "not pagan," or at least "less pagan," and that over time Catholicism in Italy became degraded with superstitious and magical encrustations even more than—in the Protestant view—had happened to Christianity generally. I suggest that the Standard Story remains popular, despite its flaws, partly because its overall structure is consistent with a Protestant master narrative that has shaped and continues to shape the academic study of religion in Europe and North America.

I am well aware that most scholars who tell the Standard Story about Italian American Catholicism are not Protestant, and I am certainly not suggesting that they have consciously set out to spread a Protestant message. The fact is that such decisions as which arguments seem reasonable and which do not, what seems worth publishing and what does not, are often influenced by historiographical biases that have crept into scholarly culture as the result of particular historical circumstances and which rarely become the object of critical examination, even by those who do not benefit from that bias. The degradation narrative is an entrenched scholarly bias of just this sort. In other words, the degradation narrative has shaped and still influences more than just our understanding of pagan religions in ancient Rome (which is Smith's argument). Among American scholars studying American religion, it has affected the study of an exotic Other (Italian American Catholics) who is much, much closer to home.

CHAPTER FOUR

Were the Acadians/Cajuns Really Good Catholics?

The study of Cajun Catholicism in Louisiana has not attracted much attention from scholars concerned with the general history of religion in America. Mark Noll's *A History of Christianity in the United States and Canada* (1992), for example, makes a few passing references to Acadians in Canada but says nothing about Cajuns in Louisiana. Gaustad and Barlow's *New Historical Atlas of Religion in America* (2001) devotes only a single sentence to Cajun Catholics. Further, even though there has been a historiographical turn towards a greater appreciation of religious diversity in America (something that we will discuss in detail in Chapter 6), books concerned with documenting and discussing that diversity typically take no notice of Cajun Catholicism. None of the essays in the books on American religion edited by Robert Orsi (e.g., 1999) and by Thomas Tweed (e.g., 1997) have anything to say about Cajun Catholicism, even though the essays in these books do discuss Irish American Catholicism, Italian American Catholicism, and Hispanic Catholicism. Even authors concerned specifically with the history of American Catholicism tend to ignore Cajun Catholicism. Jay Dolan, for example, makes no mention of this variant of Catholicism either in *The American Catholic Experience* (1992) or in his more recent book *In Search of American Catholicism* (2002). Cajun Catholicism, in short, is likely the one form of "ethnic" Catholicism that has been overlooked in the scholarly study of American religion; and, for that reason alone, it seems appropriate to include a chapter on this variant in this book. Examining Cajun Catholicism is also important because a close inspection of what *has* been written on the subject—usually in specialized works devoted specifically to the study of Cajun history—reveals at least one pattern similar to what we encounter in the literature on Irish American Catholicism and Italian American Catholicism: a historiographical predisposition to construct Cajun Catholics as clinging tightly to religious traditions acquired outside the

United States. In this case, as in those others, there are grounds for believing that this construction is problematic.

The Acadians as Devout Catholics

French Catholics began settling in Acadia, a region associated with Nova Scotia and New Brunswick in Canada,[1] during the late 1600s, when the region was under French control. Acadia was ceded to Britain by the Treaty of Utrecht in 1713, and in 1755 British authorities systematically expelled from the colony 6,000–7,000 Acadians, roughly half the population (Lockerby 2001, 4). Thus began the *Grand Dérangement* (the Great Dispersal), and over the next few years other Acadians were also sent into exile. These exiled Acadians found themselves scattered to a variety of locations, including the British colonies along the Atlantic seaboard, Britain, southern Louisiana, French possessions in the Caribbean, and France itself.[2]

Some time ago, Norbert Robichaud (1955), Archbishop of Moncton, posed a question to a visiting historian who specialized in the history of the exiles who ended up in France. Why was it, asked Robichaud, that these exiles had worked so hard to return to North America? After all, said Robichaud, only a century and a half separated them from their French ancestors. The historian's response, according to the good archbishop, was simple. The Acadians were deeply attached both to their religion and to Mother Church, and yet, in a France that was on the threshold of revolution, this was a troubled period for both Catholicism and the church. Local churches were being closed and burnt, priests were being imprisoned or exiled, and the practice of Catholicism was often interdicted by the state. The Acadians returned to North America, this historian continued, so they could more freely practice the Catholicism to which they were so deeply devoted. Robichaud not only accepted this interpretation but went on to assert that this deep Acadian attachment to Catholicism was something that dated from the earliest days of Acadian settlement in North America.

It is easy to criticize the version of history that Robichaud was promoting here. Certainly, there are grounds for believing that attacks on local churches in France during the mid-eighteenth century were less a matter of the state attacking "religion" than a matter of local resentment against the church as the institution that controlled much of the land in France. Then, too, there are other ways to explain the return of the Acadian exiles living in France. Naomi Griffiths (1992, 122–123), for example, suggests that these exiles were dissatisfied with life in France because they had lived for so long in a land marked by relatively greater material abundance and because they were unused to the restrictions and obligations imposed by the French bureaucracy. Even so, the archbishop's claim that the Acadians generally (not just those that had been exiled to France) had a deep and continuing attachment to Catholicism is a claim with a long history.

The earliest and (seemingly) most authoritative statements depicting the Acadians as devout Catholics appear in the correspondence that Acadian leaders themselves sent to various authorities during the seventeenth and eighteenth centuries. These early self-characterizations, however, need to be approached with caution. As Carl Brasseaux (1989, xiv–xv) points out, when they were writing to French authorities after 1755, Acadian leaders routinely stressed that their expulsion had been occasioned mainly by their loyalty to the French crown; but when writing to Spanish authorities (who governed in Louisiana from 1766[3] to 1803), they suggested that it had been occasioned by their deep attachment to the Catholic tradition. In other words, it would appear that Acadian leaders stressed whatever seemed most likely to elicit support from the particular authority to whom they were writing. Since historians now recognize that the first claim (that the Acadians were deeply loyal to the French crown) was likely untrue (Griffiths 1973), there are certainly grounds for skepticism concerning the second claim (that they were good Catholics). Modern skepticism notwithstanding, this early Acadian depiction of themselves as devout Catholics would come to be accepted at face value, though this acceptance was less the result of what Acadians wrote about themselves than of what was written about them by an English-speaking New England poet.

Although Henry Wadsworth Longfellow had been born in Maine, and so not far from the Acadian homeland, he did not show any interest in the Acadian expulsion until the mid-1840s. Then, during a dinner conversation, his friend, the novelist Nathaniel Hawthorne, told him about "a legend of Acadie" in which a girl had sought the lover from whom she had been separated during the expulsion (Johnston 2004a, 77). It was shortly after having heard this story from Hawthorne that Longfellow wrote his famous *Evangeline* (1856). In that poem, the Acadians of Grand Pré (in pre-1755 Acadia) were honest and hard-working rural folk who freely shared their material goods and delighted in singing ballads and telling tales. They were also devout Catholics who regularly attended church, prayed the Angelus daily, yearly celebrated the festival of the village's patron saint, and obeyed the gentle but firm admonitions of their local priest, Father Felician. Indeed, the Acadian attachment to Catholicism and to their local priest is made central to the story that Longfellow tells.

Knowing of this devotion, says Longfellow, the British chose to march into

Grand Pré on a festival day, when the local men were packed into the church and the women were attending outside in the churchyard. The British commander entered the church with his men, promptly strode to the altar, and from the altar announced that the men standing in front of him would be expelled from the colony. Longfellow tells us that several of the assembled men became visibly upset and tried to leave but were prevented from doing so by the soldiers. Tensions in the church were rising to a boiling point, but then, "in the midst of the strife and tumult of angry contention, Lo!, the door of the chancel opened and Father Felician entered, with serious mien." The good father talked of his forty years laboring in their midst, and asked if they had still to learn what he had taught them, namely, to love and forgive and most certainly not to profane the house of the Prince of Peace. With that, Father Felician asked his flock to join him in a prayer of forgiveness, which they did. After this, says Longfellow (p. 42),

> came the evening service. The taper gleamed from the altar. Fervent and deep was the voice of the priest, and the people responded, not with their lips alone, but with their hearts; and the Ave Maria sang they, and fell on their knees, and their souls, with devotion translated, rose on the ardour of prayer, like Elijah ascending to heaven.

The men remained prisoners in the church for four days, and on the fifth were marched off to the shore to be put on boats, all the while comforting themselves, the poem tells us (p. 47), by singing "a chant of the Catholic Missions—*Sacred Heart of the Saviour!*"

The immediate and immense popularity of the original 1847 edition of *Evangeline* quickly led publishers in Boston and London to put out illustrated editions in the 1850s (Johnston 2004b), and those illustrations, like the poem itself, conveyed to readers the suggestion that the Acadians had been good Catholics. Evangeline herself was depicted as a demure lass with downcast eyes wearing a cross and holding a prayer book in one hand and a rosary in the other; kindly Father Felician is shown instructing young children in Bible study or receiving deference from adults who have come to call (see Figure 5).

Longfellow did not invent the idea that pre-1755 Acadia had been a peaceful and idyllic society. The image of it as a type of paradise lost had appeared in several works published in France and England during the late eighteenth and early nineteenth centuries (Johnston 2004a). Still, although these earlier accounts certainly acknowledge that the Acadians were Catholic, they do not suggest, as did Longfellow, that the Acadians were *devout* Catholics. For example, in the account of Acadian life written by Abbé Raynal (1812, 212–218), who did much to popu-

Fig. 5. Kindly Father Felician instructing young Acadian children in Bible study in an illustration by John Gilbert from an edition of Longfellow's *Evangeline* published in 1856. Although illustrations like this suggested that Acadians had regular contact with priests, and by extension the Catholic Church, from an early age, the fact is that priests were scarce in Acadian communities.

larize the motif of paradise lost (see Johnston 2004a), we are told (p. 216) that the priests living among the Acadians drew up their public acts, wrote down their wills, and conducted religious services, but beyond this he nowhere suggests that Acadians were especially devout. By contrast, a few pages earlier (p. 213), when discussing the Abenaki Indians, who also lived in Acadia, Raynal says that the missionaries working among the Abenaki had not simply inculcated in them the tenets of Catholicism but also made them "enthusiasts" in regard to their new religion. Pierre Maillard, a missionary who worked among the Míkmaq in Acadia in the first half of the eighteenth century, was even more explicit, assessing the state of Acadian Catholicism relative to the Catholicism of the aboriginal population. Not only were the Míkmaq better Catholics, Maillard said, but the bulk of the Acadians led "a life that is completely discordant with the Evangelical maxims" (cited in Faragher 2005, 191)

In the end, however, these earlier accounts of Acadia never captured the public imagination in the way that Longfellow's did. The first edition of *Evangeline* was published in Boston in 1847, and Johnston (2004a, 77) estimates that it would eventually go through 270 editions and 130 translations. More than any other previous work, Longfellow's poem shaped nineteenth-century perceptions of the Acadians. Given this, it is hardly surprising that Longfellow's strong emphasis on the Acadians as devout Catholics quickly found its way into scholarly histories. Edme Rameau de Saint-Père (1889, 89), for example, called the Acadians "a decent people—very mindful of one for the other, very religious and very devoted to their families, living happily in the midst of their children without a lot of worries. One can characterize these people in two words: they were happy and they were honest." Similar depictions can be found in general histories of Acadia straight through to the 1960s. In his *Acadia* (1968, 13), for example, Andrew Clark—in a line that sounds as if it could have been written by Longfellow himself—declares that the Acadians were "devout in their attachment to the ancient church." Generally, as regards Acadian Catholicism, scholarly histories differed from Longfellow's account in only one respect: historians, unlike Longfellow, knew that priests were scarce in Acadia. This, however, was (and is) seen as *reinforcing* the claim that the Acadians were devout, in that the Acadians were good Catholics *despite* the scarcity of priests (see Dorman 1983, 37; Sigur 1983, 127–129).

Acadian exiles started to settle in what is now southwestern Louisiana during the early 1760s, when the entire Louisiana Territory was still under French control. This Acadian influx continued through the period of Spanish rule in Louisiana (which effectively began in 1766) and reached its peak in 1785 when the Spanish and French governments collaborated in arranging the transportation of more than 1,500 Acadian exiles from France to Louisiana. We now have several accounts of the Cajun[4] communities and traditions that developed in Louisiana, and these accounts routinely suggest that Cajuns retained that deep attachment to Catholicism that had been so much a feature of life in Acadia (see Baker 1983, 102; Bezou and Guidry 2003; Conrad 1983, 12; Dorman 1983, 37).

Anyone who searches for concrete evidence of this longstanding depiction of the Acadians and their Cajun descendants as devout Catholics quickly encounters disappointment. I see no details on what might be called the "the lived experience of Catholicism" in any of the standard reference works on Acadian history (including Clark 1968; Dorman 1983; Griffiths 1973). In her more recent work on the Acadians, Naomi Griffiths (2005) does occasionally discuss what she calls "the strength of Catholic belief" (p. 272) among the Acadians, but only to make the point that their Catholicism was more a basis for social solidarity than a matter of religious devotion (see pp. 311–312). Nor is there much (if any) evidence that the Acadians were good Catholics once they moved to Louisiana; ethnographic accounts of Cajun life are generally silent on what the lived experience of Catholicism was like in Cajun communities. Certainly, there is nothing, for instance, in Lauren Post's widely cited *Cajun Sketches* (1990), which deals with Acadian life on the prairies of southwestern Louisiana in the late 1800s and early 1900s, to suggest that Acadians were especially religious.

Studies of "Acadian Catholicism" do exist, but these studies also devote little if any attention to the lived experience of religion in Acadian and/or Cajun communities. Mainly this is because most of these studies have been written from the perspective of the institutional church and so have been concerned mainly with the things of greatest importance to church leaders. John Howard Young's (1988, 5–6) review of the "classic" literature on Acadian Catholicism prior to 1755, for example, suggests that it is concerned overwhelmingly with the activities of missionary orders like the Jesuits and the Sulpicians in Acadia. Even now, the vast majority of articles dealing with religion in a journal like *La Société historique acadienne: Les Cahiers* are still articles concerned with things like the careers of particular priests, bishops, or nuns or the early history of particular missionary or teaching orders in Acadia.[5] Charles Nolan's (1993) review of "Louisiana Catholic historiography" makes it clear that exactly this same emphasis on the activities of particular religious orders and particular bishops has also been a feature of the scholarship on Cajun Catholicism.

In part, the strong emphasis on the institutional church in studies of Acadian Catholicism derives from the fact that many of the scholars who have written these studies have strong personal ties to the institutional church. Even now, a relatively large proportion of the articles on a religious subject published in *La Société historique acadienne: Les Cahiers* are written by scholars who are also priests. On the subject of Louisiana, scholars like Alexander Sigur and Jules Daigle, both of whom wrote extensively on Cajun Catholicism, were priests. But even the authors who are not priests often have strong ties to the church. Roger Baudier, for instance, was the associate editor of the New Orleans archdiocesan newspaper when he was writing his monumental and authoritative *The Catholic Church in Louisiana* (1939). Baudier, I might add, also makes it clear in the very first paragraph of that book (p. 10) that he began writing it at the suggestion of John W. Shaw, Archbishop of New Orleans, and that one of his (Baudier's) goals was quite explicitly "to bring before the public these pioneer workers of the Church of Louisiana, many of whom have been too long buried in oblivion and the epic of their heroism too long unsung." Baudier, I grant, wrote several decades ago, but the linkage between the scholarly study of Catholicism in Louisiana and the institutional church persisted into recent years. *Cross, Crozier and Crucible* (1993), a collection of more than three dozen essays on the institutional church in Louisiana, edited by Glen Conrad, director of the Center for Louisiana Studies at Lafayette, was copublished by that center and the Archdiocese of New Orleans, and it carries an *imprimatur* and a *nihil obstat*. This means that the manuscript was submitted to a church censor for examination and that the censor, and subsequently the local bishop, found nothing objectionable in the book. At the very least, the foreknowledge that a work is going to be submitted to church authorities for vetting makes it likely that interpretations that might otherwise arise in the course of scholarly investigations will be precluded.

Apart from the activities of religious orders and the actions of particular priests, bishops, or nuns, the only topic considered at length in existing studies of Acadian Catholicism is the matter of "priestly influence." Concern with this topic has a long history. It was common for British colonial administrators after 1713 to suggest that the Acadians were overly influenced by French priests whose loyalty was to the French crown, and British apologists for the expulsions that occurred in the late 1750s routinely cited such "priestly influence" as among the things that justified those expulsions. Of course, this is simply a variant on an even older tendency among English Protestants to see Catholic priests as promoting disloyalty to the English crown by encouraging obedience to a foreign ruler. In the usual case, the fear was that priests promoted obedience to the pope in Rome (and, as we shall see in Chapter 6, a similar fear would come to shape the scholarly study of American Catholics in the mid-nineteenth century), and the implicit assumption always made here was that Catholics did what their priests told them to do. This is precisely why, as Lawrence McCaffrey (1997, 92) reminds us, the victory of William of Orange in 1688 (which would have been fresh in the minds of British administrators in Acadia) was so routinely seen by British Protestants as eliminating "an alien threat to British constitutionalism." Given this view of Catholics, as mindlessly obedient to their priests, it would have made sense to British administrators in Acadia that if local priests were committed to the French crown then disloyalty to England would be correspondingly high among their parishioners.

This political concern with "priestly influence" became a staple element in scholarly assessments of the Acadians (Griffiths 2005, 272–273). Scholars writing on Acadian history have always felt obliged to assess the British claim, that is, to determine if the Acadians really were under priestly control. Even Carl Brasseaux (1987), whose work is now central to all accounts of the Acadian experience, devotes most of his chapter on religion (pp. 150–166) to the matter of priestly influence. In regard to the issue itself, scholars now think that the influence exerted by priests on the Acadians was either variable, being highly dependent on the personality and ideology of the priest involved (Griffiths 1973, 46–47), or generally minimal (Brasseaux 1987; Griffiths 2005, 273). The main point, however, is that this longstanding scholarly concern with priestly influence is little more than an intellectual inheritance from English Protestant fears dating back to the Reformation.

John Howard Young: The Two Reasons for Believing that the Acadians Were Good Catholics

John Howard Young (1988) is one of the few investigators who constitutes an exception to the historiographical patterns noted above. Young's primary goal was to defend the popular stereotype that the Acadians were deeply and devoutly Catholic. In doing this, he sets up this claim against a counter-claim, that the Acadian attachment to Catholicism was primarily a matter of identity politics, that is, that they saw themselves as Catholic mainly because this was a way of distinguishing themselves from other groups with whom they competed for scarce resources. Young's argument, in a nutshell, is that, while this second hypothesis might explain Acadian attachment to Catholicism in pre-1755 Acadia (where their Catholicism was a way of distinguishing themselves from British Protestants), it cannot explain why the Acadians remained good Catholics in Louisiana, where they regularly interacted with other Catholics (notably Spanish and French Creole Catholics).

Young never once doubts that the Acadians *were* good Catholics. What is interesting are the two (and only two) pieces of evidence that he brings forward to support this claim. First, he says, one of the recurring themes in the correspondence that Acadian leaders directed to local authorities (French and English officials in Acadia, Spanish officials in Louisiana) was a request to send them priests. Second, the Acadians, in both Acadia and Louisiana, practiced lay baptism of their children, despite the disapproval of this practice by the official church. For Young, both patterns are evidence that the Acadians had a deep desire to participate in the sacramental life of the church on a regular basis and thus fully justify the view that they were devout Catholics. Unfortunately, although the patterns identified by Young are solidly attested to in the historical record, they can be explained in more than one way. Take, for example, the recurrent Acadian demand for priests.

In his analysis of the relationship between priests and people in Acadian communities, Carl Brasseaux (1987, 155) amasses much archival evidence indicating that Acadians regarded their priests as administrators whose job was to record information (relating to property ownership, for example) and occasionally to administer sacraments (mainly marriage). In the end, then, Brasseux's conclusions seem little different from the already-cited account of what priests did among the Acadians written by the Abbé Raynal (1812, 216) more than two centuries earlier. For Brasseaux, the fact that the Acadians saw priests as functionaries, expected only to perform certain tasks on an occasional basis, explains why the Acadians so often requested priests (the pattern that is so important for Young) and why they were willing to contribute toward the initial establishment of a church; *but*, it also explains, for Brasseaux, why the Acadians routinely resisted (as they did) contributing to the ongoing maintenance of their local church and why they responded with hostility (as they did) whenever local priests tried to exercise anything more than a loose control over their daily life.

Brasseaux's account, I might add, seems generally consistent with another pattern: despite their requests for priests, the Acadians themselves—in both Acadia and Louisiana—were always a poor source of priestly vocations. Young (1988, 187–189) himself recognized that this might be seen as undermining the suggestion that the Acadians were attached to their faith, and he explains (or, really, explains away) the lack of Acadian vocations by claiming that the great distance of Acadian communities from the nearest available seminary would have made a seminary education prohibitively expensive for most Acadian families. The fact is, however, that plans to establish a seminary in New Orleans in the late 1700s came to naught mainly because church authorities concluded that the French-speaking families, both Creole and Acadian, simply had no inclination to send their sons to such an institution (Curley 1940, 169–171). This Acadian disinclination to enter the priesthood persisted well into the twentieth century (Ancelet 1985, 26; Sigur 1983, 131).

The main point is that, if Brasseaux is correct in saying that the Acadians regarded their priests as functionaries expected to perform only occasional tasks, then there is nothing in the recurrent Acadian demand for priests which is necessarily indicative of a strongly internalized desire to participate in the sacramental life of the church on a regular and recurrent basis. In the end, then, while the requests for priests proves that they were Catholic, it cannot be taken as clear evidence that they were particularly good or devout Catholics.

What about Young's second piece of evidence, that Acadians routinely practiced the lay baptism of infants? In interpreting this practice, Young takes it as self-evident that Acadian parents baptized their children themselves only because priests were not available to do it, implicitly assuming that parents would have their children rebaptized "officially" when a priest did visit the community. Yet, in fact, although the evidence is fragmentary, it would appear from Brasseaux's (1987, 160) analysis of baptismal records in selected Cajun communities that many, and perhaps most, Cajun children were *not* eventually rebaptized by a priest, even though a priest might have subsequently visited the community. What such data hints at, I suggest, is the possibility that the lay baptism of infants may have had a meaning for Cajun parents that was unconnected to the Catholic sacrament of Baptism. What might that meaning have been? While any answer here must be highly speculative, there is one possibility that comes to mind.

Cajun infants were not the only individuals sprinkled with holy water; it would appear that holy water was also sprinkled on the corpses at Cajun funerals (Daniels 1990, 111). Establishing a symbolic association between infants and corpses by means of a common folkloric practice, which often involves the use of water in some way, is in fact a well-attested pattern in a variety of European cultures. The usual explanation for this (see for example Lombardi Satriani and Meligrana 1982, 107–116) is that infants and corpses both lie at a boundary between "this world" and "the other world" and so both need help in making a successful transition between the two.

In the end, then, there are other ways of interpreting the two bits of evidence that Young brings forward in support of his contention that the Acadians were devout Catholics. Does this mean that the Acadians were not devout Catholics? Not at all. It simply means that the case is not proven. How then to proceed in investigating Acadian Catholicism? One option, I suggest, is to recognize that the standards associated with the official church (regular attendance at Sunday Mass, fulfillment of the Easter duty, knowledge of church doctrine, etc.) are not the only meaningful criteria that might be used to assess Catholic religiosity. In particular, Acadian religiosity might be assessed by looking to see if those things that are routinely taken as indicators of popular Catholic religiosity in other sociocultural contexts were or were not present in the Acadian case.

The Stuff of Popular Catholicism in Other Areas

Although the practices of popular Catholicism have varied over time and across different cultural contexts, there are certain practices that appear regularly in the historical record. In areas like Spain, the Spanish Americas, France, and Italy, for example, rituals centered on a miraculous image (usually of the Virgin) have typically been an important element in the lived experience of Catholicism. Something else central to popular Catholicism is pilgrimage, that is, traveling to a site that is thought to be sacred for some reason. Sometimes the site is thought to possess a particularly powerful miraculous image or a particularly important set of saintly relics; in other cases, a supernatural personage, usually the Virgin Mary, is believed to have made an earthly appearance there. Pilgrims have often traveled some distance from their local community, making the pilgrimage both difficult and time-consuming. The shrine dedicated to St. James at Santiago de Compostella, Spain, for example, has drawn pilgrims from all over Europe since the Middle Ages, and the shrine dedicated to Our Lady of Guadalupe has drawn pilgrims from all over Mexico since the late colonial period.

More usually, however, Catholic pilgrimage has involved traveling to sacred sites relatively close to home. In early modern Spain, the countryside around towns and villages was dotted with chapels and outdoor shrines; and community-sponsored pilgrimages (*romerías*) to these sacred sites, often involving an overnight stay, were central to the lived experience of Catholicism there (Christian 1981, 70–91; Kamen 1993, 194–198). Local pilgrimages to nearby churches containing especially important images was also common in Bavaria in the early modern period (Lepovitz 1991, 116–121), while in pre-Famine Ireland Catholics routinely made pilgrimages to nearby holy wells, natural springs with sacred significance (Carroll 1999, 19–44). Yet, despite the centrality of such phenomena as image cults, apparitions, and pilgrimage to the experience of Catholicism in other parts of the Catholic world, including France and Spain, I know of no reports suggesting that any of these things played a significant role in the experience of Acadian Catholicism, either in Acadia or in Louisiana.

The fact that "the stuff of popular Catholicism" was absent in Acadia during the seventeenth and eighteenth centuries is all the more striking given that during this same period miraculous images and pilgrimage (though not, it would appear, apparitions) *were* part of the lived experience of Catholicism in colonial New France (Cliché 1988). As early as the late 1600s, for instance, the Church of St. Anne de Beaupré in Quebec had become an important pilgrimage site associated with miracles; by the 1730s the number of pilgrims flocking to this shrine was enough to keep four priests busy hearing confessions, celebrating mass, and leading the faithful in prayer (Choquette 2003, 128). St. Anne de Beaupré was certainly the single most popular shrine in New France, but other important pilgrimage sites also existed in and around Montreal and Quebec City (Choquette 2003). In other words, the lived experience of popular Catholicism in New France shared much in common with the lived experience of popular Catholicism elsewhere. This is precisely what cannot be said of the Catholic experience in Acadia.

The Effects of Priestly Scarcity: A Folkloric Experiment

One thing we know for certain about Acadian Catholicism is that priests were scarce. What sort of Catholicism might reasonably have developed in Cajun communities given this relative absence of priests? Some time ago, Ron Bodin (1990) came to wonder about precisely this question. In his own words: "For some 130 years rural Louisiana was often without the services of Catholic priests [and] one wonders what became of the church, and of people's religious beliefs and practices when there was either no priest or only a few circuit rider priests to visit rural areas every few years (p. 2). To answer this question, Bodin devised what might be called a "folkloric experiment": he sought out and interviewed Cajun informants over the age of 65 who were from one of two communities in Vermilion Parish that had not been served by a resident priest until the late 1920s. Using the information provided by these informants, Bodin was able to reconstruct a variant of popular Catholicism that, it would appear, had existed in both communities and that had been built around the use of sacramental objects and lay versions of certain official rituals.

Bodin's data show clearly that the rosary was the single most important Catholic sacramental in these Cajun communities and that "praying the rosary" was central to the lived experience of Catholicism there. He also found that most homes had family altars, which might include a crucifix, pictures of a saint, candles, holy water, and the like, and that these altars served as the focus for family prayer. Finally, he found that the ritual activities associated with the rosary and other sacramentals had for the most part been administered by Cajun women.

In regard to ritual activities, Bodin's informants also reported that Cajun communities developed lay equivalents for a number of official sacraments, and that here too women had been central. Lay baptism, for example, was common; and most often, an infant would be baptized by a mother, grandmother, or aunt.

Women also officiated at weekly "white masses" held in private homes. Sometimes the woman only led the assembled group in prayer; at other times, she would distribute bread, simulating Holy Communion. Finally, these Cajun communities had practiced a form of lay marriage in which jumping the broom was the central ritual act, and here too, Bodin found, the ritual had been administered by women.

There are many elements in the variant of Catholicism reconstructed by Bodin which hint at continuing traditions that date from the earliest years of Acadian culture. As already mentioned, there is solid evidence that lay baptism had long been widespread in Acadian communities. There are also scattered references in the documentary record suggesting that Acadians attended weekly white masses administered by a layperson both in pre-1755 Acadia and post-1760 Louisiana (Brasseaux 1987, 153, 156), as well as in the Acadian communities that sprang up in Cape Breton during the late 1700s (Chiasson 1962, 107–108). Then too, at least in the eighteenth century, it was common for Acadian leaders in Louisiana to note (in the reports they sent to government officials) that a visiting priest had married several different couples during his short stay (Brasseaux 1989, 103, 105); it is easy to imagine that such "clustered" marriages involved the church giving official approval to unions that had previously been established by a folk ceremony.

Still, for Bodin himself, the single most important finding to emerge from his study is that *women* were central to the maintenance of Cajun Catholicism. This is reflected in the title of his article, which suggests that the Cajun woman functioned as "unofficial deacon of the sacraments [and] priest of the sacramentals." It turns out, however, that the centrality of women to Cajun Catholicism is a more complex issue than first appears. Reading Bodin's report carefully, it becomes clear that women were central not simply because they provided leadership but because religiosity itself was gendered. Cajun males apparently did not have much interest in religion. Bodin found that Cajun men did not attend mass even when it was available (Ancelet 1985, 28; Brasseaux 1989, 163), nor were they much interested in the sacramentals and lay sacraments that were so central to the experience of Catholicism for Cajun women. On the contrary, Bodin notes (p. 9), Cajun males identified more with local Haitian-influenced *traiteur* (healer) traditions than with any aspect of the Catholic tradition.

The fact that Cajun religiosity, at least during the late nineteenth and early twentieth centuries, was gendered is—once again—a familiar pattern. As noted in Chapter 2, there is now a relatively large literature documenting the feminization of religion in the United States in both the Catholic and Protestant traditions. In the Cajun case, however, none of the three hypotheses considered in Chapter 2 as possible explanations for this feminization would seem to apply.

First, some scholars have asserted that feminization was caused by the erosion of lay male authority and subsequent "male flight," that is, as local congregations increasingly came under the control of a professional ministry, lay males—who previously had exerted much authority and influence in these congregations—increasingly abandoned religious activities, leaving them to women by default. But since there is no evidence (Longfellow aside) that Cajun males were *ever* active participants in the religious life of Cajun communities, and certainly no evidence that lay males had ever exercised authority in the religious sphere, the "male flight" hypothesis seems of little value in this case.

Another way of accounting for the feminization of religion is the "female sociability" hypothesis offered by Robert Orsi and others. In this argument, women gravitated toward the institutional church because it provided them with a "safe haven" outside the confines of their homes where they would discuss issues of common concern with other women. Whatever the value of this argument in the contexts of concern to Orsi and others, it seems not to apply in the Cajun case, because the institutional church had such a minimal presence in Cajun communities and female religiosity was centered in the home.

Finally, feminization in some cases can be explained by an affinity between the values being promoted by the institutional church and the values that women have adopted, or wanted to adopt, for nonreligious reasons, an example being the affinity between the values promoted by the American church in the mid-nineteenth century and the middle-class values that Irish American women needed to acquire to work in middle-class households. But affinity arguments of this sort would seem to be of little use in the Cajun case because, again, the institutional church had only a minimal presence in Cajun communities and there is no evidence that the sort of "official" Catholicism being promoted by the church elsewhere would have been widely known in these communities.

The Cajun case, then, forces us to search for an explanation for the feminization of religion that goes beyond the three formulations that have so far been considered. With that in mind I would like to turn to a theoretical framework which, although it has wide visibility among feminist scholars, is not one that has been much used by scholars concerned with the study of religion.

"Doing Gender"

Over the past two decades, many feminist theorists have suggested that gen-der is less about a fixed set of psychological attributes that are invariant from one situation to the next, and more about particular things that individuals *do* in interaction with others in order to establish a gendered identity.[6] Jill Dubisch (1995, 204) sums up the new approach succinctly:

> Gender [is best viewed] not as a rigid set of rules about male and female nature or about how men and women should behave, but as a framework for discourse and negotiation, worked out in the dynamic context of social life. . . . To perform [gen-der], then, is to present the socially constructed self before others, to in a sense *argue* for that self [and] thus to convince and draw recognition from others of one's place and one's satisfactory performance of that role.

One advantage of the "doing gender" approach, and the one that has so far been stressed the most by those investigators using this approach, is that it allows us to understand how and why the meaning of gender can vary from situation to sit-uation, depending upon the particular audience observing the activity (see Thorne 1999). But another advantage of the doing gender approach, and the one that seems most relevant to the academic study of religion, is that it provides us with another way of explaining religious behavior. Simply put: in certain situa-tions, engaging in overtly religious behavior can be a way of validating a gendered identity.

One of the very best studies demonstrating how religious behavior can be a way of doing gender is Dubisch's (1995) own account of pilgrimage activity at a Greek Orthodox shrine on the Aegean island of Tinos. Dubisch calls attention to the fact that many female pilgrims to this shrine engage in behaviors (like mov-ing up the shrine's steep stairs on their knees) that to outsiders seem extreme and emotionally excessive. Dubisch rejects (p. 223) those interpretations that explain such behaviors by invoking an essentialist view of women (e.g., women are more emotional than men) or by suggesting that Greek women are more pious than Greek men. Both explanations, she argues, fail to explain why the emotionalism observed at the shrine evaporates quickly when the same women engage in other activities or why, when underlying attitudes are probed, women often seem *less* attached to the Orthodox tradition than their male counterparts.

Given that religiosity at Tinos is gendered (pilgrimage activity being mainly a female activity), Dubisch argues, the pilgrimage site is a public space in which female pilgrims can act out the "poetics of Greek womanhood" (Dubisch's term) for an audience consisting mainly of other women, that is, women can engage in a number of performative acts that validate their gendered identity in the eyes of other women. Thus, since "being a mother" and "an idiom of suffering" are both central to the poetics of womenhood in Greek culture, women who appear to suffer at the pilgrimage site (by moving up the stairs of the shrine on their knees, for example), especially if this suffering is part of a vow made on behalf of their family, are engaging in behaviors that demonstrate that they are "good at being a woman." This does not mean, Dubisch (1995, 218–219) notes, that their religiosity is insincere; on the contrary, every aspect of the religious rituals in which these women engage is pervaded by a deeply felt emotion. However, their religiosity derives principally from a desire "to create expressions of their own identity," and they use materials from Orthodox religion (p. 219). It is their desire to validate their gendered identity in the eyes of others, in other words, rather than a strongly interiorized or innate piety, that fuels their religiosity.

Although Tinos is a long way from southern Louisiana in a number of ways, Dubisch's underlying theoretical argument provides us with a new way of interpreting those few bits and pieces of information we do have about Cajun Catholicism during the nineteenth century. For example: when a Cajun wife and mother maintained a home altar, very visibly prayed the rosary in front of others in her family, instructed children in the sacraments, orchestrated a "jumping the broom" marriage in front of the local community, and so forth, it seems entirely possible that she may have been doing exactly what a female pilgrim at Tinos is doing when she moves up the stairs of the shrine on her knees: engaging in behaviors, which happen to be religious behaviors, that establish her as "good at being a woman" in a culture where the maintenance of family and marital solidarity, caring for and instructing children, and other wifely and maternal duties were the things that a woman did.

Do I mean to suggest here that Cajun women should not be regarded as "good Catholics"? Well, it depends. If by "good Catholic" is meant someone characterized by a deeply interiorized piety that motivates them to seek union with God, to engage in Catholic rituals, and to participate in the sacramental life of the church in order to garner spiritual benefits, then the answer would probably be no. On the other hand, given that Cajun Catholicism was gendered (associated mainly with women), it seems entirely plausible to suggest that "being good at being a woman" and "being a good Catholic" might very well have been conflated, that to be "good at being a woman" was what "being a good Catholic" *meant* in Cajun communities.

CHAPTER FIVE

Hispanic Catholicism and the Illusion of Knowledge

In their book on New Mexico, Marta Weigle and Peter White (1988) list four "focal places" that epitomize modern New Mexico's multiethnic identity, and the only one of the four that is distinctively associated with New Mexico's Hispano Catholic population is the small church at Chimayó, located about thirty miles northeast of Santa Fe.[1] This church, it happens, is also a well-known Catholic pilgrimage site and attracts thousands of visitors annually as either tourists or pilgrims or both. Ramón Gutiérrez (1995) estimates that anywhere from five to ten thousand people visit this church on weekdays during the spring and summer, and that the number is higher on the weekends, when people from the local community attend church services there. Both Gutiérrez (1995; 2000) and Enrique Lamadrid (1999) state, though without citing any comparative data, that Chimayó is the single most popular Catholic pilgrimage site in the United States.

One of the recurring themes in both popular and scholarly discussions of Chimayó is the suggestion that the shrine there is associated with supernatural cures and favors in the same way that, say, the shrine at Lourdes is associated with supernatural cures and favors. Indeed, typing "santuario de Chimayó" into an Internet search engine quickly leads to more than a dozen websites, including one maintained by the Archdiocese of Santa Fe, which describe Chimayó as "the Lourdes of America." This characterization of Chimayó as the Lourdes of America is also found in guidebooks aimed at tourists visiting the Southwest (Knight 1999; Ward 1997), in scholarly articles (Lane 2001), and in early accounts of Chimayó addressed to the general public (De Huff 1931; Walter 1916). Unlike Lourdes, however, where supernatural cures and favors are associated with water from the spring that flows there, the cures and favors at Chimayó are associated with "holy dirt" from the *posita* (dry well) within the shrine. Phrased slightly differently, Chimayó is the sort of pilgrimage site you might expect Lourdes to be if it had emerged—like Chimayó—in a land where water is a scarce resource.

There are several origin legends associated with the Chimayó shrine (Gutiér-rez 1995; Nunn 1993), and although these legends differ in many of their details, they generally agree in suggesting that the shrine emerged sometime in the period 1810–1815 through the efforts of a local resident, Bernardo Abeyta. Abeyta is a known historical figure who would become an important and influential member of the Penitente Brotherhood. We know for certain that in 1813 Abeyta sent a petition to Fray Sebastían Alvarez at Santa Cruz de la Cañada (the commu-nity where the nearest parish church was located) for permission to build a small chapel in Chimayó that would be dedicated to Nuestro Señor de Esquípulas. The title Nuestro Señor de Esquípulas was originally associated with a miraculous crucifix that had been enshrined in a church at Esquípulas, in eastern Guatemala, during the late 1500s. By the early nineteenth century, and so at the time of the Abeyta petition, satellite churches dedicated to Nuestro Señor de Esquípulas had been established throughout Central America and Mexico.

Something else found in almost all accounts of Chimayó is the claim that cen-turies before Abeyta erected his chapel, the Chimayó site had been sacred to the Tewa Indians who lived in the area. As far as I can tell, however, this idea is rooted entirely in oral traditions collected from Pueblo Indian communities in the twen-tieth century (see for example Gutiérrez 1995; Kay 1987) and I know of no arche-ological or pre–twentieth century ethnographic evidence to substantiate it. What this means is that, while it is certainly possible that Chimayó may have been a sacred Tewa site, it is also possible that this is a story that developed among Pueblo Catholics in response to the establishment of the *santuario* as a way of allowing Pueblo Catholics to explain their involvement with a sacred site that was other-wise ostensibly Spanish in origin. Nevertheless, the simple fact that this claim is now routinely made is in itself evidence that it is an important part of the story that scholars and lay Catholics (both Hispano and Pueblo) tell about Chimayó.

The matter of origins aside, another important element in the Chimayó story is always a description of the physical structure of the *santuario* itself. Entering through the main door of the modest-sized church at Chimayó, visitors first en-counter a picturesque interior dominated by five altar screens. These screens contain *retablos* (painted wooden panels) and *bultos* (carved figures) created by three well-known nineteenth-century *santeros* (men who made religious art). The screen behind the main altar is the work of Antonio Molleno, while the others (two along each side of the church) are usually credited to José Aragón and José Rafael Aragón of Córdova. Since all three *santeros* are discussed at length in books about the religious art of New Mexico (see, for example, Cash 1999; Frank 1992; Steele 1994), it seems likely that many of the tourists who come to Chimayó come to see their work. For the pilgrims who come to Chimayó out of religious devotion, however, the most important part of the shrine lies through a small doorway to the left of the altar.

Moving through that doorway brings you first to the sacristy, a room lying alongside the main body of the church. Here you find an image of the Santo Niño (Holy Child) enclosed in a small wooden shrine (which appears to be an old confessional). Throughout the sacristy—hanging on the walls or from the ceiling, inside the Santo Niño shrine, sitting on shelves—are objects usually identified as *ex voto* (these will be discussed in detail below). Adjoining this room is a smaller room in which is found the *posita* that contains the holy dirt. Incidentally, it is common knowledge that the dirt in the posita is replenished regularly by church staff using dirt from the local area, but this does not seem to affect the regard in which the dirt in the shrine is held.

Today, the high point of the pilgrimage experience at Chimayó occurs during Holy Week, and more specifically on Good Friday (see Figure 6). Holmes-Rodman (2004) estimates that in the late 1990s about 2,000 pilgrims were visiting Chimayó on Good Friday; my own sense is that the number is likely a bit higher. Many Good Friday pilgrims arrive by car or bus, but many others arrive having made a long journey on foot. Indeed, anyone driving along the highways near Santa Fe in the days leading up to Good Friday will encounter "sanctuary walkers" moving along the side of the road toward Chimayó. In recent years, the New Mexico Department of Transportation has facilitated the Chimayó pilgrimage by closing one lane of selected highways to automobile traffic, and the State Police have assigned several dozen officers to help ensure the safety of the walkers.

Although Chimayó attracts a fair number of Anglo (English-speaking non-Hispanic) tourists, most of the pilgrims who go there for religious reasons are Hispano Catholics, that is, Catholics who claim descent from the Spanish colonists who settled in New Mexico during the seventeenth century. Gutiérrez (1995) estimates that more than 80 percent of the pilgrims who come to Chimayó for religious reasons are Hispanos. One result of this Hispano predominance, given the visibility and popularity of the Good Friday pilgrimage to Chimayó, is that this pilgrimage has become an important element in what it means to *be* a Hispano in contemporary New Mexico. (On the centrality of the Chimayó Good Friday pilgrimage to modern Hispano identity, see Carlson 1990.)

Because Chimayó will already be well-known to many readers, and because it

Fig. 6. Pilgrims entering the sanctuary at Chimayó on Good Friday 1999.

is so strongly associated with Hispano religiosity, a close analysis of the scholarly literature on Chimayó—it seems to me—can serve as a useful first step in making the overarching argument that I want to make in this chapter. That argument, simply, is this: much of what we "know" about Hispanic Catholicism derives less from the evidence than from what American scholars studying religion want Hispanic Catholicism to be. Existing scholarly knowledge about Hispanic Catholicism, in other words, is often more an illusion, though undeniably an appealing illusion, than anything else.

"A Veritable Museum of Material Culture Artifacts Associated with Spanish Catholic Spirituality"

Because it is central to all accounts of Chimayó that the pilgrims see it as a place of supernatural power, these accounts (see, for example, Gutiérrez 1995; Kay 1987) routinely mention three things: the holy dirt in the posita, the Santo Niño (through whose intercession favors are granted), and the *ex voto* brought to Chimayó by the devout. The *ex voto*, that is, items left in the sacristy as testaments to a favor that has been granted, are especially important within the logic of these accounts because they provide tangible evidence that the pilgrims who go to Chimayó truly associate the *santuario* with miraculous cures and favors. Ramón

Gutiérrez (1995, 80), for example, provides a detailed description of the *ex voto* in the sacristy:

> In contemporary times, despite the centrality of the statue of the Santo Niño de Atocha and its grotto, what gains most attention in the ex-voto room (the Sacristy) are the numerous votive offerings that have been left there by pilgrims. Every wall space and every shelf space in the room is covered with religious statues of various sizes, with equally varied pictures of Christ, the Virgin Mary, the saints and angels, with very personal missives and poems, as well as canes, crutches, limb braces, and glasses. It is not uncommon for a person to vow a pilgrimage to the Santuario if they recover rapidly from a broken bone, surgery or an illness. Thus, in the ex-voto room one finds, as I did in 1990, twenty-five crutches, five canes, two leg braces, and two pairs of eyeglasses. The room had over 170 religious pictures [on] the wall. . . . The religious statuary that pilgrims had left as offerings was also immense, numbering around 150.

Other investigators have provided similar, if briefer, accounts:

> Various offerings [hang] from the wall of the sacristy such as crutches, canes, a corset, etc., left by pilgrims who had been cured by the blessed earth. (de Borhegyi 1956, 26)

> [The] small sacristy [is] filled with a veritable museum of material culture artifacts associated with Spanish Catholic spirituality. Multiple statues of Our Lady of Guadalupe and Santo Niño, the child Jesus, are dressed in doll clothes, slips of paper pinned to them with requests for prayer. Abandoned crutches and prosthetic devices hang from the walls with testimonial letters speaking of experiences of healing. (Lane 2001, 61–62)

> Pilgrims, who often arrive (on Good Friday) on crutches or in wheelchairs and carry large wooden crosses on their shoulders, post small votive images of ailing body parts in the room called El Pocito (the little hole), which houses medicinal sand. (Holmes-Rodman 2004)

Notice that all these accounts mention items, like crutches and canes, which, when abandoned, become emblems of healing and so reinforce the suggestion that at Chimayó, as at Lourdes, there are miraculous cures to be had. Unfortunately, or so I now want to argue, the image of Chimayó and the Chimayó experience conveyed in most scholarly accounts, including all those cited to this point, is fundamentally flawed.

Visiting Chimayó during Holy Week

While writing a book on the history of the Penitentes (Carroll 2002), I made several trips to northern New Mexico to do archival research, and on each trip I made a point of visiting Chimayó. Partly, this was because Chimayó is a pleasant place to visit; but in addition, I had developed an interest in *santero* art, and the *ex voto* room did remind me of the many shrines that I had visited in Italy and Spain, and obviously something significant *was* happening at Chimayó.

Entering the sacristy on most of these occasions, I found it to contain exactly the sort of objects that Gutiérrez and others describe. One thing that was mildly puzzling to me was that most of the objects—the statues on the shelves and the pictures on the walls in particular—seemed more "generically Catholic" than Hispanic; notwithstanding a few statues and votive candles depicting the Virgen de Guadalupe, most of the statues and pictures seemed the sort of devotional objects that might be purchased in a Catholic religious supply store in any American city. Missing entirely was anything resembling the painted *ex voto* usually found in Mexican churches. These paintings, made on rectangular pieces of tin, often using house paint, depict a person (who is usually named) being delivered from danger as the result of an appeal to some madonna or saint. These painted *ex voto* have been a part of the Mexican Catholic tradition since the early nineteenth century (Giffords 1974; Luna 2000) and are still commissioned by migrant workers who have been delivered from some danger associated with the migrant experience (Durand and Massey 1995). Painted *ex voto* of this sort are also commonly found in churches in Central and South America and in Spain and Italy (though painted on wood rather than tin). But they are not found at Chimayó. At first, this seemed a minor detail. After all, the fact that pictures and statues were being brought to Chimayó as *ex voto* seemed more important than the type of pictures and statues involved.

In 1999, however, my visit to New Mexico coincided with Holy Week, and so afforded me the opportunity to visit Chimayó during the period when, everyone agrees, the pilgrims are most numerous. Because it had never been done, I wanted to do a before-and-after assessment of the *ex voto* in the sacristy, comparing the contents of that room on Holy Thursday (before the arrival of the thousands of pilgrims on Good Friday) with the contents of the room at the end of the day on Good Friday. So, on Holy Thursday I entered the sacristy around 8 PM (there were few people around and so getting inside was a simple matter) and, using a hand-held counter in my coat pocket, counted the number of items in cat-

TABLE 6
Objects Left by Pilgrims in the Sacristy at Chimayó,
Holy Thursday Evening and Good Friday Evening, 1999

Type of Item	Holy Thursday (as of 8 PM)	Good Friday (as of 8 PM)	Net Change
Religious pictures and paintings	89	100	+11
Religious statues	99	104	+5
Crucifixes	13	15	+2
Rosaries	5	10	+5
Glass-enclosed votive candles	72	19	−53
Crutches	22	24	+2

egories that more or less matched the categories used by Gutiérrez (crutches, rosaries, religious pictures, religious statues). This count is given in the first column of Table 6.

The next day, Good Friday, I visited the sanctuary in the morning, afternoon, and evening. It was packed with pilgrims on each occasion (notwithstanding the cold weather that year). By my calculation, it took someone joining the end of the line about 90 minutes to reach the church entrance. I joined the line in the evening, around 6:30, so that I would get to the sacristy around the same time I'd been there the night before. When I reached the sacristy, I was confronted with a display for which I was completely unprepared.

Stuck into every nook and cranny of the sacristy were hundreds, possibly thousands, of small photos. Most were wallet size, either school photos or the sort of photos taken at coin-operated photo machines, and depicted a single individual. There had been maybe half a dozen photos like this the night before, each stuck into the frame of a religious picture, but I hadn't bothered counting them because I had assumed that they had been put there by the people who had brought the pictures (which I was counting). Obviously, however, depositing a photo of this sort was an important part of the pilgrimage experience for many Good Friday pilgrims, even though it was something unmentioned in all existing accounts. But there was a second surprise.

While in the sacristy, I did another count of the items I had counted the previous evening. The results of this count are presented in column 2 of Table 6. I should note that there was no wholesale replacement of items, that is, as far as I could tell, the vast majority of the "*ex voto*" counted in column 2 had been there the night before. What is significant, then, comparing the two columns, is that the overall number of these items had *decreased* slightly. This slight decrease, however, was the result of 53 candles[2] being taken away. Still, the number of new objects is relatively small given the number of pilgrims who went through the sacristy on Good Friday and considering the hundreds of small photos deposited. The significant pattern, in other words, is that the number of objects in the *ex voto* room—at least the sorts of objects given special attention in existing accounts of Chimayó—had increased little despite the thousands of pilgrims who had come to the sanctuary on Good Friday.

What did the hundreds of photos deposited at the sacristy on Good Friday mean? I didn't know and still don't. Possibly they were brought in fulfillment of a promise to do so if a favor was received. Possibly they represent a request made on behalf of the person in the photo. Possibly too, however, they represent an attempt to secure protection from danger or to identify with Chimayó by leaving a bit of "yourself" there. And possibly, they are put there for all these reasons. One reason we don't know what they mean, however, is that all previous investigators, in their rush to make Chimayó the "Lourdes of America," have focused on those objects that "seem" like *ex voto* but which (apparently) are unrelated to the Good Friday pilgrimage and have ignored the photos that Good Friday pilgrims themselves prefer to leave at the shrine.

The focus on crutches, statues, and religious pictures is not the only way existing accounts of Chimayó have misrepresented the pilgrimage experience there. Typically, these same accounts give a distorted view of the history of the shrine since its founding in the early 1800s. Most existing accounts (in particular de Borhegyi 1956; Gutiérrez 1995) employ a common formula in presenting the history of the Chimayó shrine: they start by identifying it as a popular pilgrimage site and then go on to discuss (1) the founding of the original chapel by Bernardo Abeyta c. 1813, (2) its links to the Guatemalan shrine in honor of Nuestro Señor de Esquípulas established during the late sixteenth century, and (3) the Santo Niño cult installed at Chimayó in the late 1900s. The strong implication that flows easily out of all this is that Chimayó has been a popular pilgrimage site *since* the early 1800s (i.e., right from the time it was founded) and that it is heir to a continuing tradition of pilgrimage associated with the Spanish Americas. The addition by some writers that the site had previously been sacred to the Tewa Indians only reinforces this emphasis on longstanding and continuing traditions. Indeed, Ramón Gutiérrez (1995, 1) does this when he reports that "legend holds that pilgrims have been traveling to Chimayó for at least six hundred years" (p. 71) and that "during the early nineteenth century, the shrine constructed at Chimayó . . . became the northernmost shrine in an extensive network of shrines that extended from New Mexico all the way south to Central America" (p. 74). Gutiérrez goes on to suggest that this "network of shrines" included such well-known shrines as Nuestra Señora de San Juan de los Lagos in San Juan de Los Lagos, Nuestra Señora de Talpa in Talpa, and Nuestra Señora de Guadalupe in Mexico City. However, the suggestion that Chimayó was a popular pilgrimage site during the nineteenth century, and—in particular—that it was part of a "shrine complex" that included other undeniably popular shrines like those listed by Gutiérrez, is a claim unsupported by the historical evidence.

It is true that during the early 1800s, church authorities in Durango (New Mexico being part of the Diocese of Durango in Mexico at the time) issued a license permitting public masses to be celebrated in the chapel at Chimayó and that this license was renewed several times in succeeding years (Chávez 1957). This was not done, however, because large numbers of people were visiting Chimayó. On the contrary, as Fray Alvarez, the parish priest at Santa Cruz de la Cañada, made clear in his letter of support, the license was needed mainly because the residents of Chimayó found it difficult to get to the parish church at Santa Cruz de la Cañada to hear mass.[3]

Things changed a bit after Abeyta's death in 1856. Sometime in the late 1850s, another resident of Chimayó, Severiano Medina, fulfilled a vow to make a pilgrimage to the shrine of Santo Niño de Atocha in Plateros, Mexico, if he were to be cured of rheumatism (which he was). Medina returned with an image of the Santo Niño, and a chapel was erected to house this image very near the santuario. The Santo Niño cult proved popular, and shortly the newer chapel was attracting far more pilgrims than the *santuario*. In response, the Abeyta family installed their own Santo Niño image, in the *santuario*. Although the image they used was really an image of the Infant of Prague (de Borhegyi 1956), it was *seen* to be an image of the Santo Niño de Atocha and began to attract pilgrims on that basis. Very quickly the Santo Niño cult at the *santuario* eclipsed the Esquípulas cult in popularity (Nunn 1993). Although the number of pilgrims to the *santuario* became greater than earlier in the century, it did not become the sort of pilgrimage site it is today.

For example, one of the earliest accounts of a visit to the *santuario* that we have comes from the Pueblo potter María Martínez (c. 1887–1980), who in later life recalled a visit to the *santuario* that she had made during the 1890s (Marriott 1948). Martínez's account is interesting mainly because of what's missing. First, although Martínez mentions the Santo Niño image on the main altar, she says nothing about the Esquípulas cult—thus reinforcing the conclusion that it was the Santo Niño cult, not the Esquípulas cult, which attracted pilgrims in this period. Also missing from Martínez's account is the suggestion—routinely made in modern accounts of Chimayó—that the holy dirt had curative properties in the same way that water from Lourdes is said to. Martínez had been severely ill with a fever several months before their pilgrimage, and her mother had promised the Santo Niño that she would bring Maria to the *santuario* if Maria survived the illness. But it was only when Maria had recovered fully and regained enough strength to walk to Chimayó that she and her family made the pilgrimage. At the *santuario*, Maria did rub dirt from the posita over her body; but since she was fully recovered, the purpose, as her mother told her (Marriott 1948), was to secure the continuing protection of the Santo Niño over the rest of her life. Most importantly, what is also missing from Martínez's account—even though it is central to the modern experience of pilgrimage at Chimayó—is any association of pilgrimage to Chimayó with Holy Week, and in particular, any suggestion that large numbers of Hispano Catholics went to Chimayó during Holy Week.

If the church at Chimayó (at best) attracted only a very limited number of pilgrims from outside the local area during the late nineteenth and early twentieth centuries, that would explain why there is no mention of Chimayó in accounts that almost certainly would have taken note of a popular pilgrimage site in the Santa Fe area if such a site had existed. There is, for instance, no mention of Chimayó in the pastoral letter that Antonio de Zubaría, Bishop of Durango, issued from Santa Cruz de la Cañada during his 1833 visitation to New Mexico. Nor is there anything in the documentary record to suggest that Jean Baptiste Lamy, Bishop and then Archbishop of Santa Fe from 1852 to 1885, ever discussed Chimayó as a pilgrimage site (see, for example, Steele 2000). Nor is Chimayó mentioned in the ecclesiastical history of New Mexico and Arizona written by John B. Salpointe (1898), who succeeded Lamy as Archbishop of Santa Fe in 1885.

True, a few stories about Chimayó were published over the period 1880 to 1920. The focus of these stories, which were always addressed to the general public, however, was the "holy dirt" and the people who traveled to Chimayó in search of a miraculous cure. Thus, on October 3, 1885, the *Santa Fe New Mexican* reported,

> Perhaps it is not generally known that there is a spot of consecrated ground within a few day's drive of Santa Fe, where there is not a day in the year but that some distressed (person) applies the consecrated dust to his or her body. . . . the writer was told by the devout layman that has officiated in the chapel for thirty years that not a case that has visited the holy place, in good faith, but has recovered. (reproduced in La Farge 1970, 125)

A few years later, another report about Chimayó (Walter 1916, 2) made the same point:

Stories are told of the cures effected by the holy clay from the little chapel. . . . A few weeks ago, a woman from Galisteo who had been a paralytic for ten years (and) who had been pronounced incurable by physicians (came) to Chimayó. She had been unable to walk for years, but upon her return from the Santuario, while near Pojoaque, she leaped from the wagon to the great joy of her relatives with her, and since then has been able to walk and work as she did before she had been stricken with paralysis.

What is still missing from these reports is anything suggesting that Chimayó was a place of mass pilgrimage that attracted thousands of people each year, that it had some special appeal to Hispano Catholics, or that pilgrimage to Chimayó was associated with Holy Week (an association now central to the pilgrimage experience at Chimayó).

Additional evidence for believing that Chimayó was not a particularly important pilgrimage site until relatively recently is to be found in the reason that the Abeyta family gave for selling the chapel in 1929 to a group of Anglos: too few people were visiting the chapel and making donations (Kay 1987). This, incidentally, was *not* because outsiders never came to Chimayó. On the contrary, recollections collected from people who had grown up in the Chimayó area in the early part of the twentieth century suggest that a great many outsiders did come to Chimayó, but they came for the annual celebration in honor of Santiago (St. James), Chimayó's patron saint (Usner 1995); they did not come to visit the Abeyta chapel. Nor is there anything in a story about Chimayó published in the mid-1930s (Hurt 1934) which suggested that the chapel was at that time a popular pilgrimage site or in any way associated with Holy Week.

Finally, as far as I can determine, there is no mention of a pilgrimage to Chimayó in any of the stories that the *Santa Fe New Mexican* published during Holy Week for the years 1938–1946. This is true even though the newspaper did routinely alert its readers to church services (both Catholic and Protestant) in and around Santa Fe during Holy Week and did pay attention to popular Catholic practice during this period. Quite often, for example, the *New Mexican* published stories about the Penitentes around this time of the year. In some years the *New Mexican* also described a type of pilgrimage (their term) that took place in Santa Fe on Holy Thursday. In its Good Friday (March 23rd) edition for 1940 the paper reported (p. 8):

Yesterday, Holy Thursday, there took place in Santa Fe the observance of a custom probably not observed anywhere else in this country on such a scale. The streets were filled with persons, marching from one Catholic church to another—to pay a visit to each. It was the pilgrimage done once a year by many of those of the Catholic faith and one that apparently never grows old for them.   .

The story goes on to note that on this occasion church authorities opened many churches normally closed to the public ("like the little buttressed chapel of St. Michael's College"). A similar story about this Holy Thursday pilgrimage published on the *New Mexican*'s front page on April 21, 1943, reports that "thousands" of Catholics participated. But although the *New Mexican* reported on this Holy Week pilgrimage, there is no mention of a pilgrimage to Chimayó during these years.

So, just when *did* Chimayó become the truly popular pilgrimage site that it is today? As far as I can tell, it is only in the week following Easter in 1946 that we first encounter evidence of anything resembling the modern pilgrimage to Chimayó. A story in the April 24th issue of the *Santa Fe New Mexican* in 1946 announced that there would be a mass said on Sunday in the *santuario* at Chimayó "as a culmination of a pilgrimage which a number of Bataan survivors are planning." Ten men, the story continues, would be making the trek from Santa Fe to Chimayó on foot, and buses would be provided for others. A few days later another story (published on the front page on Saturday April 27th) revealed that this pilgrimage was the result of a vow that the Bataan survivors had made while in a Japanese prisoner-of-war camp. The event on Sunday was described in a front-page story published on Monday, April 29th:

> More than 500, probably the largest congregation ever to attend services in El Santuario, Chimayó's famed chapel, were present at 10 a.m. High Mass yesterday which culminated the weekend pilgrimage of veterans to that tiny community.... Twenty-three veterans—all but two members of New Mexico's 200th Coast Artillery which was captured on Bataan—made the 26 mile march.... The crowd overflowed until the 50 ft. patio in front of the church was more than half-filled. The narrow streets and yards of the rolling hillside confronting the church were filled with other groups and autos parked every which way.... After the service with its sermon in Spanish had been completed, those in the patio surged into the chapel and the little side shrine was crowded with a patient stream of supplicants who gathered handfuls of the soil from the dry well, which supposedly has curative powers.

This story is significant for at least two reasons. First, although the writer takes it as obvious that readers will know about Chimayó, he or she is also suggesting that a crowd of 500 or so people at the sanctuary is something unusual. Second, although Easter had been a week earlier, and although this pilgrimage was clearly rooted in what had happened to these men after the fall of Bataan (which happened on April 9, 1942), the fact remains that this is one of the earliest reports that even comes close to linking a pilgrimage to Chimayó with Holy Week.

Interestingly, the slight lack of fit between this 1946 pilgrimage and Holy Week has been "adjusted" in the retelling. Thus, in the preface to a photo-essay on Chimayó, Enrique Lamadrid (1999, 23) tells us:

> Pilgrimage to the Santuario exploded after the end of World War II, and the newly paved roads were an important factor in improving communication and transportation. The *tremendous Holy Week celebration of 1946* with its thousands of veterans and former prisoners of war on the road to Chimayó is still a powerful living memory. (Emphasis added.)

While this account does at least acknowledge that the modern pilgrimage experience is a product of the postwar period—and setting aside the fact that the *dozens* of veterans who made the 1946 pilgrimage have now become *thousands*—Lamadrid has the original pilgrimage occurring during Holy Week, and so *before* Easter, even though the reality is that it was staged after Easter. I don't fault Lamadrid for the chronological error. On the contrary, his reference to "powerful living memory" makes it likely that he is presenting what the older participants in the Chimayó pilgrimage now truly believe: that this pilgrimage has been associated with Holy Week since its postwar inception.

In the end, then, there are two models of Hispanic spirituality associated with Chimayó. The first, the model promoted in existing scholarly accounts, claims that Chimayó has been a popular pilgrimage destination for centuries, that the pilgrimage is a continuation of pilgrimage traditions common throughout the Spanish Americas, that the pilgrims who go to Chimayó go there because they associate the holy dirt at Chimayó with miraculous cures of the sort ascribed to the spring water at Lourdes, and that, in gratitude for these cures, the pilgrims leave crutches, canes, and objects that are distinctively religious but generally impersonal. The problem with this model is that it is unsupported by the historical record. The second model is the one that has emerged in the discussion here: both Chimayó's popularity with Hispano Catholics and the association of the Chimayó pilgrimage with Holy Week are relatively recent phenomena, having emerged only after World War II, and the Hispanic pilgrims who come on Good Friday leave objects (wallet-sized photos) that are not overtly religious or obviously indicative of miraculous cure but which are indisputably tied to some particular individual.

I grant that there are many gaps in this second model that need to be filled in.

What, for example, do the pictures brought to Chimayó on Good Friday mean? Was Chimayó's postwar popularity the result of something happening in the Hispanic community or was it part of that more general religious revival that has been documented (Noll 1992) for both Catholic and Protestant groups in the aftermath of World War II? But questions such as these cannot begin to be addressed until the first model is set aside. After all, we will never come to understand why Hispano pilgrims leave gifts on Good Friday if we continue to focus on the *wrong ex voto*, on the objects that are clearly NOT the ones left by these particular pilgrims. Nor will we be able to answer questions about Chimayó's postwar popularity if we continue to believe—à la Gutierrez and others—that it has been a popular pilgrimage site for centuries.

But all of this raises a question that is more historiographical than historical: if the first model of Hispanic piety associated with Chimayó is so easily discredited and so easily shown to be an obstacle in coming to understand the modern experience of pilgrimage at Chimayó, then why has this model been so popular for so long with scholars and their audiences? A clue to the answer, I suggest, is to be found by looking more closely at something that has already been mentioned: the Abeyta family's sale of the chapel in 1929.

Preserving an Imagined Past

During the 1920s, a group of Anglos in the Santa Fe area—whose most prominent members included Mary Austin, Frank Applegate, and John Gaw Meem—formed the Society for the Revival of Spanish-Colonial Arts (later to be formally incorporated as the Spanish Colonial Arts Society).[4] The stated goals of the organization were to preserve Spanish-Colonial (Hispanic) art and to educate the general public about the important role that such art has played in the history of New Mexico. Writing in *Commonweal*, Mary Austin (1928c, 574) made it clear why such a society was needed and why Anglos needed to take the lead:

> [The] lovely arts of weaving and carving and painting and dyeing fell into disuse [after Annexation]. . . . Slowly the natives surrendered to the lure of the mail order catalogue. Only just in time to save them from oblivion, within the last fifteen years, artists and people of a more sophisticated culture began coming to New Mexico, and discovered that there were still reminders of the Spanish culture worth saving.

The implication is that enlightened and sophisticated Anglos like herself had to preserve the Hispano heritage of New Mexico because the Hispanos themselves had no interest, in Austin's view, in doing so.

Although Austin herself seems to have been interested mainly in preserving traditions associated with *bultos, retablos*, weaving, and the like, others in the Society—notably Frank Applegate and the architect John Gaw Meem—were proponents of the Pueblo Spanish architectural style that became fashionable in the Santa Fe and Taos areas during the 1920s and 1930s.[5] The defining features of this architectural style are an emphasis on rounded corners, on walls made of material that simulated adobe both in texture and color (which usually meant stucco over reinforced concrete), and on buttresses. Although the Pueblo Spanish style was very much a reversal of the sort of architectural designs that had flourished in New Mexico over the period 1875–1910, it was promoted as the continuation of traditions dating from the colonial period, and it functioned to create a romanticized impression of the past that very much appealed (then and now) to the Anglo tourists flocking to Santa Fe and Taos.

Architects like Meem designed new structures, including both public buildings and private homes, which conformed to the new style. But because the style was sold as the continuation of something that had long been in place, a number of older buildings which should have conformed to the style (because they dated from the pre-Annexation period) but didn't were renovated to create the image that tourists wanted to see. The tourists who now flock to Taos to see the rounded adobe walls and flowing back buttress of San Francisco de Asís church—an image immortalized in one of Georgia O'Keeffe's best-known paintings—would, I think, be quite surprised to see the more angular church that existed around the turn of the century. But older church buildings were also important to Austin and her group for reasons that went beyond architectural design.

In three articles she wrote for *Commonweal* (1928a; 1928b; 1928c), Austin asserted that colonial New Mexico had been a society in which the "whole of its aesthetic and social life [was] centered around the living church," with the result that the "relations of the colonists and the Indians were better adjusted humanly than in other pioneer settlements" (she dismisses the Pueblo Revolt in 1680 as an aberration!), and that "Catholicism saved the colonies of New Mexico from what happened everywhere else in the United States—the separation of the economic life of the community from beauty, grace and suavity."

Given their view of New Mexico's past (as regards both architecture and culture), it was natural that Austin and her group in Santa Fe would take an interest in the nearby church at Chimayó. For proponents of the Pueblo Spanish style like Meem, it epitomized what they were trying to promote and preserve: not only was the church itself made of adobe, but it had a front courtyard surrounded by rounded adobe walls and an *acequia* (irrigation ditch) flowing in front of the courtyard. Indeed, writing a decade earlier, Paul Walter (1916, 6) had identified the church at Chimayó as "probably the most charming bit of primitive Santa Fe architecture in existence." But this church was also important because it could be taken as a living reminder of the role that Catholicism had (supposedly) played in structuring New Mexican life during the colonial period. Elizabeth Willis De Huff (1931, 39), a member of Austin's circle, made this clear in an article on Chimayó she wrote for the *New Mexico Highway Journal:*

> Though the faith of their fathers may die, the Santuario beneath the old cotton-woods whose myriad branches droop like protecting arms before it, with the *acequia madre* running around it as if in motherly embrace, stands as a monument and a memorial to those earlier beliefs of the simple-living weavers of Chimayó.

Given all that Chimayó stood for, then, it is hardly surprising that Austin and her group became alarmed when they learned that the church at Chimayó might lose some of its connections to the past.

Sometime in the late 1920s, María de los Angeles Cháves, Bernardo Abeyta's granddaughter, offered many of the artifacts found at Chimayó (including the carved wooden doors and an old *bulto* of Santiago) for sale to antique dealers. These sales came to the attention of Austin and her group, who got the editor of the *Santa Fe New Mexican* to publicize the situation. Eventually, Austin was able to raise money from a private donor to purchase the church,[6] and the deed transferring title to the archdiocese was signed by Cháves at her home on October 15, 1929. John Gaw Meem's signature appears on the deed as a witness (Kay 1987).

Understanding why Chimayó was so important to Austin and her group helps us see why the usual story scholars tell about Chimayó has been so uncritically accepted, despite the fact that it is historically inaccurate. Simply put, the idea that Chimayó has been an important pilgrimage site for centuries and that it had links to Spanish colonial traditions of pilgrimage that are even older fits well with the romanticized vision of New Mexico's past that Anglos like Austin and Meem were selling—a vision that continues to sell well with the hordes of non-Hispanic tourists who come to the Santa Fe–Taos region each year. Phrased differently, the usual story about Chimayó uses faux history to establish the same sense of continuity with a Spanish colonial past that architects like Meem have tried to promote using faux adobe. The fact that Anglos often hear this appealing story about Chimayó from Hispanic commentators like Ramón Gutiérrez only adds to its seeming authenticity.

The Hispano Catholic population of New Mexico is, I grant, only a small segment of the Hispanic Catholic population of the United States, and the Holy

Week pilgrimage to Chimayó—as important as it is—cannot alone represent the Hispano Catholic experience. In the end, then, the misperceptions about Chimayó that have been discussed to this point might seem to be of only marginal relevance to the more general concern of this chapter, which is to identify what is problematic in the scholarly literature on Hispanic Catholicism in the United States. What makes the Chimayó case relevant to that more general concern, however, is that when we do turn to more wide-ranging discussions of Hispanic Catholicism, we find just what we found in the Chimayó case: American scholars telling stories that are widely accepted but little supported by the available evidence. Consider, for example, what social scientists—mainly sociologists—say about Hispanic Catholicism.

What Makes Hispanic Catholicism Distinctive?

The word *Hispanic*, like *Latino* and *Latina* (preferred by some commentators), subsumes into a single category people who are undeniably diverse. Although most Hispanics in the United States are Chicano (Mexican American), the rest come from a variety of other national origins. Data derived from the 1990 U.S. census, for example, show that Mexico is the national origin of 61 percent of all Hispanics in the United States, with the corresponding percentages for other national origins being Puerto Rico, 12 percent; Cuba, 5 percent; and other countries in the Caribbean or Central or South America, 13 percent (Moore 1994). The remaining 9 percent are classed as "other Hispanic" by the Census Bureau, a term that refers mostly to Hispanics living in the Southwest who are descended from the Spanish who settled in this area during the colonial period (Moore 1994).

For a few social scientists, the diversity that exists within the Hispanic population precludes talking about a generic "Hispanic Catholicism" and necessitates a focus on particular national traditions. This point is made by Timothy Matovina and Gary Riebe-Estrella, for example, in introducing their collection of essays (2002) on Mexican traditions within American Catholicism. One result of this diversity is that there are now many studies, several of which I will be citing, that investigate popular Catholicism within individual Hispanic subcommunities— Mexican American, Cuban American, and so forth. However, the view that Hispanic diversity *precludes* talking about a generic Hispanic Catholicism is very much a minority position.

Most social scientists writing on Hispanic Catholicism first make passing acknowledgment of the diversity within the Hispanic population but then go on to suggest that, nevertheless, there are numerous elements that distinguish Hispanic Catholicism from the sort of Catholicism that prevails in other Catholic groups in the United States. Indeed, for scholars in this category, focusing on popular Catholicism within some particular Hispanic community *without* attempting to assess the extent to which the findings can be generalized to all Hispanic Catholics is considered a deficiency. In her review of Thomas Tweed's (1997a) study of religious practice at a Cuban exilic shrine in Miami, for example, Ana María Díaz-Stevens (1999) makes just this point, finding that Tweed's failure to make clear to what extent his conclusions do or do not apply to other U.S. Latino groups was the most serious flaw in his book.

Although different investigators come up with slightly different lists when identifying what is distinctive about Hispanic Catholicism, the one element that appears on almost all such lists is the claim that Hispanic Catholicism has a "matriarchal core." The following remarks are typical:

> It is to be noted that both in Spain and America, women who are barred from the ordained ministry play a very important role in *religiosidad popular*. The mother (or grandmother) is the great leader of prayer and transmitter of religious lore and values. *Rezadoras* are much more common than *rezadores*. (Vidal 1994, 85)

> . . . [T]he leadership of prayer life in the Hispanic community has traditionally been a feminine role. The main practitioners and promoters of popular religiosity are women. The first ways and words of prayer are taught by the *abuelas* (grandmothers), mothers, women religious and catechists. It is from them that the feeling of prayer, the holy, the love of God, Mary and the saints is transmitted. (Peréz 1994, 380)

> Family life is stronger among Latinos than among other Catholics. Women (Latinas) are more active in parish life and devotional life than Latino men, and commonly religion is defined among Latinos as being the women's domain. (D'Antonio, Davidson, Hoge, and Meyer 2001, 154)

> I believe that special attention must be paid to the role women have played in the maintenance of our [Hispanic Catholic] faith. Consecrated religious women have been present to the people in our neighborhoods in ways that other institutional religious leaders have not. . . . They often have greater influence and can claim higher levels of loyalty than the ordained clergy, basically because the common folk recognize wisdom when they see it. (Díaz-Stevens 2003, 176)

> For the most part, Latino rituals are preserved and led by the laity, especially lay women. The center of religious life is the home, where one finds private shrines or

home altars. In effect, Latino Catholicism embodies the ongoing influence of a "domestic church." Often a grandmother becomes the religious leader of the home and of the community. (Goizueta 2004, 2)

The claim being made in passages like these is not only that women are more likely to participate in religious activities (the feminization that is quite common in both the American Catholic and American Protestant traditions) or that women take charge of activities within the household unit, including those relating to religion; rather, the claim is that women, older women in particular, have been especially likely to take on leadership roles in connection with *communal* religious activities in Hispanic communities.

The "matriarchal core" hypothesis is of course entirely plausible. It is not difficult to imagine that under certain circumstances (say, for example, a scarcity of priests) women in a Catholic community might well take on such roles, both within the household and in regard to communal events. Indeed, that is exactly what seems to have happened in the Cajun communities discussed in the previous chapter. But suppose we ask the same sort of question that we have asked in earlier chapters in connection with Irish American Catholics, Italian American Catholics, and Cajun Catholics: What is the empirical basis for *believing* that Hispanic Catholicism has a matriarchal core? The answer, as I now hope to demonstrate, comes close to "there isn't any basis."

Searching for the Evidence

Searching for studies relevant to the matriarchal core hypothesis immediately turns up one important case that directly falsifies this hypothesis: the Penitentes of New Mexico, mentioned in passing in the discussion of Chimayó. The Penitentes were a lay brotherhood that emerged in northern New Mexico in the early nineteenth century. By mid-century, most villages and towns in the area were home to at least one local Penitente *morada* (a term that refers both to the local organizational unit of the brotherhood and to the meeting house that the local unit maintained). Importantly, at least for our purposes here, only males could become officers in the *morada* and participate in its core rituals. And yet, the public rituals sponsored by the Penitentes—especially those staged during Lent and Holy Week—were central to the experience of popular Catholicism for all members of the community, women and children included.[7] In this particular Hispanic context, in other words, there was clearly no matriarchal core to the lived experience of Hispanic Catholicism.

More usually, however, what we find in looking at studies of Hispanic Catholic practice is that the matriarchal core hypothesis is not so much falsified (as in the Penitente case) as unsupported. Consider, for example, Richard Flores's (1994a; 1994b) study of the Los Pastores skits. These dramatic presentations relate the story of Christ's nativity from the perspective of the shepherds and are performed at private homes in San Antonio, Texas. Typically, Flores found, a family invites a Los Pastores troupe to perform at their home in order to fulfill a vow made to the Virgin or to the Christ Child. The audience at these events consists of adults and children of both genders drawn from the sponsoring family and their neighbors, and there is a fairly traditional division of labor among the audience: the women of the household prepare a communal meal and serve it to the performers and attendees, and men from the household help the male performers lift the heavy props into place. The skit itself, however, is organized mainly by the performers, and it is the performers who decide when and where to perform.

What Flores found in the 1990s was that a majority of the performers, about two-thirds, were female. While at first sight this seems to lend support to the matriarchal core hypothesis, there are two additional gendered patterns that must also be taken into account. The first is that women of high school age were about as numerous as women who were 35 or older. But the second and more important pattern is that when these traveling troupes were first introduced into the San Antonio area from Mexico, they were dominated by males just as such troupes had been in Mexico. Photographs taken in the 1890s of a Los Pastores troupe that performed in San Antonio (presented in Cole 1907—see, for example, Figure 7) make it clear that, except for the character of Mary, the roles were all played by men. The inclusion of more females is a relatively recent phenomenon (and so not at all traditional); and in any event, there is no predominance of *older* women (which is what proponents of the matriarchal core hypothesis typically suggest is the case). On balance, the evidence from Flores's study provides no support for the claim that "older women known for their piety" have traditionally taken the lead in organizing and promoting communal religious rituals in Hispanic communities.

Thomas Tweed's (1997a) study of the Miami shrine in honor of Our Lady of Charity is another instance where the matriarchal core hypothesis fails to be substantiated. This shrine, established by Cuban exiles in Miami in 1973, is now the sixth most popular Catholic pilgrimage site in the United States. More importantly, it is also—to use Tweed's words (p. 3)—"the sacred center of the Cuban Catholic community in exile." Thousands of individual pilgrims come to the

Fig. 7. Players who performed in a San Antonio Los Pastores troupe in the 1890s. Note that all the players with the exception of the young girl who played Mary are male. From Cole 1907, 12.

shrine to petition the Virgin for a variety of favors or to fulfill a vow after a favor has been granted, and the shrine is also associated with a number of well-attended communal festivals that function to maintain a Cuban national identity. Tweed does report that participation in the religious events associated with the shrine is gendered: females usually outnumber males (both as pilgrims and among those attending the communal rituals). He also reports that (1) overall rates of religious participation are higher within the exilic community than they were in Cuba both before and after the revolution, and (2) that males, in particular, take a more active role in religious activities in Miami than was the case in Cuba. On the other hand, there is nothing in Tweed's discussion of the lay groups that organize the popular rituals and festivals associated with the shrine suggesting that the *leadership* of these groups is "matricentered" in the way that the matriarchal core hypothesis dictates. Generally, Tweed's sense of things is that, although women are probably a bit more involved in planning these public rituals than are men, planning is often joint (as when public rituals are organized by a married couple), men are slightly *more* likely to take the lead in public rituals (e.g., they are usually the ones who carry the statue of Our Lady of Charity from place to place during public ceremonies), and women are disproportionately the ones associated with support roles (like answering phones, providing flowers).[8] Here again we have a case study—done by an investigator very sensitive to the matter of gender—that provides no compelling evidence for the view that older women are the ones who generally take the lead in communal religious rituals in Hispanic communities.

In his study of the Mexican American community in Houston over the period 1911–1972, Roberto Treviño (2006) did find that women were especially likely to have charge of the *altarcitos* (small altars) constructed in private homes. But, again, finding that women are especially likely to be associated with the domestic sphere and so the things in that sphere (like *altarcitos*) hardly seems to support the sort of claim that scholars like Díaz-Stevens are making about the distinctiveness of Hispanic Catholic traditions. In any event, there is nothing in Treviño's discussion of parish societies or of popular religious activities staged outside the home—like the *pastorelas* or *las posadas* performed at Christmas time—which suggests that women, let alone older women, took the lead.

The studies mentioned so far—involving the Penitentes, Los Pastores troupes in San Antonio, Cuban-exilic Catholicism, the Mexican American community in Houston—might be dismissed as exceptions to the rule except for the fact that those promoting the matriarchal core hypothesis never present evidence that *establishes* the rule in the first place. On the contrary, many scholars who advance the matriarchal core hypothesis, including many of the scholars cited earlier in this discussion, simply *assert* that hypothesis without providing anything in the way of supportive evidence. Furthermore, in those cases where a scholar promoting this hypothesis does cite a study that supposedly provides supporting evidence, tracking down the cited study usually reveals that the evidence is less impressive than implied.

For example, one of the articles most often cited in support of the matriarchal core hypothesis is Ana María Díaz-Stevens's (1994) contribution to Jay Dolan and Allan Figueroa Deck's *Hispanic Catholic Culture in the U.S.* Thus, Milagros Peña (2002, 283–284) tells us:

> Ana María Díaz-Stevens (1994: 241) has documented that within the Latino/a community "religion has oftentimes given Latinas affirmation as leaders, especially at the grassroots level." In her research Díaz-Stevens asked young Latinos/as in New York City aged 15–25 who was the person they most respected in their community aside from their parents. Two thirds of them mentioned an elderly woman in the community known for her piety and her role as the leader of non-ecclesiastical religious communal rituals and prayer.

Up to a point, Peña's summary here is an accurate account of what Díaz-Stevens does report in her 1994 essay, but Peña leaves out some critical details. For example, Díaz-Stevens's respondents were all Puerto Rican, and so Peña's leap to "Latinos/as" *generally* is pure inference. Also, Díaz-Stevens interviewed only 30 people in total, and so the conclusion about matricentricity rests upon the responses given by 20 people ("two thirds" of 30). But the most serious problem is that Díaz-Stevens (1994) was only providing a brief summary of a study she did as a graduate student in 1980, and that study—as she herself tells us—was never published. This is important because there is nothing in her summary indicating how she reached the conclusion that the women "most respected" by these 20 respondents were also women known for their piety and/or women who took the lead in communal religious rituals. For that matter, there is nothing in her summary that tells us how many of the 20 women named by these respondents were simply seen to be "pious" (which might mean no more than that they participated in religious activities more than men or other women) nor how many were identified as being both pious *and* as taking the lead in communal religious activities (which is clearly the claim most relevant to the matriarchal core hypothesis). In principle, this sort of information might be retrieved by looking at the original interview data, to find out just what the critical 20 respondents did and did not say in answer to particular questions. Unfortunately, the relevant records were destroyed when a basement was flooded several years ago (information obtained from Professor Díaz-Stevens in a telephone call in April 2005). The net result: at this point, it is simply not possible to know if the conclusions that Díaz-Stevens reached about matricentricity—and which have been repeated by Peña and many others—were reasonable given the interview data she collected in 1980.

Interestingly, given that Professor Díaz-Stevens is one of the leading exponents of the matriarchal core hypothesis and given that her work is so often cited in support of that hypothesis, an argument can be made that if we read her own account of growing up in a Puerto Rican mountain village (presented in Díaz-Stevens 1993) as ethnography, then we have yet another case study that fails to provide support for this hypothesis and, indeed, even seems to falsify it. She describes several religious activities in her natal community in which laity took the lead—and in some of these cases, undeniably, women did clearly play a more active role than did men. We are told, for example, that one of the respected people in the village was the local midwife and that she baptized children right after birth. Díaz-Stevens also tells us that her own mother asked for God's blessing each day as she opened the windows and doors of their house. On the other hand, we are also told that she and her siblings always asked for a blessing "from our parents" (i.e., from both father and mother) when they left the house to go to the fields or to school and when they returned. But most importantly, perhaps, given the matriarchal core hypothesis, the only gendered pattern that Díaz-Stevens mentions when discussing *communal* religious rituals in her natal community are patterns that associate lay religious leadership with older males, not older females. During Holy Week, for example, it was her father who led the family in prayer. Her father also had a reputation for being both a good *rezador* and a good *cantador,* we are told, and so was regularly asked to participate in wakes and in village-wide Christmas celebrations, by people in both his own village and neighboring villages. Finally, we are told that her father became the village catechist "by public acclamation" (1993, p. 8) after her uncle, who had previously performed that role, migrated. The fact that her father and her uncle are the only people she mentions as associated with communal religious life is the reverse of what the matriarchal core hypothesis would lead us to expect.

Yolanda Tarango is another example of a scholar who advances the matriarchal core hypothesis and yet whose own history undermines that hypothesis. Toward the end of her essay on the role of Hispanic women in the church, Tarango (1995) tells us that "Hispanic women [have] always been identified with religious leadership in the community." Earlier, however, in describing her grandmother and the women of her grandmother's generation, she recounts (p. 41):

> I feel I entered the church at my grandmother's side through the stories she would tell me of her childhood. These were usually narratives of family and communal events framed in liturgical celebrations, such as patronal feasts and holy days. When she described encounters with the official church, *the men of my family were usually the principal actors. Many stories included accounts of my great-grandfather and uncles and their confrontations with the foreign priests in an effort to preserve cultural rituals.* (Emphasis added.)

While this account certainly supports the view that older women were key agents in the religious socialization of children within Hispanic households, it also suggests that lay *men,* not lay women, were the ones who exercised leadership in regard to religious events at the community level.

Roberto Goizueta also cites evidence in support of the matriarchal core hypothesis that turns out to be something less than supportive when examined carefully. Goizueta (2002, 135) says:

> Mexican American popular Catholicism has its principal locus in the home, the family, and the neighborhood rather than the geographical parish. As a consequence, everyday religious authority and leadership are exercised by the persons who have historically carried out those functions in the domestic sphere, namely,

women—especially the *abuelas,* or grandmothers, whose age and experience give them a special claim to authority. . . . This is not to say that the *padrecito,* or parish priest, is not respected or recognized as a religious leader; on an everyday basis, it is the women of the family who function as religious teachers or as liturgical leaders. Thus, Matovina cites the influential role played by the Hijas de María in the historical development of San Fernando Cathedral.

The reference in the final sentence is to Timothy Matovina's (2002) study of devotion to the Virgen de Guadalupe at San Fernando Cathedral in San Antonio, Texas, over the period 1900–1940. Matovina's study, I must note, is the *only* study that Goizueta cites in support of the matriarchal core hypothesis. Yet, when we consult the Matovina study, does it indeed provide the support this hypothesis implied by Goizueta? No, it does not.

Matovina (p. 28) is very clear in saying that "parishioners exerted their strongest leadership and influence at San Fernando through the numerous pious societies that they established and developed." Furthermore, Matovina's analysis of parish records does indicate that the Hijas de María (Daughters of Mary)—the society mentioned by Goizueta—"surpassed all other pious societies in organized plays, concerts, dinners, picnics, booths for parish festivals and other fundraising events" (p. 31). The problem here is the Hijas de María was an association composed of unmarried *younger* women. Hence, the fact that this group organized so many activities provides no support for Goizueta's (and Díaz-Stevens's) "leadership by *abuelas*" claim. Further, although there were several pious societies active in the parish, including, in addition to the Hijas de María, the Vasallos de Cristo Rey (composed of males) and the Vasallas de Cristo Rey (composed of females), there is nothing in Matovina's discussion suggesting that female associations, on balance, took more of a lead in organizing important communal celebrations than did the male associations. Here again, in other words, as in Tweed's study of the Our Lady of Charity shrine in Miami, we do encounter gendered patterns when looking carefully at the practice of popular Catholicism in a Hispanic community, but what we find is a mix, with males and females both involved but doing slightly different things. What we do *not* find is evidence that the individuals who took the lead in organizing popular religious activities outside the home, that is, in the community at large, were predominantly older women—which is what the matriarchal core hypothesis leads us to expect.

But, if it is so easy to locate studies that either falsify or at least fail to support the commonly advanced suggestion that Hispano Catholicism has a matriarchal core, and if proponents of that hypothesis fail to present convincing evidence in its favor, then we are once again confronted with a historiographical puzzle: why has a claim like this enjoyed such wide popularity within the American academic community? I think there are two answers here, and the first emerges when we look carefully at the meta-concerns shaping the work of those Hispanic scholars who have most forcefully advanced this claim.

Pervaded by Confessional Bias

During the 1970s, a number of historians, including Eric Cochrane (1970), Denys Hay (1977), and Giovanni Miccoli (1974), leveled some strong criticisms at the academic study of church history in Europe, especially in Italy. Too often, they argued, church history had become the preserve of scholars affiliated with the church or a church-sponsored university, which usually meant affiliation with one or another of the religious orders (Franciscans, Dominicans, Jesuits, etc.) within the church. While these scholars were in the main undeniably intelligent, thorough, and diligent, their scholarship—so the criticism went—was often shaped by their confessional orientation. Sometimes this meant only that they tended to focus on events of interest to the religious order of which they were a part but the larger historical significance of which was nil. "How many man-hours have been spent," bemoaned Hay (p. 6) in identifying the place and time of Savonarola's ordinations? . . . [H]ow many periodicals list similar details for thousands of dim and insignificant friars?" But mainly, the critics argued, the strongly confessional orientation of so many church historians in Italy meant that Italian church history was pervaded by apologetics (a desire to defend the church against criticism) and homiletics (which in this case meant a desire to use history for spiritual edification). As examples of this, Cochrane pointed to books on Italian church history that were concerned with demonstrating that the church had always been committed to the "defense of liberty for all men" and to books that used the concrete events of history to support assertions like "the well-being of the human personality results from the harmony with which body and soul . . . contribute the vital efficiency of the human composite." In a similar vein, Miccoli pointed to well-known church historians who worked hard to establish the claim that popes had treated Jews more favorably than other European leaders had or that the atrocities associated with the Crusades must be balanced against the pious works performed by many Crusaders—in this latter case conveniently forgetting, Miccoli adds, that the Crusaders saw their massacres to *be* pious works.

Fortunately, the confessional bias that Cochrane, Hay, and Miccoli saw as pervading the study of church history in Europe during the 1970s is less in evidence today. Unfortunately, a similar confessional bias seems alive and well among those social scientists who have written on Hispanic Catholicism, and in particular, among those social scientists who have advanced the matriarchal core hypothesis in their work.

As a start, a great many of these scholars have strong ties to the institutional Catholic Church. Just to take people already mentioned: Ana María Díaz-Stevens was associated with the Maryknoll Sisters and later worked for the Archdiocese of New York (Díaz-Stevens 1993); Anthony M. Stevens-Arroyo is a former priest and during the 1970s was assistant to Father Robert Stern, the director of the Office of Spanish Community Action for the Archdiocese of New York; Roberto Goizueta is a professor of theology at Boston College, an institution whose web page affirms the college's continuing commitment to its "Catholic and Jesuit heritage"; Allan Figueroa Deck is a Jesuit theologian. Similarly, of the eleven contributors to Jay Dolan and Allan Figueroa Deck's *Hispanic Catholic Culture in the U.S.* (1994), three are priests, one is a "consultant on pastoral and ministry education issues that arise from the multicultural Church," and another is editor-at-large of *Maryknoll Magazine*. In more recent scholarship, of the nineteen contributors to *El Cuerpo de Cristo: The Hispanic Presence in the U.S. Catholic Church* (Casarella and Gómez 2003), twelve are priests and/or members of a religious order and/or Catholic theologians.

I am not suggesting that these strong ties to the institutional church are problematic in and of themselves; what I am suggesting is that these ties help explain why a set of three interrelated claims appears over and over again in the social scientific literature on Hispanic Catholicism, namely,

- the claim that over the past several decades, Hispanic Catholics have come to account for a larger and larger proportion of the American Catholic Church;
- the claim that it is imperative that the church develop pastoral strategies that recognize and embrace this increasing Hispanic presence; and
- the claim that getting the official church to recognize and embrace this increasing Hispanic presence is the key to revitalizing the American Catholic Church.

Representative statements encapsulating all these claims would include:

This book is written with the conviction that what is done to promote the effective pastoral care of Hispanics today will determine to a degree still not fully appreciated the vitality and effectiveness of the U.S. Catholic Church of the twenty-first century.

There can be no greater priority for the Church, her priests, pastoral ministers, and teachers than the flesh and blood people who will constitute the majority of the Catholic faithful in the United States in the very near future. Those people shall be of Hispanic origin. (Deck 1989, 2)

It scarcely needs repeating that the future of Catholicism in the United States will be shaped by Hispanics, who at 34 million are already the most numerous "minority" in the country and constitute a majority of Catholics in many dioceses. The religious affiliation of these Hispanics will largely determine which churches grow and which ones wither in the 21st-century United States. (Stevens-Arroyo 2003, 16)

Latino traditions can save the Church in the United States. . . . Of course, the term "Latino" is artificial; there are Cuban Americans, Mexican Americans, Puerto Ricans, Hondurans, and so on. Nevertheless, they all share characteristics beyond their common language-traits with the potential to influence U.S. Catholicism's future. The two most significant of these are the broad experience of *mestizaje* or *mulataje*, racial and cultural mixing; and a tradition of popular Catholicism. (Goizueta 2004)

The confessional orientation of these scholars, who are themselves usually Hispanic, and their commitment to the belief that revitalization of the U.S. Catholic Church requires that the church treat Hispanic Catholics and Hispanic Catholicism more favorably than it has in the past, helps to explain, I contend, many of the things that make the literature on Hispanic Catholicism distinctive.

This confessional orientation helps explain why works by these scholars—just like the literature on church history criticized decades ago by Cochrane, Hay, and Miccoli—so often comingles social science, theology, and homiletics. Roberto Goizueta (Goizueta 2002, 1), for instance, sees no problem with mixing statements describing Via Crucis and Día de los Muertos celebrations in Hispanic communities with statements like "popular religion does indeed affirm life and expresses a hope-against-hope that, in the long run constitutes the very foundation of the struggle for justice" (p. 137) and "in a world that, as we have seen, refuses to separate the physical from the spiritual, and understands the personal as inherently communal, what is healed is not only the body of an individual but the person's whole world" (p. 138). Similarly, Virgilio Elizondo (1994), himself a priest in San Antonio, concludes a section on the critical importance of devotion to Virgen de Guadalupe in the maintenance of a Mexican American identity with the suggestion that the sacrament of baptism is "the complementary symbol of Guadalupe" (p. 123) because "through baptism a child not only becomes a child of God . . . but equally are children of our common mother of the Americas, Nuestra Señora de Guadalupe" (p. 125).

Nor is this tendency to merge social science and theology accidental or the result of sloppy conceptualization. Quite the contrary, for these scholars it is something that is both legitimate and desired. Díaz-Stevens and Stevens-Arroyo (1998, 6), for example, tell us that "the analysis of religion requires examination from two perspectives." The first of these looks at how religion is shaped by its social environment, and that is the task of social science. But, they continue, "we also need to recognize that . . . religion challenges the social context [and often] the best window on religion's challenges to society is theology" (p. 8). Furthermore, although this latter statement talks only about "religion's challenges to society," Díaz-Stevens and Stevens-Arroyo go on (see especially pp. 212–238) to make it clear that this entails both reform of society in general and reform of the church in particular, and that theology is important to reaching both goals.

Something else that is a common feature of the existing social scientific literature on Hispanic Catholicism, and that likely flows from the confessional orientation of many of the scholars who have produced this literature, is an emphasis on pastoral outreach programs—even when it means ignoring things that might otherwise seem important. To take a particularly clear example: the term "oxcart Catholicism" in Ana Maria Díaz-Steven's *Oxcart Catholicism on Fifth Avenue* (1993)—which as far as I can tell is one of the monographs cited most often in sociological accounts of Hispanic Catholicism—refers to the sort of popular Catholicism that Díaz-Stevens knew while growing up in Puerto Rico. What the title implies, in other words, is that the book will be about Puerto Rican popular Catholicism as it developed when transplanted to New York city. In fact, as at least one reviewer (Kane 1996) noted, Díaz-Stevens says virtually nothing about the nature of Puerto Rican Catholicism in New York. Rather, the book is almost entirely concerned with the institutional programs established by the Archdiocese of New York in response to Puerto Rican immigration and with Díaz-Stevens's analysis of the ways in which these programs were flawed.

Finally, the confessional orientation that pervades so much of the social scientific literature on Hispanic Catholicism also explains why so many scholars have accepted or even promoted the matriarchal core hypothesis despite the lack of supporting evidence for it. Remember that many of these scholars are committed to the view that revitalization of the American Catholic Church depends upon the official church's embracing Hispanic Catholicism. For this premise to make sense, Hispanic Catholicism must be constructed not only as something *different* from the sort of Catholicism currently in place but also as something *better*—and this is precisely the argument that these scholars have been making for decades. They have contrasted the prominent role that the laity have (supposedly) played in Hispanic Catholicism with the sort of leadership-from-above associated with the mainstream church. While he was still a priest, Stevens-Arroyo gave an interview to the *New York Times* (Blau 1976) that explained the absence of Hispanics in the church hierarchy this way: "The church's image of a bishop is 'someone a little pompous, an administrator, a canon lawyer,' asserted Father Stevens-Arroyo, adding that the 'more people-oriented' Spanish-speaking Catholics were thus excluded." Decades later, this same message—that Latino Catholicism places more emphasis on lay leadership and less emphasis on the institutional church than Euro-American Catholicism and is for that reason more in tune with the sort of Catholicism that American Catholics want—continues to pervade Stevens-Arroyo's sociological writing. But lay leadership *per se* is not the only reason that Latino Catholicism is seen to be different (and better). It is also different (and better) because it accords lay women a leadership role that is denied to women in the institutional church.

Positing a traditional matriarchal core to Hispanic Catholicism, in other words, permits Hispanic Catholicism to be seen as having the potential to transform American Catholicism by balancing the church's tradition of vesting institutional authority overwhelmingly in males against a pattern of lay leadership that vests it primarily in females. Under this construction, embracing Hispanic Catholicism would have the effect of producing a type of Catholicism that is far more in tune with the cultural emphasis on gender equality that has increasingly come to characterize American society over the past several decades. Díaz-Stevens (2003, 179), who is the leading exponent of the matriarchal core hypothesis, is in fact quite clear that Hispanic Catholic's matriarchal core is critical to the revitalization of U.S. Catholicism:

> As I see it, the competition from other Christian denominations, plus a downsizing of the clergy, will push the Roman Catholic Church once again towards "innovative" approaches, which will incorporate what in fact the people at the local, grassroots level have found effective for hundreds of years in their land of origin. The role of lay persons, and most especially the role of women—ordained or otherwise—will continue to increase in importance. The end result of all these activities will be transformative.

What I am suggesting is that the matriarchal core hypothesis is very widely accepted, despite the lack of supporting evidence, because it allows Hispanic Catholicism to be what the many Hispanic scholars who are also Catholic activists want it to be: the best hope for revitalizing and improving the American Catholic tradition.

But I said that there were likely *two* reasons why the matriarchal core hypothesis has proven to be so popular. Its appeal to Hispanic scholars who are also Catholic activists seems insufficient by itself to explain its uncritical acceptance within the American scholarly community generally. After all, there are certainly many scholars studying Hispanic Catholicism whose work could not by any stretch of the imagination be seen as being pervaded by confessional bias. Moreover, the matriarchal core claim has been embraced by many non-Hispanic scholars who are not Catholic activists. Its continuing popularity must rest upon something beside Hispanic Catholic activism, and for the key to understanding what that something else might be, I must return to an argument advanced earlier, namely, that the academic study of religion in the United States is still being shaped by Protestant narratives and by historiographical predispositions that flow from those narratives.

Catholics and Other Primitives

In his presidential address to the Society for the Scientific Study of Religion, Robert Orsi (2003) conceded that in the past the academic study of religion in the United States had implicitly taken "modern religion" to be a denominationally neutral version of liberal Protestantism and that this approach had defined religions that deviated from the liberal Protestant norm as both premodern and threatening. Thus, he argued (p. 170),

> Fear was central to the academic installation of religious studies [around the turn of the twentieth century]. Religious difference, moreover, overlapped with ethnic and racial otherness, and this combination produced the pervasive and characteristically American idea that dangers to the republic were germinating in the religious practices of dark-skinned or alien peoples. . . . Practitioners of the emerging discipline of religious studies were among the most assiduous guardians of the boundary between the modern and the premodern.

In the thinking of these scholars, Orsi continues, what *made* certain religions a threat to the social order in advanced societies like the United States was the fact that they were pervaded by "primitive" elements—which usually meant anything that seemed emotional or exotic against the implicit middle-class Protestant norm. Although some of the religious traditions possessing the "primitivism" that posed this threat were from non-Western (and colonized) cultures, they also included—Orsi (p. 170) argues—religions within the United States, including Pentecostalism, Mormonism and Roman Catholicism. The rest of Orsi's address was taken up with his thoughts on the increased "othering" of Islam in the aftermath of the September 11, 2001, attacks. A year later, however, in his presidential address to the American Academy of Religion, Orsi (2004) returned to the matter of Protestant bias in the academic study of religion in America, but only to assure us that such an orientation had eroded. Protestant Christianity, he said, was "no longer the hidden norm of the academic study of religion, its secret telos or its horizon, the authoritative ground for the assessment of all religious traditions" (p. 399). Orsi would later borrow ideas from these two presidential addresses in order to make these same arguments in the final chapter of his most recent book (2005) on the sort of Catholicism that he himself experienced while growing up. Unfortunately, the demise of Protestant influence that Orsi posits, like Mark Twain's death, is much exaggerated.

In fact, the historiographical patterns that have been brought to light in this and previous chapters suggest that there are at least two ways in which Catholics are still being constructed as the Other in the American academy. The first is the historiographical predisposition to see most variants of American Catholicism as having emerged in a foreign location. Such a predisposition is evident, for example, in the widely held belief that Irish American Catholicism is somehow linked to the devotional revolution in Ireland, that Italian American Catholicism was brought to America in the hearts and suitcases of Italian immigrants, and that Cajun Catholics cling tightly to traditions formed in Acadia. Although, as we have seen in earlier chapters, there is little foundation for any of these beliefs, they do function to associate Catholicism with a non-American Other. Seeing Catholicism as having a foreign origin also functions to discourage consideration of evidence suggesting that many of the things which are distinctive of, say, Irish American Catholicism or Italian American Catholicism came into existence as a creative response by the communities involved to their experiences in America.

Catholicism is also Othered within the American academic community by the historiographical predisposition to take ethnicity (which is always something different from "American") into account mainly in connection with Catholicism but not Protestantism. Thus, for example, "Irishness" is almost always considered when studying Catholicism but almost never when studying Protestantism—even though, as we saw in Chapter 1, Irish American Protestants outnumber Irish American Catholics.

Even granting this longstanding and continuing predisposition to associate

Catholicism with Otherness, it seems clear that Hispanic Catholicism presents some special difficulties for scholars writing under the influence of this predisposition. First, as commentators like Díaz-Stevens and Stevens-Arroyo keep reminding us, Hispanic Catholicism is not associated with a "foreign" location in the way that Irish American Catholicism or Italian American or Cajun Catholicism is. Although Hispanic Catholicism derives in some ways from Spain, it is more appropriately seen as having emerged in the Americas and as a type of religious practice that predates the emergence of a distinctively American Protestant tradition. Furthermore, some variants of Hispanic Catholicism—notably those associated with Hispanos in New Mexico and Tejanos in Texas—emerged centuries ago in areas that are now part of the United States. The problem for these scholars, in other words, is how to cast as Other a type of Catholicism that cannot be characterized as "foreign" as easily as most other types of Catholicism. I suggest that the second reason the matriarchal core hypothesis is so popular, despite the lack of evidence, is because it provides a solution to this problem.

Quite some time ago, Edward Said (1978) argued that Western discourse about Oriental cultures (by which he meant mainly cultures in the Middle East) depicted these cultures as being simultaneously "different from" and "inferior to" Western culture. Difference was established by focusing on things that Western audiences would find exotic or strange. Although inferiority was established in many ways, Said argued, one of the most important of these involved constructing ethnographic accounts implying that Oriental culture was in some essential way *feminized*. Such accounts, he argued, established a contrast between an implicitly masculinized West that was active and innovative and a feminized Orient that was passive and submissive. Later investigators have subsequently argued that this sort of ethnographic "feminization" has also been used in other contexts to establish the inferiority of a non-Western Other. Barbara Babcock (1990; 1997), for example, has looked at the ways the Pueblo cultures of New Mexico have been feminized in Anglo discourse.

I believe that the matriarchal core hypothesis functions in exactly the same way as the ethnographic accounts examined by Said and by Babcock; it feminizes the Hispanic Catholic tradition in an essential way. The result is the same sort of invidious comparison that Said uncovered in Orientalist discourse, which in this case is a contrast between Hispanic Catholicism, where leadership is vested mainly in females, and the official variant of Catholicism, where leadership is vested mainly in males.

But, legitimizing the matriarchal core hypothesis (by accepting it uncritically) is not the only way that mainstream scholars have Othered Hispanic Catholicism—and this brings us to a commonly made claim about Hispanic Catholics that I have so far ignored.

The (Missing) Pentecostal Connection

In reviewing the literature on Hispanic Protestantism published since 1980, Larry Hunt (1999) points out that a common theme is that there has been a dramatic increase in the number of Hispanics who have abandoned Catholicism and become evangelical or Pentecostal Christians. Sometimes, scholars who make this claim do so quite explicitly. Allan Figueroa Deck (1994, 413–414), for example, says

> Despite some gains on the part of Justo L. González's United Methodists, however, it is not they who are attracting impressive numbers of Hispanics. . . . Today when one speaks of Hispanic Protestantism one is not usually taking about the "histori-cal" churches at all but, rather, about some strains of evangelicalism and especially Pentecostalism.

In other cases, the claim is implied rather than stated outright, as when—for example—Díaz-Stevens and Stevens-Arroyo (1998) devote several sections of their book on Latino Catholicism to the matter of Latino Pentecostalism but have virtually nothing to say about other forms of Protestantism. Although the "Pentecostal defection" claim is usually made most forcefully by Hispanic scholars, it has been accepted at face value by non-Hispanic scholars concerned with the study of American religion (see Hunt 1999 for examples here). But, *are* large numbers of Hispanic Catholics in fact becoming Pentecostals?

Certainly, there are many surveys (reviewed in Hunt 1999) which seem to establish that since 1980 the proportion of Hispanics who identify themselves as Catholic has been decreasing[9] while the proportion who identify themselves as Protestant has been increasing. But, there are three things that must be kept in mind when evaluating these patterns. The first is that almost half of all Hispanic Protestants are associated with moderate or liberal Protestant denominations, not Pentecostal churches (Greeley 1997). The second is that estimates of the proportion of Hispanics who are Protestant are strongly influenced by survey methodology. For example, surveys conducted in English only tend to find a higher proportion of Hispanic Protestants in the sample being surveyed than do bilingual surveys (Perl, Greely, and Gray 2006). This is relevant to the issue at hand because most studies that report an increase in the proportion of Hispanics who are Protestant use data from English-only surveys (Perl, Greely, and Gray 2006). Finally, conversion is not the only explanation for why there are relatively fewer Hispanic Catholics and relatively more Hispanic Protestants. Hunt's own (1999) statistical analysis indicates that the increase in Hispanic Protestants is the result of an *inter-generational*, not an intragenerational, process. What is happening, he argues, is that the "Protestant children of Protestant parents" category is expanding far more rapidly than the "Catholic children of Catholic parents" category. Phrased differently, Hispanics raised by Protestant parents are more likely to remain Protestants than Hispanics raised by Catholic parents are to remain Catholic.

So, once again we have a puzzle: why—even now—do scholars writing on Hispanic Catholicism focus so much on Hispanic Pentecostals when almost half of Hispanic Protestants are not Pentecostal and when there is little evidence to support the contention that Hispanic Catholics are converting to Pentecostalism? The answer is to be found in the argument typically offered to explain *why* Hispanics are becoming Pentecostals, which is that, in becoming Pentecostals, they are not moving far from their cultural roots.

Deck (1994, 421–422) elaborates on this explanation. Under the heading "The Unanalyzed Affinity: Popular Religiosity and Evangelicalism," he explains the supposed appeal of Pentecostalism to Hispanic Catholics this way:

> [Hispanic Catholicism] eschews the cognitive in its effort to appeal to the senses and the feelings. . . . Its main qualities are a concern for an immediate experience of God, a strong orientation toward the transcendent, an implicit belief in miracles, a practical orientation toward healing, and a tendency to personalize or individualize one's relationship with the divine. . . . The point I want to make here is that . . . [i]n a certain sense the movement of Hispanics to evangelical religion is a way to maintain continuity with their popular Catholic faith.

In short, this argument says that Pentecostalism is appealing to Hispanic Catholics because its characteristics are the same or similar to those of the premodern forms of Catholicism to which Hispanics have clung for centuries. Other versions of this same argument can be found in Espín (1994) and Davis (1994). This "affinity explanation," I might add, tends *not* to be offered by scholars who have studied in some detailed way Latino Pentecostals whose families have been Pentecostal for generations; these scholars are instead more likely to see Latino Pentecostalism as a creative adaptation to the new social and cultural conditions that Hispanic immigrants encountered in the United States (see, for example, Sánchez-Walsh 2003).

As an *explanation*, the argument that there is an essential similarity between Hispanic Catholicism and Pentecostalism offered by Deck and others fails, if only because there is nothing *to* explain—Hispanic Catholics are *not* defecting to Pentecostalism in especially large numbers. But, in making this argument, scholars like Deck are in effect constructing Hispanic Catholicism in the same way that Catholicism generally, and Pentecostalism, were constructed at the turn of the twentieth century, as a religion that is primitive and premodern by virtue of its emotionalism and its emphasis on visual imagery, mystery, mysterious healing, and so forth. Thus, this argument, just like the matriarchal core hypothesis, functions to construct Hispanic Catholicism as Other relative to an implicit mainstream Protestant norm in the scholarly literature on American religion; and this, I suggest, is why the "massive Hispanic defection to Pentecostalism" claim—just like the matriarchal core hypothesis—has been so popular despite its lack of evidence.

CHAPTER SIX

Protestantism and the Academic Study of American Religion

An Enduring Alliance

As I indicated in the Introduction, and as now should be clear, this book is about several things at once. One goal has been to offer answers to questions that have not previously been raised about American religion (like "How did the Irish become Protestant in America?"). Another has been to provide new answers to old questions (like "Why did Irish American Catholics become the mainstay of the American church?" and "Why did Italian American Catholics stage festas in honor of the saints and madonnas associated with their villages in Italy?"). Still another has been to show the value of theoretical perspectives—like the "doing gender" approach—that have so far been underutilized in the study of American religion. And in some cases, the goal has been to show that much of what we think we know about American religion is illusory and not at all rooted in the evidence.

In pursuing all these goals, what has also emerged is an argument—made most forcefully at the end of Chapter 3 and in Chapter 5—that the wrong turns and blind alleys we have encountered in reviewing the scholarly study of American religion derive from a longstanding and continuing intellectual orientation that is ultimately Protestant in origin. The claim being made is that the scholarly study of American religion is still very much in the grip of a Protestant imagination. In this chapter, I want to look at the historical origins of this Protestant imagination and at the ways it continues to shape the academic study of American religion, even when there are no Catholics in sight.

During the late nineteenth and early twentieth centuries, the academic study of American religion was shaped by two distinct but mutually reinforcing intellectual traditions. The first was a social evolutionary perspective that had been imported from Europe and that was concerned with two questions, namely: how had religion come into existence, and how had it developed with the advance of civilization? The European scholars working in this tradition proposed a range of answers to the first of these questions. John Lubbock, Herbert Spencer, and Edward Tylor, for example, suggested that religion had first come into existence as primitive peoples sought to make sense of the dream experience; Max Müller suggested that religious belief (at least, Indo-European religious beliefs) had developed when metaphors describing natural phenomena had come to be taken literally; and Emile Durkheim argued that primitive religion was a response to the feelings of psychic effervescence generated when clan members gathered to engage common rituals.[1] But, while they gave different answers in explaining the origin of religion, these same European theorists were in general agreement on the answer to the second question: primitive religion, they all believed, had been pervaded by an emphasis on the concrete and on this-worldly concerns, and social evolutionary progress in the religious realm meant movement away from what was concrete and this-worldly toward forms of religion that emphasized a transcendent God and deeply internalized ethical codes.

Social evolutionary arguments in general were popular in Western societies during the nineteenth century, as Robert Connell (1997, 20) and others have suggested, because the always-present distinction between "primitive" and "advanced" cultures functioned to legitimize the overseas colonization projects of European powers like France, England, and Germany and the internal colonization projects of countries like the United States. But this particular social evolutionary argument, which saw reliance on material objects as a sign of *religious* primitiveness, was also appealing, at least in Protestant societies like Britain and the United States, because of its affinity with the Protestant worldview. After all, from the time of the Reformation forward, the Protestant degradation narrative (encountered in Chapter 3) portrayed Christianity as originally a pristine religion strongly focused on a transcendental God and ethical teachings but claimed that over time the Roman Catholic Church had allowed superstition and pagan elements to creep into Christian practice. Further, in pointing to examples of Catholic activities that were pervaded by superstitious and pagan elements, Protestant commentators had always pointed most of all to Catholic cults focused on physical objects (like images and relics) and the rituals (like pilgrimages) associated with these cults. The social evolutionary perspective on religion, then, in seeing movement away from an emphasis on the concrete as a sign of religious progress, gave a theoretical legitimacy to this older Protestant narrative. Phrased differently, the social evolutionary approach to religion in effect transformed the Protestant degradation narrative, originally just a historical account about Christianity, into an ahistorical and universal theory that functioned to validate Protestant superiority over both Catholicism and most of the (other) religions flourishing in the non-Western world.

In American academic circles, the social evolutionary approach to religion had the greatest impact in the newly emerging discipline of psychology, especially through the work of G. Stanley Hall (1844–1924), president of Clark University, and Edwin Starbuck (1876–1947).[2] What allowed social evolutionism to creep into their psychology of religion was the view, held by both scholars, that ontogeny recapitulates phylogeny. Thus, said Starbuck (1907, 193), "The study of the mental life of children and the epochs through which they pass is doing its part in making indubitable the law that the individual recapitulates in itself the history of the race." Hall routinely said the same thing (see especially the Introduction in Hall 1915). In regard to religion, what this meant is that the religious development of the individual went through stages similar to those associated with the transition from the religion of primitive societies to the religion of advanced societies. Both Hall and Starbuck asserted that religious sentiment in children was characterized by an emphasis on the self and self-interest, on the concrete, and on rules and regulations imposed externally. By contrast, religious sentiment in the mature adult consisted in a deeply internalized "craving for righteousness, a desire to be all and do all for the glory of God and the service of man" (Starbuck 1912, 394). In retrospect, of course, it seems clear that what both Hall and Starbuck saw to be "mature" religiosity was little more than the sort of religiosity being promoted by liberal Protestant denominations of the period.

Starbuck, it should be noted, sometimes came close to understanding the Protestant roots of his conceptualization. He studied the "conversion experience"— which is what he and Hall called the process by which individuals made the transition to mature religiosity—by distributing a questionnaire to a sample of 1,265 people. To his credit, he noted that since almost all his subjects were Protestant, his conclusions about the conversion experience might or might not apply to other religious groups (Starbuck 1912, 25). Even so, neither Starbuck nor Hall ever questioned the implicit premise that pervaded all their work, namely, that liberal Protestantism, with its emphasis on a transcendent God and service to humanity, epitomized the endpoint of both social evolution and psychological development.

Still, although the social evolutionary perspective on religion developed by European theorists, and the corresponding theories of religious development formulated by American psychologists like Hall and Starbuck, helped to create an academic climate in the United States that privileged Protestantism in the study of religion, it was really another and far more home-grown approach to religion which most ensured that Protestantism became, to borrow again from Robert

Orsi (2004, 399), "the hidden norm of the academic study of religion" in the United States. This second approach is what Catherine Albanese (2002; 2004) has called the "consensus model of American religion."[3]

The consensus model stated, first, that the Protestant traditions that had developed in America, especially those that derived from the Puritan experience, were quite different from what had existed in Europe and, second, that these American Protestant traditions had from the beginning contributed to the rise of American democracy. Books typically taken as exemplars of this tradition include Robert Baird's *Religion in the United States of America* (1844), Daniel Dorchester's *Christianity in the United States* (1888), Leonard W. Bacon's *A History of American Christianity* (1897), and William W. Sweet's *The Story of Religions in America* (1930). Most commentators (see Albanese 2002; Hackett 1995; Wilson 2003) also suggest that Sydney Ahlstrom's *A Religious History of the American People* (1972) can reasonably be regarded as the last comprehensive work written under the influence of the consensus model.

Because the consensus model put Protestantism and its links to American democracy front and center in academic discussions of American religion, scholars writing under the influence of this model paid little attention to groups outside the Protestant mainstream. Baird's (1844) *Religion in the United States of America*, for example, a book which is more than 700 pages in length, devotes only four pages to American Catholics. Bacon's (1897) *A History of American Christianity* devotes a bit more attention to Catholics here and there throughout his discussion but nothing like what you would expect, given the number of Catholics living in the United States at the time. But perhaps the most important consequence of the consensus model for the study of Catholicism was that the model's logic dictated *how* the study of American Catholics should proceed, to the extent that Catholics were mentioned at all.

Starting from the premise that there was a perfect fit between American Protestantism and American democracy, the obvious question to ask in the case of other denominations and religions—especially in the case of Catholicism, which was accounting for a larger and larger share of the American population—is to what extent these other groups fell short of this perfect fit. Within the logic of the consensus model, the question that had to be asked of American Catholics was whether they could be good Americans or whether, instead, their Catholicism and their growing numbers posed a threat to the Republic.

Interestingly, when discussing whether or not Catholics were a threat to American institutions, Protestant scholars took notice, at least implicitly, of the changing composition of the Catholic population in the United States. Baird was writing at a time (1844) when nativist groups saw Catholics—Irish Catholics in particular—to be a threat to democratic institutions, mainly because they saw Catholics as unthinkingly obedient to their priests, who in turn followed orders issued by the pope. During the period of increasing Irish immigration, Catholics were popularly seen, in other words, to have an allegiance to a foreign ruler. Accordingly, this was the only issue that Baird raised when discussing the Catholic threat. Thus, he (p. 616) says, the suggestion that Catholics "can never be safe citizens of a republic . . . must rest, I should think, on the presumed hatred of the priests to republican institutions and the impossibility of controlling the influence they possess over their people." While Baird went on to express some skepticism about the matter of priestly influence over ordinary Catholics, the point is that he, like the nativists, framed the issue in these terms.

By the turn of the century, however, while the Irish were still a plurality within the American Catholic Church, other groups—notably the Italians—were looming larger and larger in popular thinking about American Catholicism. Whatever they might think about the Irish, even the most hostile Protestant commentator could not construct Italian American Catholics as a threat to American democracy on the ground that they owed their allegiance to the pope. Quite the contrary, as we saw in Chapter 3, the "Italian problem" within the American Catholic Church was precisely that they were seen not to be under the control of their local priests or the pope. As a consequence, the emphasis on priestly influence when discussing the relationship between Catholicism and American democracy (and this issue did remain central to academic discussions of Catholicism) gave way to a more general assessment of the fit between Catholicism and American cultural values. Bacon (1897, 320–332), for example, declared that while the Catholic Church in other areas (he names Spain, Mexico, and Italy) was clearly antidemocratic, Catholics in America had the potential to "revolutionize" (his term) their Catholicism by putting less emphasis on symbols and sacrament and more on the figure of Christ (read: by becoming more like the Protestant sects who took up most of Bacon's discussion).

Turning Points and the New/Old Approach to American Religion

All commentators agree that the consensus model, with its focus on mainstream Protestantism and its tendency to ignore other groups, became less popular during the 1960s and 1970s and that, simultaneously, scholars came more and more to focus on religious diversity when studying American religion. The issue of *why* this happened is a matter of debate. Early on, Sydney Ahlstrom (1970, 234–235) suggested that historians during the 1960s were sensitized to the matter of religious diversity partly because religious diversity had become more of a fact in American society and partly because of the many and various changes (some having little to do with religion) taking place in American society during that period. Thomas Tweed would later make the same argument (1997b). For David Hackett (1995) the breakdown of the consensus model derived from the influence of social historians like E. P. Thomson and Eugene Genovese and anthropologists like Clifford Geertz, whose works collectively fostered a greater interest in popular religion as opposed to the older interest in formal theology and established churches. Charles Cohen (1997, 697) suggests that the shift to an emphasis on diversity occurred when historians turned their attention from books and diaries written by New Englanders to more mundane sources (like court depositions, inventories, pottery, etc.) associated with other American regions. For Catherine Albanese (2002, 6) the shift was prompted mainly by the distrust of grand narratives bred into younger scholars by postmodernism and postcolonialism. Needless to say, these various explanations are not mutually exclusive.

But, if the consensus model is gone, what has emerged to take its place? Nothing yet, at least no new model. Instead, as Wilson (2003, 33) observes, the academic study of American religion over the past two decades has been guided by two separate impulses:

> One is the approach to American religious history that undertook to make the case that multiple narratives should replace a master narrative; the other is the approach that took seriously studies of religion among social scientists that propose how useful generic mechanisms or common dynamics can be to interpret American (as well as extra-American) religious phenomena.

The goal of scholars writing in what Wilson here calls the "multiple narratives" approach (his "social science" approach will be considered later) is to create accounts of particular groups that are very much tied to particular social and historical contexts. In introducing a collection of readings intended to present the new multiple narratives scholarship as forcefully as possible, Hackett (1995, ix) makes clear just how diverse the literature in this area has become:

> During the 1980s, and up to the present, the thrust of this [new] work has dramatically expanded the area of research. Regional religious stories of the West and the South are coming into view. Native American religious history, non-existent as a field until the 1980s, is an exciting and rapidly emerging new discipline. Dramatic

revisions are being made in our understanding of the African American past. Mormons, Masons, Pentecostals, ethnic Catholics, sunbelt Jews, followers of Islam, Asian religions, and Haitian Vodou are now on the scene.

And indeed, each of the groups that Hackett mentions here (and others) are the subject of one or more of the twenty-six essays included in his reader. Other popular readers organized around the new multiple narratives tradition include Tweed's (1997b) *Retelling U.S. Religious History* and Orsi's (1999) *Gods of the City.*

And yet, although an emphasis on diversity is now undeniably central to the study of American religion, have the underlying conceptual frameworks being used really changed all that much? As regards the study of American Catholics, which has been a special concern in this book, there are grounds for doubt. As a start, it is still the case that Catholics are not taken as the object of study in mainstream journals dealing with American religious history as often as their numbers in the United States would seem to dictate. But even more important, I suggest, is that when Catholics do become the object of study in American academic circles, the questions asked still show the influence of the old and supposedly discredited consensus model. Consider the matter of Jay Dolan, professor emeritus of history at Notre Dame.

Dolan has long been the dean of American Catholic studies. His books—including *The Immigrant Church* (1975) and *The American Catholic Experience* (1992)—are standard reference works in the study of American Catholicism and have always earned him high praise. The founder of the Cushwa Center for the Study of American Catholicism and its director from 1975 to 1993, Dolan edited or co-edited a number of books dealing with topics like Hispanic Catholicism, women in the church, and the history of American Catholic parishes. And yet, what is the central issue in his recent *In Search of American Catholicism* (2002)? Very simply, it is what Robert Orsi, in a review that appears on the dust cover of Dolan's book, calls "the tense and conflicted but ultimately creative encounter of the church of migrants and immigrants with the challenges and opportunities of American democracy." Dolan's recent book, in other words, is about the fit between Catholicism and American democracy. True, Dolan does provide a more nuanced account of this issue than was done in the heyday of the consensus model. He considers not simply Catholic leaders who opposed democratization of the church in the nineteenth century but also those who promoted democratization, and in the closing chapter he assesses the ways in which Catholic concerns may have shaped American culture since the 1960s. Nevertheless, the fact remains that Dolan frames his discussion of American Catholicism using exactly the same issue—the fit between Catholicism and American democracy—that was so important to Baird, Bacon, Sweet, and others. I am not suggesting that this fit shouldn't be *an* issue in discussing American Catholicism, but making it *the* issue—as Dolan does—betrays the lingering influence of the supposedly defunct consensus model. To understand why this is so problematic, imagine how we would react if authors writing in the new multiple narratives tradition of religious historiography invariably made "fit with American democracy" *the* central issue in discussing the Mormons, Sunbelt Jews, Pentecostals, native Americans, and black Americans.

But what most of all demonstrates the continuing presence of the consensus model lurking beneath the stories told by scholars writing in the multiple narratives tradition are the analyses described in earlier chapters of this book. The vast majority of the studies that we have considered in discussing Irish American Catholicism, Italian American Catholicism, Cajun Catholicism, and Hispanic American Catholicism are exactly the sort of studies that commentators like Albanese and Tweed cite as indicative of the new approach to American religion, that is, they are studies that individually provide a localized narrative of some particular group and collectively reflect the diversity characteristic of the American religious experience. And yet, what we have found in all cases is, first of all, that many of the claims made in these narratives—such as Famine immigrants were devout Catholics when they arrived; Italian immigrants were deeply attached to the madonnas and saints associated with their natal villages; Hispanic Catholicism is matricentered—although widely accepted, rest on little or no empirical evidence. We have also found that these narratives have systematically ignored patterns suggesting that the religious practice of many "ethnic" Catholics was more a creative response to their experiences in America than something they brought from their country of origin. Finally, we have found that these two patterns taken together function to construct American Catholicism as an Other that is foreign, passive, and exotic relative to an implicit American Protestant norm. A great many of the studies written in the "new" multiple narratives tradition, in other words, far from undermining the logic of the "old" consensus model, actually reinforce it.

But, if an implicit Protestant norm still lurks beneath the surface of so many studies that are part of the multiple narratives approach, what about the second impulse that, according to commentators like Wilson, has shaped the study of American religion in recent decades, namely, the increasing use of social scientific arguments that treat religion as a generic phenomenon? Phrased differently, have American social scientists studying religion avoided using the sort of hidden Protestant norm that has structured historical studies of American religion? Unfortunately, the answer here would seem to be no. Consider first, for example, how American psychologists typically measure religion.

Psychologists and Their Measures of Religion

As several commentators have pointed out (Ladd and Spilka 2006; Slater, Hall, and Edwards 2001; Wulff 1997, 233–241) the two psychological measures used most often over the past several decades to assess a person's religious orientation are (1) some version of the Intrinsic/Extrinsic (I/E) Scale developed by Gordon Allport (Allport and Ross 1967) or (2) some version of the Quest Scale developed by C. Daniel Batson and his associates in the early 1970s (Batson, Schoenrade, and Ventis 1993). Both scales are still in widespread use and quite often are used together (see, for example, Salsman and Carlson 2005).

In discussing the I/E Scale, Ralph Hood (1971, 370) provides a succinct account of the difference between an extrinsic religious orientation and an intrinsic religious orientation:

> While [Allport] never clearly defined these terms, it is apparent that the extrinsic dimension was primarily conceived to reflect an explicit, utilitarian orientation to generally institutionalized aspects of religion while the intrinsic dimension was primarily conceived to reflect an implicit, personal, "devout" orientation to more experiential aspects of religion.

The underlying conceptualization, in other words, is rooted in the contrast between someone attached to an institutional church for utilitarian (read: selfish) reasons and someone with deeply internalized religious beliefs that play an important role in determining how they conduct their life. Given this underlying conceptualization, then, it makes sense that in a widely used version of the I/E Scale (Gorsuch and McPherson 1989) an extrinsic orientation is operationalized as agreement with items like:

— "I go to church because it helps me to make friends."
— "I pray mainly to gain relief and protection."
— "I go to church mostly to spend time with my friends."

while an intrinsic orientation is operationalized as agreement with items like:

— "It is important to me to spend time in private thought and prayer."
— "I try hard to live all my life according to my religious beliefs."
— "My whole approach to life is based on my religion."

Although the intrinsic/extrinsic distinction supposedly refers only to two different religious orientations, psychologists studying religion have always, at least implicitly, seen the intrinsic orientation as more positively valued. Allport himself, for example, tells us that he first developed the intrinsic/extrinsic distinction in order to disentangle the relationship between religion and prejudice (Allport and Ross 1967, 432). He argued that, although church attenders are on average more prejudiced than nonattenders, this general finding masks the fact that a certain subset of attenders—namely, those characterized by an intrinsic orientation—are significantly less prejudiced than people with an extrinsic orientation. Although subsequent research would not always sustain the negative correlation between an intrinsic orientation and prejudice that Allport found in his initial studies, the number of studies which have found this negative correlation, combined with studies (reviewed in Wulff 1997, 234) that have found a correlation between an extrinsic orientation and a wide variety of negatively valued traits (like prejudice, dogmatism, authoritarianism, ethnocentrism), has ensured that the intrinsic orientation was seen to be the "better" sort of religiosity.

Although Wulff (1997, 231–237) and others have criticized the I/E distinction as simplistic, and have seen particular versions of the I/E Scale as tapping into personality variables that have little to do with religion per se (like dogmatism and a desire to look good in the eyes of others), the fact is that the I/E conceptualization and its associated scales are still widely popular. Why? For Wulff himself (1997, 594), that the I/E Scale "remains popular is testimony both to its conceptual appeal, especially to those who share Allport's wish to preserve genuine piety from the opprobrium attached to religious bigotry, and to the lack of equally convenient alternatives." But if, as Wulff suggests, the I/E distinction is popular because of its "conceptual appeal," we need to ask if that appeal extends beyond a desire on the part of some psychologists to disassociate pure religion (Wulff's "genuine piety") from prejudice. And this again leads us to the issue of Protestant bias.

Christopher Burris (1999, 147) has already suggested that Allport's personal and familial ties to a "North American Protestant articulation of Christianity" undoubtedly influenced his conceptualization of the I/E distinction. In the same vein, Cohen, Hall and Meador (2005) have more recently pointed out that the emphasis upon individualism and internalized piety in conceptualizing the more-valued intrinsic orientation reflects an implicitly Protestant norm and that people belonging to religious traditions that are less individualistic and more given to communal rituals (like Catholicism and Episcopalianism/Anglicanism) would almost certainly score high on the less-valued extrinsic orientation scale. Cohen et al. go on to observe (p. 58) that, while the I/E Scale was "culturally sensible" in the period when it was developed by Allport, "American culture [at that time] retained a significant element of nascent Protestant Christianity," and we have now moved into a post-Christian era that requires a different measure. A quite different interpretation, however, but one equally consistent with the data, is that the Protestant norm implicit in the I/E Scale has *always* made it an inappropriate tool for assessing religion as a generic phenomenon (which is what its proponents claimed it was) and that it became the norm *because* of its implicit Protestant bias. What makes this alternative explanation all the more plausible is that a similar Protestant norm is implicit in the measures that have been proposed as alternatives to the I/E Scale.

The Quest Scale developed by Batson and his associates has for some years now been almost as popular as the I/E Scale. It was designed to measure "the degree to which an individual's religion involves an open-ended, responsive dialogue with existential questions raised by the contradictions and tragedies of life" (Batson, Schoenrade, and Ventis 1993, 168). The more an individual engages in such an ongoing and open-ended dialogue with existential questions, the higher he or she scores on the Quest Scale. The scale thus implies that a dialogue of this sort is the better sort of religion, which is why investigators using this scale are quite at ease in suggesting that a high score on the Quest Scale can be taken as evidence of religious maturity (see, for example, Leak and Randall 1995).

The examples that Batson and his associates (1993, 166–168) present as illustrating a high Quest orientation—they range from Siddhartha to Malcolm X to Mahatma Gandhi—might seem to indicate that the Quest Scale was intended to be applicable well beyond the specific case of American Christianity. Even so, one bit of evidence Batson and his associates present suggests—however inadvertently—that the Quest Scale is indeed closely tied to the American Protestant tradition. This evidence appears in the section of their book (pp. 177–179) where the authors respond to the claim, advanced by some critics, that the Quest Scale does not measure anything "religious." To establish the scale's validity, they rely heavily (see pp. 178–179) on a study comparing seminarians at Princeton Theological Seminary with undergraduates at Princeton. Since the seminarians, they argue, are "reasonably identifiable as religious" the fact that they scored higher on the Quest Scale (as they did) is evidence that the scale "is a valid measure of something religious" (p. 178). Only in passing, however, do we learn that the seminarians were all studying for the Presbyterian ministry. Once we know that, we could just as easily argue that the result (that Presbyterian seminarians scored relatively high on the Quest Scale) is evidence that the Quest Scale is a valid measure of the sort of religiosity to which Presbyterians (or, more generally, Protestants) are committed.

Still, what is most revealing of the Protestant norm implicit in the Quest Scale is the content of the items used in the scale. In the version of this scale presented in Batson, Schroenrade, and Ventis (1993, 170), we find items like:

— "I am constantly questioning my religious beliefs."
— "For me, doubting is an important part of what it means to be religious."
— "I do not expect my religious beliefs to change in the next few years." [reverse scored]
— "My life experiences have led me to rethink my religious convictions."
— "There are many religious issues on which my views are still changing."

What is being conveyed in these statements is not simply an individualistic emphasis of the sort encountered in the I/E Scale (though that emphasis is certainly present) but also the suggestion that *challenging received knowledge and thinking for yourself in religious matters is a sign of religious maturity*. An emphasis on challenging received tradition, of course, has long been a central element in Protestant perceptions of the Protestant tradition, just as the distinction between blindly obedient and unquestioning Catholics and Protestants who think for themselves without aid of priestly intermediaries has long been a stock element in Protestant critiques of Catholicism.

Moreover, the individualism and willingness to embrace change associated with Protestantism generally are emphases that have long been seen to be *especially* characteristic of American Protestantism. In 1775, for instance, in his famous speech urging conciliation with the American colonists, Edmund Burke declared:

> The people are protestants; and of that kind, which is the most adverse to all implicit submission of mind and opinion. . . . All protestantism, even the most cold and passive, is a sort of dissent. But the religion most prevalent in our Northern Colonies is a refinement on the principle of resistance; it is the dissidence of dissent, and the Protestantism of the Protestant religion. This religion, under a variety of denominations, agreeing in nothing but in the communion of the spirit of liberty, is predominant in most of the Northern provinces. (Elofson and Woods 1996, 121–122)

Burke was referring mainly to Puritanism and its various offshoots, but, as we saw in Chapter 1, an emphasis on individualism and "thinking for yourself without aid of established authority" became even more central to the American Protestant tradition when these emphases (which were part of the revolutionary ethos) were incorporated into the message preached by upstart sects like the Methodists and Baptists in the wake of the Revolution.

Something else central to the forms of evangelical Christianity that became popular in the United States during the nineteenth century was an emphasis upon the conversion experience. This is relevant to the Quest Scale because the essence of the conversion experience, as then articulated by evangelical groups, was a total transformation of the individual involved. Evangelicals in the United States, even more than Christians from other Protestant traditions, saw "embracing change" within the context of the conversion experience as a prerequisite for religious maturity—which is exactly what the Quest Scale now in use also implies.

By contrast, the emphasis on "thinking for yourself" and "embracing change" that is so much a central part of the Protestant stereotype (the American Protestant stereotype in particular) is absent from discussions of the American Catholic tradition. Indeed, as we have seen throughout this book, American religious historians have repeatedly constructed American Catholics as passive and as clinging tightly to beliefs and practices they acquired outside the United States—even when the evidence permits other interpretations. In the end, then, the Quest Scale's emphasis on the individual, on thinking for oneself, and on a willingness to embrace change reflects an implicit religious norm that is far closer to stereotypes about American Protestantism than to stereotypes about American Catholicism.

The third and final measure that I want to consider is the Faith Maturity Scale (FMS) developed by Benson, Donahue, and Erickson (1993). Although the FMS has not as yet displaced either the I/E Scale or the Quest Scale, it is worth analyzing because it has a Protestant bias that has been acknowledged, but acknowledged in a way that masks the full extent of its bias. Moreover, coming to understand more fully just why the FMS is so much a product of a distinctively Protestant worldview can, I think, serve as a useful step in the development of measures that would be more appropriate in studying, say, American Catholics.

Benson, Donahue, and Erickson were quite up front in saying that in developing the Faith Maturity Scale they first consulted with representatives from six mainline Protestant denominations and that the scale was subsequently tested and refined using data from surveys administered to samples drawn from each of these six denominations. Moreover, they were also quite clear about what they sought to measure and the ways in which their analysis was, and was not, tied to a distinctively Protestant worldview—and here it is necessary to quote them:

The core dimensions of a mature-faith measure should prominently reflect the . . . two themes found in most faith traditions, both Christian and non-Christian. One is about the self, including one's personal relationship to God, one's efforts to seek God, and the personal transformations one experiences in this divine encounter. This theme might be called vertical, agentic, or "love of God" faith. . . . The second theme is about obligation and action on the human plane. It has to do with heeding the call to social service and social justice. While all faith traditions embrace this dimension, it is particularly salient in mainline Protestantism. (Benson, Donahue, and Erickson 1993, 4).

One result of this conceptualization is that the FMS has two subscales, the FMS-Vertical (which assesses the "relationship with God" dimension mentioned in this passage) and the FHS-Horizontal (which assesses the "social service and social justice" dimension). Note, however, that while the last line in this passage suggests that the FMS-*Horizontal* subscale is especially tied to a Protestant worldview, it does not make a similar remark about the FMS-*Vertical* subscale. Left unexamined is the possibility that the FMS embraces a view of "relating to God" that is also distinctively Protestant. Does it?

Consider some of the items that Benson, Donahue, and Erickson (1993, 19) use in their FMS-Vertical subscale:

— "My faith shapes how I think and act each and every day."
— "My faith helps me know right from wrong."
— "I take time for periods of prayer and meditation."
— "I talk with other people about my faith."
— "My life is filled with meaning and purpose."
— "I have a real sense that God is guiding me."
— "I am spiritually moved by the beauty of God's Creation."

Certainly the emphasis here on the individual, and an individual's deeply internalized faith, might in itself be taken as having a distinctively Protestant flavor. But what is *most* distinctively Protestant about the FMS-Vertical, I suggest, is the implicit suggestion that faith and faith alone (to borrow from Luther borrowing from St. Paul) is what most of all establishes and shapes an individual's personal relationship with a transcendent God.

So far, I have sought to demonstrate that there is an implicit Protestant norm structuring contemporary psychologists' study of religion, by looking carefully at the content of the measures psychologists uses to assess religiosity. Another way to uncover that hidden Protestant norm is to imagine how things might be different if we approached the study of American religion from a Catholic perspective. To do that, we need to dip into a body of scholarly literature that is very much concerned with how individual Catholics relate to God but which is rarely if ever mentioned by most psychologists (or by most sociologists) studying religion in the United States.

Contrasting the Catholic Imagination and the Protestant Imagination

Some time ago (1967), Guy Swanson argued that a fundamental difference between Catholicism and Protestantism had to do with *immanence*. Catholics, he said, accepted the view that God, or more generally, the sacred, could be immanent in this world. Catholics, in other words, believed not simply that God had created the world and was a continuing and active presence in it (views also embraced by Protestants), but also that God's essence could and did pervade all aspects of the material world. In varying degrees, Protestant groups rejected this last claim. For Swanson, the Catholic belief in immanence and the Protestant rejection of immanence were fundamental, because this distinction was the basis for any number of important doctrinal differences between the two traditions, especially those relating to the nature of church, the importance of the sacraments, and the nature of the Eucharist.

Although Swanson limited his analysis to matters of official doctrine, it is not difficult to come up with examples that show how the differing Catholic and Protestant attitudes toward immanence play out in connection with popular practice. The importance of immanence in the European Catholic tradition, for example, can be seen in the central role that cults organized around miraculous images and relics have played in that tradition and in the importance to Catholics of pilgrimage to sites sacralized by the earthly appearance of a madonna or saint. Similarly, the strong rejection of immanence in the Protestant tradition can be seen in the vehemence with which Protestants—acting under the influence of the degradation narrative discussed in Chapter 3—rejected these very same things (image cults, relics, pilgrimage).

Some years later (1981), the Catholic theologian David Tracy added to the Swanson argument by asserting that the centrality of immanence in the Catholic tradition and the Protestant rejection of immanence had given rise to two distinct modes of theological thinking. Basically, what Tracy argues is that, because Catholic theologians see the created world as pervaded by the sacred, they are predisposed toward *analogical thinking*, that is, toward using familiar relationships found in the created world as analogies that can effectively convey an understanding of relationship between human beings and God. By contrast, Protestant theologians, who reject immanence, see an "infinite qualitative difference" between God and the created world (Tracy 1981, 415). Hence, Tracy argues, Protestant theologians are predisposed toward a form of *dialectical thinking* that emphasizes the preached word, which is God's message to humanity, and the way we react to that word. The result of this perspective is that in Protestant theological thought a person's relationship with God depends most of all on the degree to which that person embraces God's message.

Although Tracy's argument is well known in Catholic intellectual circles— Mark Massa (2001, 564), for example, calls it "one of the seminal works of 20th-century theology"—his discussion is not in any sense rooted in the sort of social scientific studies that we have been reviewing in this book. However, in various publications, Andrew Greeley (1994; 1995; 2000; 2004), a sociologist, has stated that what Tracy calls analogical thinking is in fact characteristic of Catholics generally (and so not just Catholic theologians), and he has marshaled much evidence indicating that, because Catholics are predisposed toward analogical thinking, they relate to God in a manner that is qualitatively different from that of Protestants.

Greeley's basic argument is similar to Tracy's in positing that, because Catholics see God (and the sacred) as immanent in all aspects of the world, they are more likely than Protestants to "think about" God using metaphors drawn from everyday life. Because Catholics see the sacred is immanent in all human relationships, for example, they are more likely to think about God using maternal as well as paternal metaphors. For Greeley, this explains the intense devotion to Mary in the Catholic tradition; he sees the devotion to Mary as simply a way of thinking about God using a maternal metaphor drawn from daily experience.

Mark Massa in turn has used the arguments developed by Tracy and Greeley to provide a fresh perspective on an issue directly relevant to the concerns of this book: the continuing tendency on the part of "many Americans in the media, the academy, and in popular culture [to] perceive Catholicism to be different, perhaps disturbingly different, from the American way of life" (2001, 568), In particular, Massa, following Greeley (2000, 111–135), argues that, in the Protestant imagination, the infinite qualitative difference seen to exist between God and humanity leads to the view that "human society is both unnatural and oppressive" (2001, 567). And in the United States, the predominance of this view has always meant a strong concern with protecting the rights of the individual against the oppression of government and social networks. In the Catholic imagination, by contrast, because God is seen to be immanent in the world, human communities are more likely to be seen as both natural and good—with the result that Catholics are less likely to share that distrust of government so central to the Protestant American worldview. It is the absence of this distrust of government, Massa argues, that really explains why Catholics came to be defined as the Other in American society.

Finally, Robert Orsi (2005) has added to this literature on immanence and the Catholic imagination in his quasi-autobiographical account of the changes and continuities associated with the American Catholic experience in the last half of the twentieth century. Orsi's special contribution is to point out that we need to study *how* the sacred becomes immanent for American Catholics. In his words (p. 73),

> the study of Catholicism in everyday life is about the mutual engagement of men, women and holy figures present to each other. But presence is a human experience; how sacred presences become real in particular times and places is a question. That is what I begin with here. How do religious beliefs become material? How do the gods and other special beings . . . become as real to people as their bodies, as substantially there as the homes they inhabit?

Although Orsi goes on to identify a number of processes that have functioned to make the sacred material for American Catholics, he emphasizes the role played by certain types of physical bodies (p. 74).

> The materialization of the religious world includes a process that might be called the corporalization of the sacred. I mean by this the practice of rendering the invisible world visible by constituting it as an experience in a body—in one's own body or in someone else's body—so that the experiencing body itself becomes the bearer of [a sacred] presence for oneself and for others.

In developing this point, Orsi goes on to argue that the visible bodies of young children (like the altar boys assisting a priest at mass; schoolchildren in the pews; young girls dressed up as Our Lady of Fatima), and the bodies of people who were physically crippled or in great pain (like his own uncle Sal, who had cerebral palsy, and Italian stigmatics like Gemma Galgani and Padre Pio) were especially important in determining how American Catholics experienced the sacred.

The Greeley/Tracy/Orsi argument needs work. For example, Greeley's (2004, 135) in-passing remark to the effect that analogical thinking was promoted by the sacramental objects and practices common in the pre–Vatican II church, organized as they were around angels, the souls in Purgatory, religious medals, the Stations of the Cross, and the like, might be read as suggesting that analogical thinking is now less common among American Catholics precisely because the use of such sacramentals has declined over the past few decades. Further, although Orsi (2005) is almost certainly correct in saying that cultic activities commonly associated with the pre–Vatican II era have not died out as completely as is commonly thought, it does seem fair to say that the emphasis on "corporalizing sacredness" in the bodies of young children or suffering saints and cripples—the emphasis that Orsi sees as having been so central to making the sacred immanent in the visible world—is likely less a part of the American Catholic experience today than it was when Orsi himself was growing up. And, certainly, Catholic commentators like David Carlin (2003) have pointed out that since Vatican II many American Catholic leaders and thinkers have increasingly embraced precisely that emphasis on religious individualism that used to be more uniquely associated with the Protestant tradition.

Nevertheless, even if a belief in immanence and use of the analogical imagination are not as common as they once were among American Catholics, there are still reasonable grounds for asserting that a belief in immanence and the resulting emphasis on analogical thinking promotes a way of relating to God that is really quite different from the way of relating to God that results from the Protestant rejection of immanence and from dialectical thinking. If we now ask what mode of relating to God seems implicit in the items used to construct the most commonly used measures of a person's religious orientation (the I/E Scale, the Quest Scale, the FMS), then clearly it seems a mode closer to the Protestant view, which emphasizes an individual's internalization of God's word, than to the Catholic view, which emphasizes relating to God by the use of metaphors drawn from everyday life or through our experience of children in church, handicapped relatives, suffering saints, and so on.

Yes, But . . .

One way of responding to the discussion to this point would be to argue that if there are problems with any of the scales that we have been considering, then these problems would become apparent when the scales are assessed for construct validity, reliability, and multidimensionality. And, certainly, there exist a very large number of studies which *do* assess these scales (especially the I/E Scale and the Quest Scale) in just these terms. Nevertheless, the point that Carol Gilligan (1982) made long ago, I suggest, is still valid: in developing theories, where you *start* often determines where you end up. In Gilligan's case, this meant that developing a theory of moral reasoning by first studying responses elicited from males leads to a theory that is quite different from the one which emerges when you start by studying responses elicited from females. What it means here, I suggest, is that studying religion as a generic process using measures that uniformly rest upon a Protestant vision will likely result in conclusions that are qualitatively different from those that might have been reached had the measures been less dependent upon a distinctively Protestant view.

Unfortunately, there is little basis for believing that the Protestant norm implicit in the measures considered here will be dislodged among academics studying religion in the near future. On the contrary, the I/E Scale, the Quest Scale, and the FMS-Vertical subscale are still popular and still being sold as measures of a generic religiosity that transcends the Protestant case. Moreover, the arguments by Tracy, Greeley, and Orsi on immanence and the analogical imagination, which at least might provide the foundation for developing measures of religiosity that are dramatically different from those currently in use, have been ignored in mainstream psychology of religion. This might be understandable in the case of Tracy and Orsi. Tracy, after all, is a theologian whose "data" consist for the most part of arguments developed by other theologians, so his work is really quite outside the social scientific mainstream. As regards Orsi's 2005 work, my own sense is that much of the autobiographical material he presents—though interesting in itself—is too often only very tenuously tied to his theoretical argument and so, if anything, functions to obscure that argument. In any event, since the argument developed in this most recent book goes beyond the arguments made in earlier ones (like 1985 and 1996), there really has not been enough time for Orsi's work on the Catholic imagination to have had a major impact on the academic study of religion.

Greeley, however, is a different matter. For decades now, Andrew Greeley—quite apart from his status as an active priest and best-selling novelist—has been one of the most visible scholars working in the sociology of religion, and his many (many) articles and books are widely cited by psychologists of religion. Wulff's (1997) textbook, for example, which is likely the most widely used in this area, mentions several of Greeley's studies. In each case, however, the study is cited by Wulff only because of some particular empirical finding it reports; Greeley's theoretical arguments on the Catholic imagination have simply been ignored.

In the end, then, not only are there grounds for suggesting that the measures of religiosity commonly used by psychologists of religion continue to rest upon an implicitly Protestant view of the sacred, but also that a body of literature which might be used to challenge this situation, and which is highly visible among Catholic intellectuals in the United States, has been steadfastly ignored.

But what about sociology? Have American sociologists been able to transcend the implicit Protestant norm that continues to structure the academic study of religion in psychology? Unfortunately, no.

The Sociology of Religion

While the study of religion is by no means a central disciplinary concern within the American sociological establishment, it is a subject that continues to attract the attention of a great many sociologists. There are, for example, a number of specialty journals devoted to the sociological study of religion (the two most important of which are the *Journal for the Scientific Study of Religion* and *Sociology of Religion*), and at least a few articles on religion regularly appear in top-ranked sociology journals like the *American Sociological Review* and the *American Journal of Sociology*. Moreover, more than five hundred sociologists are members of the Sociology of Religion Section of the American Sociological Association (ASA)—which puts this section right about in the middle (in terms of membership) of the forty or so sections in the ASA (Wuthnow 2003, 18).

It is conventional, in accounts that discuss the intellectual origins of the sociology of religion, to trace those origins back to the often-referenced "Founding Fathers" (and they were all fathers) of sociology itself; but the precise list of these progenitors varies a bit from one commentator to the next (compare, for example, Ammerman 2006; Davie 2003; Greeley 1995, 5–21; Stark and Finke 2000, 27–31; Wuthnow 2003). Most (but not all) commentators put Marx on the list, and a few (but only a few) list Freud and Simmel as well. But the only two names that appear on everybody's list are Max Weber and Emile Durkheim. Unfortunately, the often-made claim that Weber and Durkheim laid the foundations for the sociological study of religion, at least if we are talking specifically about the sociology of religion in the United States, is simultaneously correct and misleading.

While the study of religion was certainly a central concern of both Durkheim and Weber during their lifetimes, their works on religion in fact had little effect on American sociologists at the time. Connell's (1997) careful study of the published work of leading American sociologists in the early twentieth century, for example, suggests that while early American sociologists had a passing familiarity with the work of Durkheim and Weber, these two authors were not then singled out as being especially important. As Connell and others (e.g., Collins 2006) point out, it was only during the 1940s and 1950s, mainly through the efforts of influential sociologists like Talcott Parsons, Robert Merton, and C. Wright Mills, that Durkheim and Weber came to be seen as the founders of sociology and that their works, including those on religion, came to be required reading in sociology.

On the other hand, even granting that Durkheim and Weber did not rise to prominence in American sociology until the 1940s and 1950s, it is undeniably the case that, over the past several decades, acquiring a familiarity with their core arguments has been a rite of passage for graduate students training to be sociologists. Given this, it is important to point out (at least given the concerns of this chapter) that in their best-known and most widely read theoretical formulations about religion, Weber and Durkheim both privileged Protestantism.

This privileging of Protestantism is, of course, easiest to see in the case of Weber. After all, his best-known work on religion, *The Protestant Ethic and the Spirit of Capitalism* (1905/1996), associates Protestantism with nothing less than modernity and economic progress. Thus, in Weber's formulation, Lutheranism gave an impetus to the development of modern European capitalism by suggesting that secular callings (e.g., being a merchant) could be as morally legitimate as any other calling—an attitude which Weber very explicitly contrasted with the medieval (read: Catholic) view that involvement with the world put your immortal soul at risk. But even more importantly, Weber argued that the anxiety generated by the Calvinist doctrine of predestination gave rise to the "spirit of capitalism," which for Weber was a set of values (including a commitment to the rational pursuit of profit, the view that individuals had a moral obligation to make a profit, that spending money for personal pleasure was wrong) that was an essential precondition for economic progress. What all this means, as John McGreevy (2003) points out, is that when Talcott Parsons set about championing and popularizing Weber's argument, Parsons became the very first American sociologist to endorse the quintessentially Protestant claim that the Reformation, by breaking with the Catholic tradition, had marked a turning point (and a progressive move forward) for the modern West.

The privileging of Protestantism in Durkheim's work is a bit harder to see. After all, one of the central claims in *Suicide* (1897/1951) is that Catholics are less prone to suicide than Protestants—which hardly seems to put Catholicism in a bad light. But here we must keep in mind how Durkheim (pp. 157–158) *explains* the lower suicide rate among Catholics: he credited it to higher levels of social solidarity deriving from the Catholic Church's suppression of individualism and free inquiry and the church's corresponding insistence that all members hold precisely the same beliefs and engage in the same rituals. Durkheim's emphasis on "common values and rituals" is significant because of the argument he had developed earlier, in *The Division of Labor in Society* (1893/1933), which—like *Suicide*— is still required reading in most classical theory courses in sociology.

In the first half of *The Division of Labor,* Durkheim suggests that societies can be arrayed along a social evolutionary sequence that starts with societies bound together by the solidarity produced by common values and ritual and ends with modern societies that are bound together by the solidarity that derives from the mutual interdependence occasioned by a societal division of labor. Within the logic of *The Division of Labor*, in other words, an emphasis on common values and rituals, and a corresponding deemphasis on individualism, is the hallmark of a more "primitive" form of social organization. The result of this reasoning is that when *Suicide* is read against the social evolutionary argument developed in *The Division of Labor*, what *Suicide* does is suggest very clearly that Catholicism, by virtue of its strong emphasis on common values and rituals, is a far more primitive form of religion than Protestantism.

Basically, then, both Weber and Durkheim—albeit in slightly different ways—developed arguments that imported into the sociology of religion that same social evolutionary premise (that Catholicism is a more primitive form of religion, or if you prefer, that Protestantism is a more advanced form of religion) that scholars like Hall and Starr had imported into the psychology of religion.

On the other hand, although what Durkheim and Weber wrote about religion is still required reading in sociology, and so likely continues to contribute to a mindset that privileges Protestantism, the particular theoretical arguments they developed have increasingly been set aside, at least by American sociologists of religion, in favor of arguments that on the surface seem quite different from the arguments that Durkheim and Weber developed. A careful examination of these newer arguments, however, reveals that they too privilege Protestantism.

The Rise of Rational Choice Theory

Writing in the late 1980s, Robert Wuthnow (1988) concluded his assessment of the sociology of religion with this summary judgment:

> In viewing the sociology of religion as a whole many significant developments have obviously taken place over the past several decades; yet it appears regrettable that the field has grown more rapidly in inductive research and in subspecializations than in attempts to identify theoretically integrative concepts.

Basically, as I read his article, what Wuthnow was saying is that, while sociologists of religion had established what does and does not correlate with religion in a variety of empirical studies (with maybe a few words of ad hoc theorizing thrown in at the end) and had increasingly turned their attention to religious phenomena previously ignored (like the study of new religious movements), they had done little to advance the theoretical understanding of religion as a generic social process. In retrospect, however, we know that Wuthnow made this assessment at the beginning of a period during which sociologists of religion became increasingly concerned with theoretical matters. In particular, over the past two decades, sociologists of religion have been drawn into a debate over which of two specific theoretical paradigms is best suited for the study of religion.

The first of these theoretical paradigms is usually called "secularization theory," and its central contention is that religion will decline as modernity advances. This, of course, is an old argument and very much a part of the theorizing done by Marx, Durkheim, Weber, and other classical theorists. Although most commentators (see, for example, Gorski 2003b, 111) believe that secularization theory emerged during the early nineteenth century in the works of Saint-Simon and Comte, Grace Davie (2003, 69) is likely correct in suggesting that, at least to some extent, its roots are in the medieval idea that both the church and its authority are maintained by formal and informal sanctions that would be threatened by religious pluralism.

While secularization theory is likely still the dominant perspective in Europe, its popularity in the United States has waned. Davie (2003, 68) calls Stephen Warner's (1993) article assessing theoretical trends in the sociology of religion "a watershed in American understandings of their own society," because it signaled an increasing awareness among American sociologists that the older secularization thesis, whatever its applicability to Europe might be, could not be taken for granted in the American case. What has increasingly come to replace secularization theory in the United States is the theory of religious economies developed by Rodney Stark and a variety of associates (Finke 1990; Finke and Stark 1988; Finke and Stark 2003; Stark and Finke 2000; Stark and Iannaccone 1991).

Stark and Finke (2000) define the theory of religious economies in terms of several dozen propositions and definitions which they use to explain religious phenomena. Most simply, however, their core argument is this:

> Religious economies are like commercial economies in that they consist of a market made up of a set of current and potential customers and set of firms seeking to serve that market. The fate of those firms will depend upon (1) aspects of their organizational structure, (2) their sales representatives, (3) their product, and (4) their marketing techniques. Translated into more churchly language, the relative success of religious bodies (especially when confronted with an unregulated economy) will depend upon their polity, their clergy, their religious doctrines, and their evangelization techniques. (Finke and Stark 1992, 17)

Moreover, Stark et al. have always been quite clear about which religious doctrines (the "product" mentioned above) they think will sell best in an unregulated religious economy: ones that require their adherents to maintain at least a moderate level of "tension" with their environment (see especially Stark and Finke 2000, 193–217). What they mean by this is that the most appealing sort of religion will be religion that requires at least a moderate level of self-sacrifice on the part of its adherents. In explaining *why* this will be the most appealing sort of religion, Stark et al. posit that, if people pay a relatively high price for membership, they will believe that the rewards to be gained from membership will be high. In Stark's (2003, 20) words, "religions that ask more from their members are thereby enabled to give them more—in worldly as well as spiritual rewards."

The theory of religious economies has had an enormous influence on the sociological study of religion in the United States. Randall Collins (1997) finds the Stark et al. theory to be "a landmark in the sociology of religion," just as works by Durkheim and Weber were landmarks in an earlier period. In part, the tremendous success of this newer theory derives from the body of evidence Stark and his associates have amassed in support of the theory (see Stark and Finke 2000, for an overview of this evidence). The theory has its critics, of course, who themselves have collected evidence that key predictions from the theory are generally unsupported (Chaves and Gorski 2001; Gorski 2003b). Even so, the debate over the Stark et al. theory has become increasing central to the discipline—as anyone familiar with the three specialty journals devoted to the sociology of religion in the United States[4] will know.

For example, in 1999 Skerkat and Ellison (378) stated that the debate over the theory of religious economies had become the single most visible debate in the sociology of religion. Furthermore, Thomas Robbins (2001) was, and is, almost certainly correct in characterizing the theory as "the biggest game in town," because it has come to overshadow completely all possible competitors. The Stark et al. theory now likely shapes the way American sociologists think about religion more than any other single sociological theory. In what follows, then, I want to show two things: (1) that the theory of religious economies (just like the I/E Scale, the Quest Scale, etc.) rests upon a conceptualization of religion that is implicitly Protestant, and (2) that the Protestant conceptualization underlying this theory has warped Stark and others' understanding of American religion, the one case that for many people is the case where the theory works best.

The Power of the Word

In reviewing Stark and Finke's *Acts of Faith*, Robbins (2001, 334) declares that the theory of religious economies "entails a distinctly cognitivist or objectivist theory of religion, in which *beliefs* [emphasis in original] about God(s) take center stage." Robbins then goes on to contrast this theory to theoretical perspectives that emphasize "rituals or feelings" in the study of religion. While I think that Robbins's remarks here are insightful, I suggest that his conclusion is only partly correct. In fact, Stark and his associates do *not* usually investigate the actual beliefs that individuals hold. On the contrary, as Stark and Finke themselves made clear in the passage cited above, what is of central importance to the theory of religious economies are the *messages*—that is, the formal doctrines and creeds—that religious organizations market to the public. One result is that there is little or no room in the theorizing by Stark et al. for the possibility of a significant discrepancy between the official doctrines and creeds of a religious organization and the actual beliefs (and/or behaviors) of its members. Consider, for example, Stark's most recent work, which—though not about American religion per se—provides an especially clear demonstration of this problem.

Stark (2001b; 2003) starts with the premise that European Christians, both Protestants and Catholics, have been committed to a belief in an omnipotent God who is rational, responsible, and dependable and to the belief that the universe was created by this God. Stark then goes on to argue that this belief structure has been responsible for some of the master patterns in European history, including the rise of modern science, witch hunts, and the elimination of slavery. At the level of formal theological doctrine, of course, Stark is absolutely correct—this *is* the vision of God embraced by both Catholic and Protestant theologians. What Stark assumes, however, without presenting any supporting evidence whatsoever, is that these formal theological positions have been consciously held by the individuals (anti-slavery activists, scientists, witch hunters) he is studying. Ignored entirely, in other words, is the possibility that non-theologians have thought about God in ways different from those prescribed in formal doctrine. Also ignored is a possibility that will be obvious to anyone familiar with the history of European Catholicism, namely, that for ordinary Catholics, including many Catholic intellectuals, Mary and the saints have been far more central to the experience of religion than the omnipotent God postulated in formal Catholic doctrine—which in turn suggests that popular beliefs about Mary and the saints have likely been more important in shaping Catholic attitudes than the doctrines relating to God that are so important in Stark's analysis.

If there is an emphasis on formal doctrine and creed in the theorizing by Stark and his associates, where does it come from? I suggest that it derives from the sort of "dialectical thinking" which David Tracy found to be pervasive in Protestant theology and which Andrew Greeley has suggested is the defining characteristic of the Protestant imagination (see the discussion earlier in this chapter). What Stark et al., have done, in other words, is to take a Protestant theological orientation (what matters most is how people react to God's revealed message) and morphed it into a theoretical argument (what matters most in studying religion is the effect that formal doctrine and creeds, seen as coming from God, have on human behavior). The problem with this essentially Protestant orientation, whatever its value as a theological position, is that it can so easily lead us astray as we try to understand the lived experience of religion in particular contexts. And this, as I will now argue, is precisely what happened in Finke and Stark's *The Churching of America* (1992), a work that is still routinely held up (see, for example, Ebaugh 2002) as demonstrating that the "religious economies" approach is especially well-suited to the American case.

Just How Strict Were the Baptists and Methodists?

In *The Churching of America* (1992), Finke and Stark use their "high tension sells best" argument to explain some of the master patterns in American religious history. Why did the Methodists and Baptists become so popular in the aftermath of the American Revolution, at the expense of other (and older) Protestant denominations? This occurred largely, they say, because the Revolution led to disestablishment of the state church (and so to an unregulated religious economy) and because the Methodists and Baptists, with their strictures against dancing, drunkenness, public brawling, and so forth, required sacrifices not required by other denominations. And why did the Methodists lose ground to the Baptists in the latter part of the nineteenth century? Finke and Stark find that it was at least partly because the Methodists, but not the Baptists, abandoned the sort of high-tension religion that they had helped pioneer a century earlier. But where is the evidence that the Baptists and (early) Methodists were so strict? In fact, the only "evidence" that Finke and Stark present is that Baptist and Methodist clergy *preached* self-control. Finke and Stark provide no evidence bearing on the one issue that is central to their argument: the degree to which the people who flocked to hear these sermons chose to exercise such self-control in their daily life. This criticism might seem to be academic pettifogging, I grant, except that there is a body of evidence, which has been available for some time, indicating that during the late eighteenth and nineteenth centuries there was often a gap between what was preached by evangelical ministers and the actual behavior of evangelical Christians.

For example, based upon his analysis of a variety of sources, including private journals and diaries, Grady McWhinney (1988, 171–192) concludes that in the U.S. South many evangelicals were in fact fairly lackadaisical about such things as attending preaching services or sending their children to Sunday school, and that when they did attend church services, they often exhibited a level of gaiety that offended northern visitors. Why? Because, says McWhinney (p. 189) "the way to heaven, as explained by most preachers and accepted by most southerners, was simple enough—one only had to believe in the divinity of Jesus and to be baptized." This response hardly seems consistent with the claim by Stark et al. that the success of evangelical sects rested upon the fact that members were required to renounce pleasure.

Ted Ownby's (1990) *Subduing Satan* covers much the same ground as McWhinney but with greater theoretical sophistication. Ownby starts with an observation that is commonly made by historians studying southern culture (Lindman 2000; Lyerly 1998): in the South the evangelical emphasis on self-sacrifice and renunciation of physical pleasure (which was certainly there at the level of preached creed) was most problematic for males since it was so much at odds with the traditional model of masculinity, which rested upon public displays of physical prowess and participation in activities like drinking, horseracing, cockfighting, card playing, and so on. What Ownby goes on to show, however, is that, at least in the rural South, forms of social organization developed which moderated the tension that existed between the formal demands of evangelical Christianity and traditional masculinity. This was done, first, by making the home the sacred center of religious life and so implying that activities *outside* the home might be a little less evangelically upstanding than activities *in* the home. Hunting, for example, always conducted at some distance from the home, routinely provided evangelical males with a "space" in which they could be aggressive, boisterous, and—quite often—drunk. Accommodation was even made in the local church: men were allocated a separate section of the church, so that they could come in late (after socializing out front) and could engage in masculine behaviors (like spitting on the floor) during church services. Males also dominated the public squares in small towns, and here too, Ownby points out, they often engaged in some decidedly nonevangelical behaviors, especially during the extended Christmas season. Ownby's (1990, 167) summary of his argument goes like this:

The institutions of evangelical culture [in the South] allowed men outlets from a normally strict moral code. Both men and women expected men to adhere more closely to evangelical values inside the home than outside it. The church allowed men to slink into the building at the last minute, to sit on their own sides of the building and to spit tobacco. The revival meeting allowed open sinners—most of them men—to make a periodic statement of repentance, even if they tended not to live up to their momentary commitments.

On balance, it might have been true that evangelicals were more likely to engage in renunciatory activities than nonevangelicals, and this might be enough to save the Finke-Stark argument. The point, however, is that, in focusing on preached creed rather than on actual behaviors, they are ignoring what their own theorizing would otherwise suggest they need to focus on: the degree to which ordinary Baptists and Methodists engaged in the sort of impulse control that supposedly made membership in the upstart sects valuable. But if Finke and Stark's focus on preached creed introduces *possible* distortions into their account of evangelical Protestantism, it does significantly more damage to their analysis of Irish American Catholicism

The Catholic Connection

Finke and Stark (1992, 136) claim that during the nineteenth century American Catholicism was for all practical purposes an "Irish sect movement." They go on to explain that the religion which Irish Catholic immigrants brought with them after 1850 was the Catholicism that had risen to prominence in Ireland as a result of the devotional revolution described by Larkin (whose work Finke and Stark cite). This was, they argue, a type of Catholicism that was as strict as anything associated with the Baptists and Methodists and so, for that reason, popular. In their own words (1992, 138):

Without pausing to explore the cause of the Irish devotional revolution here, we may note that this revolution spread to America with successive waves of Irish immigrants (Larkin, 1972). And in combination with the immense predominance of Irish clergy, the sect-like qualities of Irish Catholicism predominated as well. Once committed to the zealous conviction of the Irish brand of faith, the average American Catholic held as many moral reservations as did the average Baptist or Methodist. Granted, Catholics did not condemn drinking and dancing . . . . But Catholics adhered to many moral and behavioral standards that were far stricter than those of secular society.

Finke and Stark then go on to list a variety of Catholic prohibitions associated with sex, divorce, contraception, Lenten practice, and so on.

As far as it goes, Finke and Stark's characterization of Catholic *doctrine* during this period is quite on the mark. As we saw in Chapter 2, the Catholicism being marketed by ultramontantist clergy in the nineteenth century (both in the United States and Ireland) was every bit as strict as Finke and Stark say. Furthermore, in Ireland itself this sort of Catholicism did become popular in the wake of the Famine—though whether that was because it was strict (which is the Finke-Stark argument) or because its values were congruent with the values of the tenant farmer class (which, remember, was Eugene Hyne's argument; see Chapter 2) is a matter of debate. Even so, where the Finke-Stark argument clearly fails is as an explanation of Irish Catholicism in *America*.

As a start, and as pointed out in Chapter 2, it was Larkin's contention that the devotional revolution occurred in Ireland largely because this was the sort of Catholicism that had long been favored by the well-off tenant farmer class and because the Famine shifted Ireland's demographic profile so that this group became more prominent. The Famine, in other words, disproportionately killed off or drove off those nominal Irish Catholics who were *not* committed to this sort of Catholicism. This is why, for Larkin, the Irish immigrants who arrived in the United States in the wake of the Famine would *not* have been especially good Catholics (which, as the material reviewed in Chapter 2 suggests, was in fact true).

Partly then, the Irish case is instructive because it poses puzzles for the theory of religious economies. For example, if indeed it is true that a general emphasis on "strictness" is what makes a religious message appealing, then why was the strict Catholicism promoted by Cardinal Cullen in Ireland appealing to only one particular stratum (well-off tenant farmers) but not to others (for example, the great mass of landless laborers)? And why did Irish immigrants, who had not found this sort of strict Catholicism to be especially appealing in Ireland, embrace it with such gusto once they were in the United States? And why was this "strict" sort of Catholicism so appealing to Irish immigrants but not to Italian immigrants? One answer to all these questions, of course, is that Stark et al. are wrong, that strictness is not a variable that anywhere and everywhere makes a religious message valuable, and that each of these patterns has to be explained in some other way (for instance, in terms of the affinity between religious values and class interests, which is the sort of argument developed earlier in this book).

Still, as with the other arguments considered in this chapter, I am less concerned with the empirical adequacy of the Finke-Stark theory than with the ways in which the Protestant underpinnings of this theory structure the research process. The implicitly Protestant emphasis in the theory of religious economies on the "content of religious messages" as being the critical element in explaining religion predisposes us to *ignore* questions (like "Just how strict were the Methodists and Baptist?" and "Were the Famine Irish in fact good Catholics?") that might otherwise lead to a more nuanced understanding of religion America. But there's more: I now want to argue that the implicitly Protestant emphasis on "message" in *The Churching of America* caused Finke and Stark to see patterns in their data that were not there. Consider, for example, their account of the increase in Baptist and Methodist "market share" in the wake of the Revolution.

The Torrential Increase That Wasn't

Using the theory of religious economies, Finke and Stark (1992) posited that, when churches in the American colonies were established, ministers had little incentive to craft the sort of high-tension messages that sell well, and so membership rates should have been low. And, indeed, their analysis shows that in 1776 the "adherence rate" (= percent of the general population, including children, that belonged to some religious group) was only 17 percent. With disestablishment, however, all this changed: the religious market was thrown wide open, and Methodists and Baptists—"upstart sects"—gained in popularity precisely because their ministers did craft and promote forms of high-tension religion. But, if we look carefully at Finke and Stark's discussion of Methodist and Baptist success, we find that they are saying more than simply that these groups gained a larger share of the religious marketplace. Generally, the imagery invoked in their discussion conveys the impression that the success of the upstart sects following disestablishment occasioned a rise in the adherence rate that was abrupt and steep. They write (p. 15), for example, that "by the start of the Civil War," the original 17 percent adherence rate "had *risen dramatically,* to 37 percent" (emphasis added). They later (pp. 56–59) describe Methodist and Baptist growth following disestablishment as "torrential." They also mention (p. 104) the "Methodist *miracle* of growth between 1776 and 1850" (emphasis added). But do the data they present really support the imagery they invoke? Do the data really show an increase in the membership rate that is *dramatic, torrential,* and *miraculous?* No.

In their Figure 1.2, Finke and Stark (1992, 16) present a bar graph giving adherence rates[5] for the period 1776 through 1980. In fact, however, it presents the adherence rate for 1776 and then the one for 1850. The rate for 1776, in other words, is the *only* rate reported for any of the years during which the American religious marketplace was noncompetitive, and there is no data on any of the

TABLE 7
Rates of "Religious Adherence," 1776–1980, as Reported by Finke and Stark

Years Used in Finke and Stark's Analysis	Adherance Rate in Each Year	Absolute Increase over Roughly Equal Intervals (about 75 years)
1776	17%	
1850	34%	+17
1860	37%	
1870	35%	
1890	45%	
1906	51%	
1916	53%	
1926	56%	+22
1952	59%	
1980	62%	

NOTE: Rate of religious adherence = percentage of the population, including children, affiliated with a formal religious group (Finke and Starke 1992, 289).

years between 1776 and 1850—an omission that is easy to miss, because their graph places the years used as charting points at equal intervals even though the intervals between the selected years are in fact not equal.

The problem should be evident in Table 7, which presents the Stark-Finke data on adherence rates over the period 1776–1980. On the one hand, these data *do* show that adherence rates increased over the century and a half following the Revolution. But remember, the imagery in Finke and Stark's discussion suggests that the rush to the upstart sects following disestablishment was sudden and dramatic, and these data simply do not support this interpretation. Quite the contrary, what these data show (see third column) is that, in the first seventy-five years following the Revolution, adherence rates rose from 17 percent to 34 percent, for an absolute increase of 17 percent, while in the next seventy-five years, adherence rates rose from 34 percent to 56 percent, for an absolute increase of 22 percent. This move looks more like a pattern of steady, linear growth. Still, if there is evidence of an "upsurge" in the Finke-Stark data, clearly that upsurge occurred in the second half of the period being surveyed, not in the first.

If there is no evidence in the data of a sudden and abrupt upsurge in adherence rates in the wake of the Revolution, which is what Finke and Stark assert in their discussion, where does that imagery come from? I suggest that it is a distortion that flows easily from the emphasis on "message" that is part of the Protestant imagination. Simply: if it is God's message that counts most of all in attracting adherents, and if the most appealing message is the sort of high-tension message that demands renunciation, then it only makes sense that there would be a torrential increase in Baptist and Methodist market share (and so a general increase in the adherence rate) fairly immediately, that is, as soon as possible after disestablishment gave Baptist and Methodist ministers the opportunity to preach that message to the public. Because the logic of Finke and Stark's implicitly Protestant orientation led to the expectation that there should have been a torrential increase in the membership of the upstart sects immediately following disestablishment, they reported such an increase even though it wasn't present in their own data.

I have given *The Churching of America* close consideration because it is regularly cited as one of the most successful applications of the theory of religious economies and because it is devoted entirely to the study of American religion. But Protestant influence can also be detected in other works in the religious economies tradition. The theory that strictness leads to an increase in religious commitment has generated a large number of studies, many (likely most) of which assess this claim using data drawn from contemporary American congregations (see Olson and Perl 2005 for a review of this literature). Yet, in examining these "strictness" studies, we continue to find that same emphasis on the "preached word" that pervades the work done by Finke and Stark.

In two studies, for example, Olson and Perl (2001; 2005) assess the "strictness" hypothesis using data from Hoge et al.'s (1996) study of financial giving in 625 congregations throughout the United States. And how was the degree of strictness associated with each congregation assessed? By the responses given to a single question that Hoge et al. had included in the questionnaire sent to a single informant, usually the pastor, in each congregation. That question was:

> Does your congregation teach that Christian life should be safeguarded through abstinence from (check all that apply)
>
> Certain kinds of food
> Alcohol or tobacco
> Gambling
> Certain kinds of entertainment such as movies, night clubs, or dancing
> Other
> No form of abstinence is stressed

Obviously, what this question assesses, and so what is central to the Olson and Perl studies, is the degree of strictness *preached* in the congregations being studied. Olson and Perl, of course, cannot be held responsible for the design of someone else's survey; the point, however, is that they see nothing problematic about the emphasis on the preached word in the Hoge et al. study.

I might note that in the original Hoge et al. study, a second questionnaire was sent out to a sample of 10,903 lay members of the congregations being studied. Unlike the questionnaire sent to pastors, this questionnaire contained no items about strictness, that is, no items that asked members about the degree to which they actually abstained from things like alcohol and gambling. One reason for this omission, it would appear, is that the original Hoge et al. analysis was concerned entirely with correlating what was *preached* with the levels of financial giving. Hoge and his associates, in other words, also took an emphasis on the preached word—and the lack of concern with actual behavior in regard to what is preached—as entirely unproblematic.

But an emphasis on the preached word is not the only element of the Protestant imagination that has shaped the theoretical arguments developed by rational choice theorists. Consider the sort of person seen by rational choice theorists as inhibiting religious growth, that is, the sort of person who makes a particular congregation downright unappealing in the religious marketplace.

The Free Rider "Problem"

In a well-known article that has provoked a lively debate among American sociologists, Laurence Iannaccone (1994) developed a slightly different version of the "strictness makes a church popular" argument advanced by other rational choice theorists (including Stark). Iannaccone took as his starting point an argument developed by Dean Kelley (1972/1977). Kelley had noted that conservative Protestant denominations were growing faster than mainline (liberal) Protestant denominations. He then explained this by hypothesizing that "the business of religion is meaning" (p. 38) and that people have a "craving for ultimate meaning [that is] very deep and ancient in human experience" (p. 155). Conservative churches are appealing, Kelley argued, because of their strictness, by which he meant a strong insistence that they alone have the truth, an intolerance of dissent, a clear sense of which lifestyle behaviors are appropriate and which are not, etc. This strictness provides meaning to people in a way that non-strict (liberal) churches do not. What Iannaccone sought to do, he tells us (p. 1181), was to "embed Kelley's thesis within a much broader rational choice approach to religion." And, as Joseph Tamney (2005) has noted, Iannaccone did this by introducing something that was not at all a part of Kelley's original argument: the idea of "free riders," by which Iannaccone meant people who attend church services and make use of church resources (like pastoral counseling and the fellowship of church members) but who themselves contribute little if anything in the way of money or volunteer effort.

Free riders are problematic for a congregation, Iannaccone (1994, 1184) argues, because

> their mere presence dilutes a group's resources, reducing the average level of participation, enthusiasm, energy, and the like. Heterogeneity can thus undermine intense fellowship and major undertakings. Lacking a way to identify and exclude free riders, highly committed people end up saddled with anemic resource-poor congregations.

And "anemic resource-poor" congregations hold little appeal to new members.

But free riders can be driven out (and kept out) of a congregation—and this is the core of Iannaccone's argument—by the personal costs associated with strictness, that is, by the costs associated with strict behavioral codes, strict rules about whom one may and may not socialize with, and so forth. With free riders driven out, says Iannaccone, the members who remain in strict congregations will be highly committed and more than willing to contribute both their time and their money in support of the congregation's communal activities. The result is that strict congregations are resource-rich, and so, choosing to join a strict congregation (or so Iannaccone's argument goes) is very much a "rational choice" because it allows access to those resources.

There has been an ongoing reaction to Iannaccone's argument in the sociology of religion that shows no signs of abating. Some scholars have focused on conceptual issues by pointing out (among other things) that, although Iannaccone begins by citing Kelley's work on the growth of conservative churches, Iannaccone himself includes no measure of growth in his analysis (Marwell 1996). More usually, however, scholars have tried to assess the empirical adequacy of Iannaccone's argument. Daniel Olson and Paul Perl have amassed evidence demonstrating that members in strict congregations do contribute more time and money than members in non-strict congregations (Olson and Perl 2001) and that strictness does drive out free riders (Olson and Perl 2005). On the other hand, Joseph Tamney (2005) has presented data indicating that there is no relationship between the perceived number of free riders in a congregation and the availability to other members in that congregation of collective rewards, and also that, while there may indeed be a correlation between strictness and church growth in certain contexts, that correlation is spurious, not causal. Finally, it seems clear that even in the U.S. context, strictness is not a necessary condition for growth. Robert Wuthnow and Wendy Cadge (2004), for example, in their own comment on Iannaccone's argument, point out that Buddhism has become more appealing in the United States in recent years even though most Buddhist groups are definitely not strict in Iannaccone's sense.

It is not my intent here to sort through the various studies available to determine if, on balance, Iannaccone's argument is more supported than undermined (or vice versa) by the available evidence. My concern instead is with the idea that was central to Iannaccone's original argument, an idea that has clearly resonated well with theorists, including Stark (see for example Stark and Finke 2000, 147–150), working within the rational choice tradition: the presence of free riders in a congregation is a "problem."

Whatever "free rider" might mean in the area of economic theory generally, what it means in the religious arena (at least in formulations by rational choice theorists like Iannaccone) sounds suspiciously like the sort of person that the upstart sects in the postrevolutionary period excluded from full membership: someone who has not truly undergone that sort of conversion experience which established a deeply internalized and personal relationship with God and who consequently was not yet committed to devoting their life fully and completely to the pursuit of the Christian ideal (however that might be defined in the congregation involved). What I am suggesting, in other words, is that scholars like Iannaccone and Stark have taken an early evangelical Protestant ideal, in this case the belief that the best sort of congregation is a congregation consisting of highly committed members willing to focus their life (and their money) on the single-minded pursuit of their vision of the desired Christian condition, and have transformed this ideal into a sociological theory, namely, that congregations *generally* (whether Protestant or not) must find ways of eliminating free riders in order to flourish in the religious marketplace.

This concern with the "problem" of free riders is still very much a part of the rational choice tradition. Brewer et al. (2006), for example, suggest—*contra* Iannaccone and others—that "market share" is critical to understanding the presence of free riders. Their core argument is that relatively large congregations are more likely to be seen as offering the social connections and social influence that free riders crave. Still, the point I want to make here is that Brewer et al. start their article by saying that "free riders can be a problem" (p. 389) and then go on to explain why be giving the sort of reasons that rational choice theorists always give. Thus, they argue, free riders have little or no interest in ministry and faith and so don't contribute money, and they are interested mainly (or only) in being part of a social network. As in the formulations by Iannaccone and Stark, defining free riders as a problem serves to reinforce an essentially evangelical vision of what a good (i.e., not problematic) member is. Notice, finally, that someone approaching the same material with the Catholic imagination—with its emphasis on immanence and so on the view that human relationships can be a metaphor for a relationship with God—might well see the "free rider's" concern with being part of a social network in a more positive light.

But if the Protestant imagination can be detected in the emphasis on the preached word which pervades studies done in the religious economies tradition as well as the claims made by rational choice theories about "free riders," it can also be detected in something else that has increasingly become important to rational choice theorists: the particular sort of relationship with a particular sort of God that makes religion matter.

The Right Kind of Relationship with the Right Kind of God

In recent publications, Stark (2001b; 2003; 2004) has advanced two interrelated claims. The first of these is that Durkheim had things backwards: whereas as Durkheim believed that ritual, not a belief in gods, was the sociologically significant element in religion, the reverse is true. Stark's contention is that the internalized beliefs we have about gods, not the rituals that we perform collectively, loom largest in the social experience of religion in all cultures. Stark's second contention is that, although gods of some sort are found in every religious tradition, it is only when people believe in a certain type of god that religion reinforces the moral order. And in his presidential address to the Society for the Scientific Study of Religion (2004, 470), Stark made clear what sort of god this was:

> Gods can lend sanctions to the moral order only if they are concerned about, informed about, and act on behalf of humans. Moreover, to promote virtue among humans, gods must be virtuous—they must favour good over evil. Finally, gods will be effective in sustaining moral precepts, the greater their scope—that is, the greater the diversity of their powers and the range of their influence. All-powerful, all-seeing gods ruling the entire universe are the ultimate deterrent.

At one level, of course, the sort of god described by Stark here (an all-powerful god who wants people to follow a moral code) is indeed the sort of god found not only in Christianity (in both its Protestant and Catholic variants) but also in Islam and Judaism; and so, at first sight there might not seem to be anything distinctly Protestant about this conceptualization. A Protestant connection, however, shows up when we look carefully at how Stark tests his theory. Using survey data from a variety of Western nations (where Christianity, Judaism, or Islam prevails), Stark

(2001a; 2003, 371–376; 2004) assesses the link between God and morality by correlating answers to the question "How important is God in your life?" with a variety of questions designed to reveal attitudes towards behaviors (e.g., buying goods known to be stolen) that violate established moral precepts. In the end, what is important in Stark's argument is not simply that one believe in an all-powerful god but *the degree to which you as an individual embrace that god and make that god an important element in your life.* What becomes central to Stark's conceptualization in this recent work is exactly that same emphasis upon an individual's direct and unmediated relationship with an all-powerful (read: transcendent) god, and on the degree to which we embrace the message (moral codes) seen as coming from this god, which David Tracy found to be the defining element of the Protestant imagination.

As far as I can tell, Stark's more recent work on monotheism has not yet influenced the sociology of religion in the way that the theory of religious economies generally has. Still, given an American society increasingly concerned with the connections between religion and political behavior, and given Stark's visibility in the field, I suspect that his recent message—which is that religion will reinforce morality only if individuals follow the evangelical Protestant model and develop an unmediated relationship with an all-powerful god—is a message that will (dare I say it?) sell well and only further cement in place the implicit Protestant norm that continues to structure the theorizing done by so many American sociologists studying American religion.

Epilogue

We have now met the cast of characters that I promised we would meet: the staunch Irish Presbyterians in colonial America who weren't very staunch, the devout post-Famine Irish Catholics who weren't very devout, Italian immigrants clinging to localized madonnas and saints who didn't cling very hard, Cajun Catholics whose Catholicism was possibly more about performing femininity than religion, and Hispanic Catholics who, well, turn out to be not what they seem even if we don't yet know quite what they are. Along the way, I hope, we have come to understand how a distinctively Protestant imagination, in particular an implicitly Protestant way of relating to the sacred, continues to shape the academic study of American religion—claims to the contrary notwithstanding. Finally, we have seen how this Protestant imagination has diverted scholarly attention from empirical patterns that might otherwise serve as the starting point for new insights into American religion.

What are the implications of the analysis presented here for the academic study of American religion? The answer, as it must, depends upon the reaction that the material in this book evokes in the minds of readers. In thinking about that reaction, one of my worries is that in some sections I may have overstated my case, with the result that some readers will see me as making blanket claims that I really did not intend to make. For example, do I mean to say that all scholars studying Italian Catholicism tell the Standard Story? That no scholars studying the Famine Irish acknowledge that they were not initially devout? That all scholars studying Hispanic Catholicism see it as a strongly matricentered version of Catholicism? The answer of course is no in each case. Indeed, this book would not have been possible had I not been able to draw upon evidence and insights from studies authored by scholars whose work is *not* susceptible to the criticisms I have raised. My intent has been only to suggest that much—but certainly not all—of the academic literature on American religion is pervaded by biases and metanarratives which in one way or the other derive from a Protestant imagination.

One response to even this limited claim might well be to simply ignore it, or at best, to file this book under a "contains some interesting stuff but I'm not convinced" rubric and *then* ignore it. Certainly, a great many academic books meet that fate. But another response would be to contest the claims being made here, to demonstrate that my analysis of, say, the academic study of Hispanic Catholicism or the Quest Scale is flawed. For me, contestation of this sort would be the best possible outcome.

This is not because I am confident that my analyses will be vindicated in every detail nor because of a commitment to some ideal that science proceeds by comparing theory with data. No, contestation would be useful because it would promote the only thing that has the slightest chance of promoting change with respect to the historiographical and other biases that have been identified here: getting scholars who study American religion to reflect critically on the conceptual toolkit they now take for granted.

Two • Why the Famine Irish Became Catholic in America

1. Margaret Anne Cusack (1832–1899), the "Nun of Kenmare," was born into a wealthy Protestant family in Dublin but converted to Catholicism. She joined the Poor Clares around 1860 and was living in a Poor Clare convent in Ireland when she wrote her *Advice to Irish Girls in America*, as well as a number of other popular works. Although she would win praise from Pope Leo XIII for her efforts on behalf of the Irish poor following the crop failures in 1879, her political activities would eventually cause her to leave the Catholic Church in the 1880s. For more on her life, see Glazier (1999, 198–199).

Three • Italian American Catholicism

1. The Dillingham Commission (1911, 215) reported that for the years 1898–1910 inclusive, 84 percent of all Italian immigrants to the United States were from Southern Italy, and scholars (see, for example, Tomasi 1975, 18–19) have generally taken this figure at face value. I suspect that, in fact, the percentage would be a bit lower, at least if by "Southern" is meant the region that is usually termed the Mezzogiorno. The reason for this lies with something usually overlooked in the commission's report: Genoa and the surrounding region were taken to be a part of the South of Italy (see Dillingham 1911, 250–252). This is because—quite in line with the racialized thinking of the time—commission members saw "Southern Italian" as more of a physical type than a geographical category.

2. The 1918 estimate is based on several sources. First, the old prayer card in front of the madonna's statue says that the Society was founded in that year. Second, in August 1988, while attending the annual festa in honor of the Madonna della Guardia (which continues to be held), I met a former leader of the Society who later showed me Society records in her possession that make reference to a twenty-fifth anniversary dinner held in 1943, suggesting a founding date of 1918. On the other hand, she also showed me a handwritten list of "original members still living" that had been drawn up in 1965 and which gave the date each person had first joined the Society. This list indicated that some people had joined the Society in 1916 and 1917.

3. The new immigration laws also had an effect on scholarship. For example, the

authors of the *Report of the Committee on Linguistic and National Stocks in the Population of the United States* made it clear that it was the new "national origins plan of restricting immigration" that had led to a greater concern with determining the national origins of the white population in the United States and so to their study (American Council of Learned Societies 1931, 107).

4. Here again, as with the discussion of the Church of Santi Pietro e Paolo, the events being described cut close to home for me. My mother still remembers the day when her mother received a phone call from my grandfather saying that he had been arrested for selling wine at his restaurant. It was the arrest, not the fact that he provided wine to his customers, that was surprising. For years my grandfather had kept bottles of homemade wine on hand, generally stored behind some loose boards on the outside wall of the restaurant (which formed part of an enclosed alleyway). Although he sold this wine only to regular customers he knew well, these regular customers had always included a number of federal agents working in San Francisco. Indeed, he put their pictures up on the wall in the restaurant. My grandfather, then, didn't hesitate at all when one of these agents asked for a glass of red wine with his meal on that particular day. Unfortunately, as the agent would later explain, my grandfather was serving wine to a friend who had fallen behind in his arrests; and so, in the contest between looking good to his superiors and honoring his friendship with my grandfather, it was the former that won out, and the agent arrested my grandfather. Although my grandmother paid a fine and my grandfather was quickly released, I've always believed that that arrest and my grandfather's desire to distance himself from the shame of it explain why he made a point of associating with police officers in later life. He had his picture taken with several chiefs of police and retired chiefs of police (these too went up on the restaurant's wall), and I can still recall days in the 1950s when the officer on the beat was always invited to share in Monday lunch (often made with leftovers but outstandingly good nevertheless), which my grandfather provided free to his friends on the day the restaurant was closed to the public.

Four • *Were the Acadians/Cajuns Really Good Catholics?*

1. As Griffiths (1992, 3–32) makes clear, *Acadia* meant different things to different groups at different times. In sixteenth-century maps, for example, *Acadie* was the label given to a region that today includes southeastern Quebec, New Brunswick, Prince Edward Island, Nova Scotia, and northeastern Maine (Griffiths 2005, 467). Nevertheless, as a practical matter, the vast majority of those who first developed a distinctly "Acadian" identity lived in and around those parts of Nova Scotia and southeastern New Brunswick that border the Bay of Fundy.

2. Delaney (2005) provides a week-by-week account of the events associated with the expulsion of the Acadians in 1755 and then follows their fate through 1816.

3. Although France ceded Louisiana to Spain in 1762, the first Spanish governor, Don Antonio de Ulloa, did not arrive in the colony until 1766.

4. The term *Cajun* came into widespread use during the latter half of the nineteenth century, mainly among English speakers in Louisiana, as a derogatory term for lower-class Acadians. Basically, as Ancelet (1997, 34) suggests, it meant something like "poor white

French-speaking trash." More recently, however, the term has tended to lose its derogatory connotations and has come to be applied to all French-speaking Louisianans who claim descent (or partial descent) from the Acadians who settled there in the late 1700s. This is the usage I have adopted here.

5. These comments are based on a reading of the articles published between 1995 and 2006 in *La Société historique acadienne: Les cahiers.*

6. For an overview of the "doing gender" approach, see Ginsberg and Tsing (1990), Kimmel (2000), and Marecek (1995).

Five • Hispanic Catholicism and the Illusion of Knowledge

1. The three other focal places identified by Weigle and White are the Shiprock and Four Corners area, Pecos Pueblo and Mission, and Carlsbad Caverns.

Hispano refers specifically to the Spanish-speaking inhabitants of northern New Mexico who claim descent from the early Spanish colonists.

2. These are 8 to 10 inch–tall candles enclosed in a glass casing on which the image of a saint or madonna has been imprinted. They are widely available in New Mexico; at the time, for example, I purchased one at a local Wal-Mart for ninety-nine cents.

3. Fray Alvarez's letter to diocesan authorities in Durango is document #2 in folder #17, Miscellaneous Church Records, New Mexico Records Center and Archives, Santa Fe.

4. On the early history of the Spanish Colonial Arts Society, see Weigle (1983).

5. On the history of the Pueblo Spanish style and its use in the Santa Fe–Taos area, see Wilson (1997).

6. The sale of the *santuario* is described in Kay (1987) and Weigle (1983).

7. On the centrality and importance of the Penitente Brotherhood in Hispanic communities, see Carroll (2002) and Weigle (1976). For an autobiographical account of just how central Penitente rituals were to the lived experience of Catholicism in New Mexican communities, even as late as the 1930s, see Sandoval (1990).

8. Email communication with Thomas Tweed, June 2005.

9. Even though the proportion of Hispanics who are Catholic is decreasing, it is still the case—just as scholars like Stevens-Arroyo and Díaz-Stevens declare—that the proportion of Catholics who are Hispanics is increasing (Harris 2002). What allows this to happen, of course, is that, as the result of both natural increase and migration, the size of the Hispanic Catholic population is increasing dramatically relative to the rest of the Catholic population in the United States.

Six • Protestantism and the Academic Study of American Religion

1. Harris (1968) still provides the best overview of the theories of religion developed by these and other social evolutionary thinkers in the nineteenth century.

2. On the influence Hall and Starbuck had in psychology, see Wulff (1997).

3. The history and nature of the consensus model is discussed at length in Albanese (2002) and Wilson (2003), and I have relied heavily on these discussions in what follows here. This use of the term *consensus* derives from this tradition's emphasis on a melting

pot ideology, that is, on the need for non-Protestant groups to become more like the sort of Protestantism that "made America great."

4. These are the *Journal for the Scientific Study of Religion, Sociology of Religion*, and *Review of Religious Research*.

5. Finke and Stark (1992) make clear in a footnote (p. 298) that they use the term *adherence rate*, rather than *membership rate*, in order to signal to readers that they have "standardized the membership data to eliminate different definitions of membership across religious bodies." Basically, in the case of denominations that do not include children as members, Finke and Stark inflated membership statistics using data on the local age profile.

Abrahamson, Harold J. 1975. "The social varieties of behavior: the Italian experience viewed comparatively." In *The Religious Experience of Italian Americans*, ed. Silvano M. Tomasi, 55–67. Staten Island, N.Y.: American Italian Historical Association.

Agnew, W. H., S.J. 1913. "Pastoral care of Italian children in America." *Ecclesiastical Review* 8:257–267.

Ahlstrom, Sydney E. 1970. "The problem of the history of religion in America." *Church History* 39:224–235.

———. 1972. *A Religious History of the American People*. New Haven: Yale University Press.

Akenson, Donald Harman. 1984a. "Commentary." *William and Mary Quarterly* 41:125–129.

———. 1984b. "Why the accepted estimates of ethnicity of the American people, 1790, are unacceptable." *William and Mary Quarterly* 41:102–119.

———. 1988. *Small Differences: Irish Catholics and Irish Protestants, 1815–1922*. Montreal: McGill-Queen's University Press.

———. 1993. *The Irish Diaspora: A Primer*. Toronto: P. D. Meany Company.

Albanese, Catherine L. 2002. "American Religious History: A Bibliographical Essay." Currents in American Scholarship Series. Washington, D.C.: U.S. Department of State.

———. 2004. "How I have changed my mind." *Religion and American Culture* 14:3–10.

Allport, Gordon W., and J. Michael Ross. 1967. "Personal religious orientation and prejudice." *Journal of Personality and Social Psychology* 5:432–443.

Almond, Philip C. 1988. *The British Discovery of Buddhism*. Cambridge: Cambridge University Press.

American Council of Learned Societies. 1931. "Report of the Committee on Linguistic and National Stocks in the Population of the United States." In *Annual Report of the American Historical Association*, vol. 1, 107–439, Washington, D.C.: Government Printing Office.

Ammerman, Nancy. 2006. "2005 SSSR presidential address: on being a community of scholars—practicing the study of religion." *Journal for the Scientific Study of Religion* 45:137–148.

Ancelet, Barry Jean. 1985. "Ote voir ta sacree soutane: anti-clerical humor in French Louisiana." *Louisiana Folklore Miscellany* 6:26–33.

———. 1997. "From Evangeline hot sauce to Cajun ice: signs of ethnicity in South Louisiana." *Louisiana Folklore Miscellany* 12:29–42.

Austin, Mary. 1928a. "Catholic culture in the Southwest," part 1 "El Dorado on the Rio Grande." *Commonweal* 8:510–512.

———. 1928b. "Catholic culture in the Southwest," part 2 "The work of the Brown Gowns." *Commonweal* 8:544–546.

———. 1928c. "Catholic culture in the Southwest," part 3 "Salvaging the old crafts." *Commonweal* 8:572–575.

Avella, Steven M. 2000. "Phelan's cemetery: religion in the urbanizing West, 1850–1869." In *Rooted in Barbarous Soil: People, Culture, and Community in Gold Rush California*, ed. Kevin Starr and Richard J. Orsi, 250–279. Berkeley: University of California Press.

Babcock, Barbara A. 1990. "A New Mexican Rebecca: imaging Pueblo women." *Journal of the Southwest* 32:400–436.

———. 1997. "Mudwomen and whitemen: a meditation on Pueblo potteries and the politics of representation." In *The Material Culture of Gender—The Gender of Material Culture*, ed. Katharine Martinez and Kenneth L. Ames, 253–280. Winterthur, Del.: Henry Francis de Pont Winterthur Museum.

Baccari, Alessandro, Vincenza Scarpaci, and Rev. Father Gabriel Zavattaro. 1985. *Saints Peter and Paul Church: The Chronicles of the Italian Cathedral of the West*. San Francisco: Alessandro Baccari.

Bacon, Leonard W. 1897. *A History of American Christianity*. New York: Christian Literature.

Baird, Rev. Robert. 1844. *Religion in the United States of America*. Glasgow: Blackie and Son.

Baker, Vaughan B. 1983. "In and out the mainstream: the Acadians in antebellum Louisiana." In *The Cajuns: Essays on Their History and Culture*, ed. Glen R. Conrad, 95–108. Lafayette: Center for Louisiana Studies, University of Southwestern Louisiana.

Barrett, James R., and David R. Roediger. 2005. "The Irish and the "Americanization" of the "new immigrants" in the streets and churches of the urban United States, 1900–1930." *Journal of American Ethnic History* 24:3–33.

Batson, C. Daniel, Patricia Schoenrade, and W. Larry Ventis. 1993. *Religion and the Individual: A Social-Psychological Perspective*. New York: Oxford University Press.

Baudier, Roger. 1939. *The Catholic Church in Louisiana*. New Orleans: Roger Baudier.

Benson, Peter L., Michael J. Donahue, and Joseph A. Erickson. 1993. "The Faith Maturity Scale: conceptualization, measurement, and empirical validation." In *Research in the Social Scientific Study of Religion*, vol. 5, ed. Monty L. Lynn and David O. Moberg, 1–26. Greenwich, Conn.: JAI Press.

Bezou, H. C., and G. Guidry. 2003. "Louisiana, Catholic Church in." In *New Catholic Encyclopedia*, vol. 8, ed. B. I. Mathaler, 808–816. Washington, D.C.: Thomson-Gale in association with the Catholic University of America.

Blau, Eleanor. 1976. "Hispanic priests veto affiliation." *New York Times*, April 25, p. 25.

Blessing, Patrick Joseph. 1977. "West among strangers: Irish emigration to California, 1850 to 1880." Ph.D. diss., University of California, Los Angeles.

Blethen, H. Tyler, and Curtis W. Wood. 1997. "Scotch-Irish frontier society in southwestern North Carolina, 1780–1840." In *Ulster and North America: Transatlantic Perspectives* on the Scotch-Irish, ed. H. Tyler Blethen and Curtis W. Wood, 213–226. Tuscaloosa: University of Alabama Press.

Bodin, Ron. 1990. "The Cajun woman as unofficial deacon of the sacraments, priest of the sacramentals in rural Louisiana, 1800–1930." *Attakapas Gazette* 25:2–13.

Bona, Mary Jo. 2004. "Confessing the self: Italian American women authors and the Catholic Church." In *Models and Images of Catholicism in Italian Americana: Academy and Society*, ed. Joseph A. Varacalli, Salvatore Primeggia, Salvatore LaGumina, and Donald D'Elia, 162–174. Stony Brook, N.Y.: Forum Italicum Publishing.

Bonomi, Patricia U. 1986. *Under the Cope of Heaven: Religion, Society and Politics in Colonial America.* Oxford: Oxford University Press.

Brasseaux, Carl. 1987. *The Founding of New Acadia: The Beginnings of Acadian Life in Louisiana, 1765–1803.* Baton Rouge: Louisiana State University Press.

———. 1989. *Quest for the Promised Land: Official Correspondence relating to the First Acadian Migration to Louisiana, 1764–1769.* Lafayette: Center for Louisiana Studies.

Braude, Ann. 1997. "Women's history *is* American religious history." In *Retelling U.S. Religious History*, ed. Thomas A. Tweed, 87–107. Berkeley: University of California Press.

Brewer, Stephanie M., James J. Jozefowicz, and Robert J. Stonebraker. 2006. "Religious free riders: the impact of market share." *Journal for the Scientific Study of Religion* 45:389–396.

Briggs, John. 1978. *An Italian Passage: Immigrants to Three American Cities, 1890–1930.* New Haven: Yale University Press.

Brown, Callum G. 2001. *The Death of Christian Britain.* London: Routledge.

Brown, Katharine L., and Nancy T. Sorrells. 2001. "Presbyterian pathways to power: networking, gentrification and the Scotch-Irish heritage among Virginia Presbyterian ministers, 1760–1860." In *Atlantic Crossroads: Historical Connections between Scotland, Ulster and North America*, ed. Patrick Fitzgerald and Steve Ickringill, 27–40. Newtownards, Northern Ireland: Colourpoint Books.

Browne, Henry J. 1946. "The "Italian problem" in the Catholic church of the United States, 1880–1900." *United States Catholic Historical Society: Historical Records and Studies* 35: 46–72.

Bryson, J. H. 1891. "The Scotch-Irish people: their influence in the formation of the government of the United States." In *The Scotch-Irish Society of America, Proceedings and Addresses of the Third Congress at Louisville, Ky., May 14 to 17, 1891*, 99–122. Louisville, Ky.: Methodist Episcopal Church.

Burchell, R. A. 1979. *The San Francisco Irish, 1848–1880.* Manchester, England: Manchester University Press.

Burris, Christopher T. 1999. "Religious orientation scale." In *Measures of Religiosity*, ed. Peter C. Hill and Ralph W. Hood, 144–154. Birmingham, Ala.: Religious Education Press.

Byron, Reginald. 1999. *Irish America.* Oxford: Clarendon Press.

Campbell, Malcolm. 2002. "Ireland's furthest shores: Irish immigrant settlement in nineteenth-century California and eastern Australia." *Pacific Historical Review* 71:59–90.

Cantelmo, Ercole. 1906. "Usi, costumi e feste degli Italiani negli Stati Uniti." In *Gli Italiani negli Stati Uniti d'America*, ed. Luigi Aldrovandi, 156–162. New York: Italian American Directory.

Carey, Patrick W. 2004. *Catholics in America: A History.* Westport, Conn.: Praeger.

Carlin, David. 2003. *The Decline and Fall of the Catholic Church in America.* Manchester, N.H.: Sophia Institute Press.

Carlson, Alvar W. 1990. *The Spanish-American Homeland: Four Centuries in New Mexico's Río Arriba.* Baltimore: Johns Hopkins University Press.

Carroll, Michael P. 1986. *The Cult of the Virgin Mary.* Princeton: Princeton University Press.

———. 1989. *Catholic Cults and Devotions: A Psychological Inquiry.* Kingston: McGill-Queen's University Press.

———. 1992. *Madonnas That Maim: Popular Catholicism in Italy since the Fifteenth Century.* Baltimore: Johns Hopkins University Press.

———. 1996. *Veiled Threats: The Logic of Popular Catholicism in Italy.* Baltimore: Johns Hopkins University Press.

———. 1999. *Irish Pilgrimage: Holy Wells and Popular Catholic Devotion.* Baltimore: Johns Hopkins University Press.

———. 2002. *The Penitente Brotherhood: Patriarchy and Hispano-Catholicism in New Mexico.* Baltimore: Johns Hopkins University Press.

———. 2003. "Were the Acadians/Cajuns (really) devout Catholics?" *Studies in Religion* 31:323–337.

———. 2004. "Upstart theories and early American religiosity: a reassessment." *Religion* 34:129–143.

———. 2006. "How the Irish became Protestant in America." *Religion and American Culture: A Journal of Interpretation* 16:25–54.

Casarella, Peter J., and Raúl Gómez. 2003. *El Cuerpo de Cristo.* Lima, Ohio: Academic Renewal Press.

Cash, Marie Romero. 1999. *Santos: Entering Images of Northern New Mexican Village Churches.* Niwot: University Press of Colorado.

Cash, Wilbur Joseph. 1941. *The Mind of the South.* New York: A. A. Knopf.

Chaves, Mark, and Philip S. Gorski. 2001. "Religious pluralism and religious participation." *Annual Review of Sociology* 27:261–281.

Chávez, Angélico. 1957. *Archives of the Archdiocese of Santa Fe, 1678–1900.* Washington, D.C.: Academy of American Franciscan History.

Chepesiuk, Ronald. 2000. *The Scotch-Irish: From the North of Ireland to the Making of America.* Jefferson, N.C.: McFarland.

Chiasson, Anselme. 1962. *Cheticamp: histoire et traditions acadiennes.* Moncton, N.B.: Éditions des Aboiteaux.

Choquette, Robert. 2003. *Canada's Religions: An Historical Introduction.* Ottawa: University of Ottawa Press.

Christian, William A, Jr. 1981. *Local Religion in Sixteenth-Century Spain.* Princeton: Princeton University Press.

Cimechella, Mgr. André-M. 1986. "Monseigneur Ignace Bourget, deuxième évêque de Montréal (1840–1876)." In *L'Église de Montréal: aperçus d'hier et d'aujourd'hui, 1839–1986,* ed. R. Litalien, 62–71. Montreal: Fides.

Cinel, Dino. 1982. *From Italy to San Francisco: The Immigrant Experience*. Stanford, Calif.: Stanford University Press.

Clark, Andrew H. 1968. *Acadia: The Geography of Early Nova Scotia*. Madison: University of Wisconsin Press.

Clarke, Brian P. 1988. "Poverty and piety: the Saint Vincent de Paul Society's Mission to Irish Catholics in Toronto, 1850–1890." In *Canadian Protestant and Catholic Missions, 1820s-1960s*, ed. John S. Moir and C. T. McIntire, 75–101. New York: Peter Lang.

———. 1993. *Piety and Nationalism: Lay Voluntary Associations and the Creation of an Irish-Catholic Community in Toronto, 1850–1895*. Montreal: McGill-Queen's University Press.

Cliché, Marie-Aimée. 1988. *Les Pratiques de dévotion en Nouvelle-France*. Quebec: Les Presses de l'Université Laval.

Cochrane, Eric. 1970. "New light on post-tridentine Italy: a note on recent Counter-Reformation scholarship." *Catholic Historical Review* 56:291–319.

Cohen, Adam B., Daniel E. Hall, and Keith G. Meador. 2005. "Social versus individual motivation: implications for normative definitions of religious orientation." *Personality and Social Psychology Review* 9:48–61.

Cohen, Charles L. 1997. "The post-Puritan paradigm of early American religious history." *William and Mary Quarterly* 54:695–722.

Cole, M. R. 1907. *Los Pastores: A Mexican Play of the Nativity*. Boston: American Folk-Lore Society.

Collins, Randall. 1997. "Stark and Bainbridge, Durkheim and Weber: theoretical comparisons." In *Rational Choice Theory and Religion: Summary and Assessment*, ed. L. A. Young, 161–180. New York: Routledge.

———. 2006. Review of *The Protestant Ethic Turns 100: Essays on the Century of the Weber Thesis. Journal for the Scientific Study of Religion* 45:297–298.

Connell, R. W. 1997. "Why is classical theory classical?" *American Journal of Sociology* 102:1511–1557.

Connolly, Sean. 1982. *Priests and People in Pre-Famine Ireland*. Dublin: Gill and Macmillan.

Conrad, Glen R. 1983. "The Acadians: myths and realities." In *The Cajuns: Essays on their History and Culture*, ed. Glen R. Conrad, 1–18. Lafayette: Center for Louisiana Studies, University of Southwestern Louisiana.

———. 1993. *Cross, Crozier and Crucible: A Volume Celebrating the Bicentennial of a Catholic Diocese in Louisiana*. Lafayette: Archdiocese of New Orleans in cooperation with the Center for Louisiana Studies.

Cosco, Joseph P. 2003. *Imagining Italians: The Clash of Romance and Race in American Perceptions, 1880–1910*. Albany: State University of New York Press.

Crehan, Joseph. 1952. *Father Thurston: A Memoir with a Bibliography of His Writings*. London: Sheed and Ward.

Cronin, Mike, and Daryl Adair. 2002. *The Wearing of the Green: A History of St. Patrick's Day*. London: Routledge.

Curley, Michael. 1940. *Church and State in the Spanish Floridas (1783–1822)*. Washington, D.C.: Catholic University of America Press.

Curtin, Nancy. 1998. "Society of United Irishmen." In *The Oxford Companion to Irish History*, ed. Sean J. Connolly, 567–568. Oxford: Oxford University Press.

Cusack, Margaret Anne. 1872. *Advice to Irish Working Girls in America.* New York: J. A. McGee, Publisher.

D'Angelo, Anthony. 1994. "Italian Harlem's Saint Benedict the Moor." In *Through the Looking Glass: Italian and Italian-American Images in the Media,* ed. Mary Jo Bona and Anthony J. Tamburri, 235–240. Staten Island, N.Y.: American Italian Historical Association.

Daniels, R. L. 1990. "The Acadians of Louisiana." *Attakapas Gazette* 25:107–115.

Daniels, Roger. 1997. *Not Like Us: Immigrants and Minorities in America, 1890–1924.* Chicago: Ivan R. Dee.

D'Antonio, William V., James D. Davidson, Dean Hoge, and Katherine Meyer. 2001. *American Catholics: Gender, Generation, and Commitment.* Walnut Creek, Calif.: AltaMira Press.

Davie, Grace. 2003. "The evolution of the sociology of religion: theme and variations." In *Handbook of the Sociology of Religion,* ed. Michele Dillon, 61–75. Cambridge: Cambridge University Press.

Davis, Kenneth. 1994. "Brevia from the Hispanic shift: continuity rather than conversion." In *An Enduring Flame: Studies on Latino Popular Religiosity,* ed. Anthony M. Stevens-Arroyo and Ana María Díaz-Stevens, 207–210. New York: Bildner Center for Western Hemisphere Studies.

de Borhegyi, Stephen F. 1956. *El Santuario de Chimayo.* Santa Fe, N.Mex.: Spanish Colonial Arts Society.

Deck, Allan Figueroa, S.J. 1989. *The Second Wave: Hispanic Ministry and the Evangelization of Cultures.* New York: Paulist Press.

———. 1994. "The challenge of evangelical/Pentecostal Christianity to Hispanic Catholicism." In *Hispanic Catholic Culture in the U.S.: Issues and Concerns,* ed. Jay P. Dolan and Allan Figueroa Deck, S.J., 409–439. Notre Dame: University of Notre Dame Press.

De Huff, Elizabeth Willis. 1931. "The Santuario at Chimayo." *New Mexico Highway Journal* (June):16–17, 39.

Delaney, Paul. 2005. "Chronologie des déportations et migrations des acadiens (1755–1816)." *La Société Historique Acadienne* 36:52–101.

Delumeau, Jean. 1977. *Catholicism between Luther and Voltaire: A New View of the Counter-Reformation.* London: Burns and Oates.

De Rosa, Gabriele. 1983. *Vescovi, Popolo e Magia nel Sud.* Naples: Guida Editori.

Díaz-Stevens, Ana María. 1993. *Oxcart Catholicism on Fifth Avenue.* Notre Dame: University of Notre Dame Press.

———. 1994. "Latinas and the Church." In *Hispanic Catholic Culture in the U.S.: Issues and Concerns,* ed. Jay P. Dolan and Allan Figueroa Deck, S.J., 240–277. Notre Dame: University of Notre Dame.

———. 1999. Review of *Our Lady of the Exile: Diasporic Religion as a Cuban Catholic Shrine in Miami. Sociology of Religion* 60:91–93.

———. 2003. "The Hispanic challenge to U.S. Catholicism." In *El Cuerpo de Cristo: The Hispanic Presence in the U.S. Catholic Church,* ed. Peter Caserella and Raúl Gómez, 157–179. Lima, Ohio: Academic Renewal Press.

Díaz-Stevens, Ana María, and Anthony M. Stevens-Arroyo. 1998. *Recognizing the Latino Resurgence in U.S. Religion.* Boulder, Colo.: Westview Press.

DiCarlo, Denise Mangieri. 1990. "The history of the Italian festa in New York City: 1880s to the present." Ph.D. diss., Graduate School of Arts and Sciences, New York University, New York.

———. 1994. "The role of the Italian festa in the United States." In *To See the Past More Clearly: The Enrichment of the Italian Heritage, 1890–1990,* ed. H. E. Landry, 198–205. Austin, Tex.: Nortex.

DiGiovani, Stephen M. 2003. "The saints in the lives of Italian-Americans: some key figures." In *The Saints in the Lives of Italian-Americans,* ed. Joseph A. Varacalli, Salvatore Primeggia, Salvatore LaGumina, and Donald D'Elia, 28–43. Stony Brook, N.Y.: Forum Italicum Publishing.

di Leonardo, Micaela. 1984. *The Varieties of Ethnic Experience.* Ithaca: Cornell University Press.

———. 1991. "Habits of the cumbered heart: ethnic community and the women's culture as American-invented traditions." In *Golden Ages, Dark Ages: Imagining the Past in Anthropology and History,* ed. J. O'Brien and W. Roseberry, 234–252. Berkeley: University of California Press.

———. 1998. *Exotics at Home: Anthropology, Others, American Modernity.* Chicago: University of Chicago Press.

Dillingham, William P. 1911. *Abstracts of Reports of the Immigration Commission.* Washington, D.C.: Government Printing Office.

Diner, Hasia R. 1983. *Erin's Daughters in America: Irish Immigrant Women in the Nineteenth Century.* Baltimore: Johns Hopkins University Press.

———. 1999. "Women, nineteenth-century." In *Encyclopedia of the Irish in America,* ed. Michael Glazier. 963–966. Notre Dame: University of Notre Dame Press.

Doherty, Gillian M. 2004. *The Irish Ordnance Survey: History, Culture and Memory.* Dublin: Four Courts Press.

Dolan, Jay P. 1975. *The Immigrant Church: New York's Irish and German Catholics, 1815–1865.* Baltimore: Johns Hopkins University Press.

———. 1992. *The American Catholic Experience: A History from Colonial Times to the Present.* Notre Dame: University of Notre Dame Press.

———. 2002. *In Search of American Catholicism.* Oxford: Oxford University Press.

Dolan, Jay P., and Allan Figueroa Deck, S.J.. 1994. *Hispanic Catholic Culture in the U.S.: Issues and Concerns.* Notre Dame: University of Notre Dame Press.

Donnelly, J. P., and M. W. Maher. 1999. *Confraternities and Catholic Reform in Italy, France and Spain.* Kirksville, Mo.: Thomas Jefferson University Press.

Doorley, Michael. 1987. "The Irish and the Catholic Church in New Orleans, 1835–1918." Master's thesis, Faculty of the Graduate School, University of New Orleans, New Orleans.

———. 2001. "Irish Catholics and French Creoles: ethnic struggles within the Catholic Church in New Orleans, 1835–1920." *Catholic Historical Review* 87:34–45.

Dorchester, Daniel. 1888. *Christianity in the United States.* New York: Phillips and Hunt.

Dorman, James H. 1983. *The People Called Cajuns: An Introduction to Ethnohistory.* Lafayette: Center for Louisiana Studies, University of Southwestern Louisiana.

Doyle David Noel. 1980. "The Irish and the Christian Churches in America." In *America and Ireland, 1776–1976: The American Identity and the Irish Connection,* ed. D. N. Doyle and O. D. Edwards. Westport, Conn.: Greenwood Press.

———. 1981. *Ireland, Irishmen, and Revolutionary America, 1760–1820.* Dublin: Mercier Press for the Cultural Relations Committee of Ireland.

———. 1999. "Scots-Irish or Scotch-Irish." In *The Encyclopedia of the Irish in America,* ed. Michael Glazier, 842–851. Notre Dame: University of Notre Dame Press.

Dubisch, Jill. 1995. *In a Different Place: Pilgrimage, Gender, and Politics at a Greek Island Shrine.* Princeton: Princeton University Press.

Dunne, Edmund M. 1914a. "The Italians again." *America* 12:144.

———. 1914b. *Memoirs of Zi Pre'.* St. Louis, Mo.: B. Herder.

Dunne, Robert. 2002. *Antebellum Irish Immigration and Emerging Ideologies of "America": A Protestant Backlash.* Lewiston, N.Y.: Edwin Mellen Press.

Durand, Jorge, and Douglas S. Massey. 1995. *Miracles on the Border: Retablos of Mexican Migrants to the United States.* Tucson: University of Arizona Press.

Durkheim, Emile. 1893/1933. *The Division of Labor in Society.* New York: Free Press.

———. 1897/1951. *Suicide.* New York: Free Press.

Eagles, Charles W. 1992. "Introduction." In *The Mind of the South: Fifty Years Later,* ed. Charles W. Eagles, ix–xii. Jackson: University Press of Mississippi.

Ebaugh, Helen Rose. 2002. "Presidential address 2001—return of the sacred: reintegrating religion in the social sciences." *Journal for the Scientific Study of Religion* 41:385–395.

Eid, Leroy V. 1986. "The Colonial Scotch-Irish: a view accepted too readily." *Eire-Ireland* 21:81–105.

———. 1997. "Irish-American backwoods culture: D. H. Fischer's *Albion's Seed.*" *New Hibernia Review* 2:83–96.

Elizondo, Virgilio. 1994. "Popular religion as the core of cultural identity based on the Mexican American experience in the United States." In *An Enduring Flame: Studies on Latino Popular Religiosity,* ed. Anthony M. Stevens-Arroyo and Ana María Díaz-Stevens, 113–132. New York: Bildner Center for Western Hemisphere Studies.

Elofson, W. M., and John A. Woods, eds. 1996. *The Writings and Speeches of Edmund Burke.* Vol. 3 of 3. Oxford: Clarendon Press.

Espín, Orlando O. 1994. "Popular Catholicism among Latinos." In *Hispanic Culture in the U.S.: Issues and Concerns,* ed. Jay P. Dolan and Allan Figueroa Deck, S.J., 308–359. Notre Dame: University of Notre Dame Press.

Faragher, John Mack. 2005. *A Great and Noble Scheme: The Tragic Story of the Expulsion of the French Acadians from Their American Homeland.* New York: W. W. Norton.

Ferrante, G. 1906. "Chiese e scuole parrocchiali italiane." In *Gli italiani negli Stati Uniti d'America,* ed. Luigi Aldrovandi, 89–94. New York: Italian American Directory.

Fichera, Sebastian. 2003. "The disturbing case of Dino Cinel." *History News Network* (online), George Mason University, posted April 28, 2003.

Finke, Roger. 1990. "Religious deregulation: origins and consequences." *Journal of Church and State* 32:609–626.

Finke, Roger, and Rodney Stark. 1988. "Religious economies and sacred canopies: religious mobilization in American cities, 1906." *American Sociological Review* 53:41–49.

————. 1992. *The Churching of America, 1776–1990*. New Brunswick, N.J.: Rutgers University Press.

————. 2003. "The dynamics of religious economies." In *Handbook of the Sociology of Religion*, ed. Michele Dillon. Cambridge: Cambridge University Press.

Fischer, David Hackett. 1989. *Albion's Seed*. New York: Oxford University Press.

Fitzgerald, Patrick. 2003. "Scotch-Irish." In *The Encyclopedia of Ireland*, ed. Brian Lalor, 969. New Haven: Yale University Press.

Fitzpatrick, David. 1984. *Irish Emigration, 1801–1921*. West Tempest, Ireland: Dungalan Press.

Fitzpatrick, Rory. 1989. *God's Frontiersmen: The Scots-Irish Epic*. London: Weidenfeld and Nicolson.

Flores, Richard R. 1994a. "*Los Pastores* and the gifting of performance." *American Ethnologist* 21:270–285.

————. 1994b. "Para el Niño Dios: sociability and commemorative sentiment in popular religious practice." In *An Enduring Flame: Studies on Latino Popular Religiosity*, ed. Anthony M. Stevens-Arroyo and Ana María Díaz-Stevens, 171–190. New York: Bildner Center for Western Hemisphere Studies.

Ford, Henry Jones. 1915. *The Scotch-Irish in America*. Princeton: Princeton University Press.

Frangini, A. 1914. *Italiani in San Francisco e Oakland, Cal*. San Francisco: Lanson-Lauray.

Frank, Larry. 1992. *New Kingdom of the Saints: Religious Art of New Mexico, 1780–1907*. Santa Fe, N.Mex.: Red Crane Books.

Gallo, Patrick J. 1981. *Old Bread, New Wine: A Portrait of the Italian-Americans*. Chicago: Nelson-Hall.

Gambino, Richard. 1974. *Blood of My Blood: The Dilemma of the Italian-Americans*. New York: Doubleday.

Gaustad, Edwin Scott, and Philip L. Barlow. 2001. *New Historical Atlas of Religion in America*. Oxford: Oxford University Press.

Gesualdi, Louis. 2004. "A comparison of the attitudes and practices of the Irish American and Italian American Catholics." In *Models and Images of Catholicism in Italian Americana: Academy and Society*, ed. Joseph A. Varacalli, Salvatore Primeggia, Salvatore J. LaGumina, and Donald J. D'Elia, 40–51. Stony Brook, N.Y.: Forum Italicum Publishing.

Gibson, Ralph. 1989. *A Social History of French Catholicism, 1789–1914*. London: Routledge.

Gibson, Rev. William. 1860. *The Year of Grace: A History of the Ulster Revival of 1859*. Edinburgh: Andrew Elliot.

Giffords, Gloria Fraser. 1974. *Mexican Folk Retablos*. Albuquerque: University of New Mexico Press.

Gilligan, Carol. 1982. *In a Different Voice: Psychological Theory and Women's Development*. Cambridge: Harvard University Press.

Ginsburg, Faye, and Anna L. Tsing. 1990. *Uncertain Terms: Negotiating Gender in American Culture*. Boston: Beacon Press.

Giovinco, Joseph Preston. 1968. "The Italian-American press and its fight against intolerance, 1918–1924." M.A. thesis, Department of History, San Francisco State University, San Francisco, Calif.

Girardot, Norman J. 2002. *The Victorian Translation of China: James Legge's Oriental Pilgrimage.* Berkeley: University of California Press.

Glazer, Nathan, and Daniel Patrick Moynihan. 1970. *Beyond the Melting Pot: The Negroes, Puerto Ricans, Jews, Italians and Irish of New York City.* Cambridge: M.I.T. Press.

Glazier, Michael. 1999. *The Encyclopedia of the Irish in America.* Notre Dame: University of Notre Dame Press.

Gleeson, David T. 2001. *The Irish in the South, 1815–1877.* Chapel Hill: University of North Carolina Press.

Goizueta, Roberto. 2002. "The symbolic world of Mexican American religion." In *Horizons of the Sacred: Mexican Traditions in U.S. Catholicism,* ed. Timothy Matovina and Gary Riebe-Estrella, 119–138. Ithaca: Cornell University Press.

————. 2004. "Old-time religion: Latino traditions can save the Church in the United States." In *Boston College Magazine* (online), Summer. Accessed June 16, 2005.

Good, Patricia K. 1975. "Irish adjustment to American society: integration or separation? A portrait of an Irish-Catholic parish: 1863–1886." *Records of the American Catholic Historical Society of Philadelphia* 86:7–23.

Goodrich, Charles A. 1851. *A Pictorial and Descriptive View of All Religions.* Hartford, Conn.: A. C. Goodman and Company.

Gorski, Philip S. 2003a. *The Disciplinary Revolution: Calvinism and the Rise of the State in Early Modern Europe.* Chicago: University of Chicago Press.

————. 2003b. "Historicizing the secularization debate: an agenda for research." In *Handbook of the Sociology of Religion,* ed. Michele Dillon, 110–122. Cambridge: Cambridge University Press.

Gorsuch, Richard L., and Susan E. McPherson. 1989. "Intrinsic/Extrinsic measurement: I/E-Revised and single-item scales." *Journal for the Scientific Study of Religion* 28: 348–354.

Greeley, Andrew. 1971. *Why Can't They Be Like Us? America's White Ethnic Groups.* New York: E. P. Dutton.

————. 1988. "The success and assimilation of Irish Protestants and Irish Catholics in the United States." *Sociology and Social Research* 72:229–236.

————. 1994. *Sex: The Catholic Experience.* Allen, Tex.: Tabor Publishing.

————. 1995. *Religion as Poetry.* New Brunswick, N.J.: Transaction Publishers.

————. 1997. "Defection among Hispanics." *America* 177:12–13.

————. 1999. "Achievement of the Irish in America." In *The Encyclopedia of the Irish in America,* ed. Michael Glazier, 1–4. Notre Dame: University of Notre Dame Press.

————. 2000. *The Catholic Imagination.* Berkeley: University of California Press.

————. 2004. *The Catholic Revolution: New Wine, Old Wineskins, and the Second Vatican Council.* Berkeley: University of California Press.

Green, Samuel Swett. 1895. *The Scotch-Irish in America.* Worcester, Mass.: Press of Charles Hamilton.

Griffin, Patrick. 2001. *The People with No Name: Ireland's Ulster Scots, America's Scots Irish, and the Creation of a British Atlantic World, 1689–1764.* Princeton: Princeton University Press.

Griffiths, Naomi. 1973. *The Acadians: Creation of a People.* Toronto: McGraw-Hill.

————. 1992. *The Contexts of Acadian History, 1686–1784.* Montreal: McGill-Queen's University Press.

————. 2005. *From Migrant to Acadian: A North American Border People, 1604–1755.* Montreal: McGill-Queen's University Press.

Gumina, Deanna Paoli. 1978. *The Italians of San Francisco.* New York: Center for Migration Studies.

Gutiérrez, Ramón. 1995. "El Santuario de Chimayo: A syncretic shrine in New Mexico." In *Feasts and Celebrations in North American Ethnic Communities,* ed. Ramón Gutiérrez and Geneviève Fabre, 71–86. Albuquerque: University of New Mexico Press.

————. 2000. "Culture knows no borders." In *Nuevo México Profundo: Rituals of an Indo-Hispano Homeland,* (no ed.), 133–141. Santa Fe: Museum of New Mexico Press.

Hackett, David G. 1995. "Introduction." In *Religion and American Culture: A Reader,* ed. David G. Hackett, ix–xi. New York: Routledge.

Hall, G. Stanley. 1915. *Adolescence, Its Psychology and Its Relations to Physiology, Anthropology, Sociology, Sex, Crime, Religion, and Education,* vol. 1. New York: D. Appleton and Company.

Hanna, Charles A. 1902/1968. *The Scotch-Irish, or, The Scot in North Britain, North Ireland and North America.* Baltimore: Genealogical Publishing.

Harris, Joseph Claude. 2002. *"The future church." America* 186:7–9.

Harris, Marvin. 1968. *The Rise of Anthropological Theory.* New York: Thomas Y. Crowell Company.

Harris, Ruth. 1999. *Lourdes: Body and Spirit in a Secular Age.* London: Penguin Press.

Hatch, Nathan O. 1989. *The Democratization of American Christianity.* New Haven: Yale University Press.

Hay, Denys. 1977. *The Church in Italy in the Fifteenth Century.* Cambridge: Cambridge University Press.

Hoffman, Ronald, and Sally D. Mason. 2000. *Princes of Ireland, Planters of Maryland: A Carroll Saga, 1500–1782.* Chapel Hill: University of North Carolina Press for the Omohundro Institute of Early American History and Culture, Williamsburg, Virginia.

Hoge, D. R., C. Zech, P. McNamara, and M. J. Donahue. 1996. *Money Matters: Personal Giving in American Churches.* Louisville, Ky.: Westminster John Knox Press.

Holmes-Rodman, Paula. 2004. "They told what happened on the road: narrative and the construction of experiential knowledge on the pilgrimage to Chimayó, New Mexico." In *Intersecting Journeys: The Anthropology of Pilgrimage and Tourism,* ed. Ellen Badone and Sharon Roseman, 24–51 Urbana: University of Illinois.

Hood, Ralph W. 1971. "A comparison of the Allport and Feagin scoring procedures for intrinsic/extrinsic religious orientation." *Journal for the Scientific Study of Religion* 10:370–374.

Hopcroft, Rosemary L. 1997. "Rural organization and receptivity to Protestantism in sixteenth-century Europe." *Journal for the Scientific Study of Religion* 36:158–181.

Hotten-Somers, Diane M. 2003. "Relinquishing and reclaiming independence: Irish domestic servants, American middle-class mistresses, and assimilation, 1850–1920." In *New Directions in Irish-American History,* ed. Kevin Kenny, 227–242. Madison: University of Wisconsin Press.

Hout, Michael, and Joshua R. Goldstein. 1994. "How 4.5 million Irish immigrants became 40 million Irish Americans: demographic and subjective aspects of the ethnic composition of white Americans." *American Sociological Review* 59:64–82.

Hunt, Larry. 1999. "Hispanic Protestantism in the United States: trends by decade and generation." *Social Forces* 77:1601–1624.

Hurt, Amy. 1934. "Chimayó, the village time has blest." *New Mexico Magazine* November: 10–12, 43–44.

Hynes, Eugene. 1978. "The Great Hunger and Irish Catholicism." *Societas* 8:137–155.

———. 1988. "Family and religious change in a peripheral capitalist society: mid-nineteenth-century Ireland." In *The Religion and Family Connection: Social Science Perspectives,* ed. Darwin L. Thomas, 161–174. Provo, Utah: Religious Studies Center, Brigham Young University.

———. 1990. "Nineteenth-century Irish Catholicism, farmer's ideology, and national religion: explorations in cultural explanation." In *Sociological Studies in Roman Catholicism: Historical and Contemporary Perspectives,* ed. Roger O'Toole, 45–69. Toronto: Edward Mellen Press.

Iannaccone, Laurence R. 1994. "Why strict churches are strong." *American Journal of Sociology* 99:1180–1211.

Ickringill, S. J. S. 1999. "American Revolution." In *The Oxford Companion to Irish History,* ed. S. J. Connolly, 13. Oxford: Oxford University Press.

Iorizzo, Luciano J., and Salvatore Mondello. 1980. *The Italian Americans.* Boston: Twayne.

Isoleri, Rev. Antonio. 1911. *Souvenir and Bouquet, ossia Ricordo della Solenne consacrazione della Chiesa Nuova di S. Maria Maddalena De-Pazzi.* Philadelphia: privately published.

Johnston, A. J. B. 2004a. "The call of the archetype and the challenge of Acadian history." *French Colonial History* 5:63–92.

———. 2004b. "Imagining Paradise: the visual depiction of pre-deportation Acadia, 1850–2000." *Journal of Canadian Studies* 38:105–128.

Jones, Maldwyn A. 1991. "The Scotch-Irish in British America." In *Strangers within the Realm: Cultural Margins of the First British Empire,* ed. Bernard Bailyn and Philip D. Morgan, 284–313. Chapel Hill: University of North Carolina Press.

Kamen, Henry. 1993. *The Phoenix and the Flame: Catalonia and the Counter Reformation.* New Haven: Yale University Press.

Kane, Paula M. 1996. Review of *Oxcart Catholicism on Fifth Avenue. Church History* 65: 317–318.

Katz, Michael B. 1975. *The People of Hamilton, Canada West: Family and Class in a Mid-Nineteenth-Century City.* Cambridge: Harvard University Press.

Katzman, David M. 1978. *Seven Days a Week: Women and Domestic Service in Industrializing America.* New York: Oxford University Press.

Kay, Elizabeth. 1987. *Chimayo Valley Traditions.* Santa Fe, N. Mex.: Ancient City Press.

Kelleher, Patricia. 2003. "Young Irish workers: class implications of men's and women's experiences in Gilded Age Chicago." In *New Directions in Irish-American History,* ed. Kevin Kenny, 185–208. Madison: University of Wisconsin Press.

Keller, Kenneth W. 1991. "What is distinctive about the Scotch-Irish?" In *Appalachian Fron-*

tiers: Settlement, Society and Development in the Preindustrial Era, ed. Robert D. Mitchell, 69–86. Lexington: University of Kentucky Press.

Kelley, Dean M. 1972/1977. *Why Conservative Churches Are Growing*. New York: Harper and Row.

Kennedy, Billy. 1995. *The Scots-Irish in the Hills of Tennessee*. Londonderry, Northern Ireland: Causeway Press.

———. 1997. *The Scots-Irish in the Carolinas*. Belfast: Causeway Press.

———. 1998. *The Scots-Irish in Pennsylvania and Kentucky*. Londonderry, Northern Ireland: Causeway Press.

Kenny, Kevin. 2000. *The American Irish: A History*. New York: Pearson Education.

Kimmel, Michael. 2000. *The Gendered Society*. New York: Oxford University Press.

Knight, Christina. 1999. "Fodor's 2000: New Mexico." New York: Fodor's Travel Publications.

Ladd, Kevin L., and Bernard Spilka. 2006. "Inward, outward, upward prayer: scale reliability and validation." *Journal for the Scientific Study of Religion* 45:233–267.

La Farge, Oliver. 1970. *Santa Fe: The Autobiography of a Southwestern Town*. Norman: University of Oklahoma Press.

LaGumina, Salvatore. 1987. "Immigrants and the church in suburbia: the Long Island Italian-American experience." *Records of the American Catholic Historical Society of Philadelphia* 98:3–19.

Lamadrid, Enrique. 1999. *Pilgrimage to Chimayó*. Santa Fe: Museum of New Mexico Press.

Lane, Belden C. 2001. "Giving voice to place: three models for understanding American sacred space." *Religion and American Culture* 11:53–81.

Larkin, Emmet. 1972. "The devotional revolution in Ireland." *American Historical Review* 77:625–652.

———. 1984. *The Historical Dimensions of Irish Catholicism*. Washington, D.C.: Catholic University of America.

Leak, Gary K., and Brandy A. Randall. 1995. "Clarification of the link between right-wing authoritarianism and religiousness: the role of religious maturity." *Journal for the Scientific Study of Religion* 34:245–252.

Lecky, William Edward Hartpole, and James Albert Woodburn. 1898. *The American Revolution, 1763–1783; being the chapters and passages relating to America from the author's History of England in the Eighteenth Century*. New York: D. Appleton and Company.

Leonard, Bill J. 2003. *Baptist Ways: A History*. Valley Forge, Pa.: Judson Press.

Lepovitz, Helena Waddy. 1991. *Images of Faith*. Athens: University of Georgia Press.

Lewis, Thomas A. 2003. *West from Shenandoah*. New York: John Wiley and Sons.

Light, Dale. 1988. "The reformation of Philadelphia Catholicism, 1830–1860." *Pennsylvania Magazine of History and Biography* 112:375–405.

Lindman, Janet Moore. 2000. "Acting the manly Christian: white evangelical masculinity in revolutionary Virginia." *William and Mary Quarterly* 57:393–416.

Lipset, Seymour Martin. 1990. *Continental Divide: The Values and Institutions of the United States and Canada*. New York: Routledge.

Liptak, Dolores. 1989. *Immigrants and Their Church*. New York: Macmillan.

Lobody, Diane H. 1993. "That language might be given me: women's experience in early

Methodism." In *Perspectives on American Methodism: Interpretive Essays*, ed. Russell E. Richey, Kenneth E. Rowe, and Jean Miller Schmidt, 127–144. Nashville, Tenn.: Kingswood Books.

Lockerby, Earle. 2001. "Île-Saint-Jean in 1745–1747: threats and indulgences." *La Société Historique Acadienne: Les Cahiers* 32:4–39.

Lombardi Satriani, Luigi M., and Mariano Meligrana. 1982. *Il Ponte de San Giacomo*. Milan: Rizzoli Editore.

Longfellow, Henry Wadsworth. 1856. *Evangeline*. London: George Routledge and Company.

Lopreato, Joseph. 1970. *Italian Americans*. New York: Random House.

Loughlin, James F. 1913. "Pius IV." In *The Catholic Encyclopedia*, vol. 12, ed. C. G. Herbermann, E. A. Pace, B. P. Conde, T. J. Shahan, and J. J. Wynne, 129–130. New York: Encyclopedia Press.

Luconi, Stefano. 2001. *From Paesani to White Ethnics*. Albany: State University of New York Press.

Luna, Sandra. 2000. "Retablos y Exvotos." Mexico City: Museo Franz Mayer / Artes de México.

Lyerly, Cynthia Lynn. 1998. *Methodism and the Southern Mind, 1770–1810*. New York: Oxford University Press.

Lynch, Rev. D., S.J. 1901. "In the Italian quarter of New York." *Messenger of the Sacred Heart of Jesus* 36:115–126.

Mangione, Jerre, and Ben Morreale. 1992. *La Storia: Five Centuries of the Italian American Experience*. New York: Harper Collins.

Mannion, John J. 1991. "Old World antecedents, New World adaptations: Inistioge (Co. Kilkenny) immigrants in Newfoundland." In *The Irish in Atlantic Canada*, ed. Thomas P. Power, 30–106. Fredericton, N.B.: New Ireland Press.

Marecek, Jeanne. 1995. "Psychology and feminism: can this relationship be saved?" In *Feminisms in the Academy*, ed. Domna C. Stanton and Abigail J. Stewart, 101–132. Ann Arbor: University of Michigan Press.

Marriott, Alice. 1948. *María: The Potter of San Ildefonso*. Norman: University of Oklahoma Press.

Marwell, Gerald. 1996. "We still don't know if strict churches are strong, much less why: comment on Iannaccone." *American Journal of Sociology* 101:1097–1103.

Massa, Mark S. 2001. "The new and old anti-Catholicism and the analogical imagination." *Theological Studies* 62:549–570.

Mathews, Donald G. 1969. "The Second Great Awakening as an organizing process, 1780–1830: an hypothesis." *American Quarterly* 21:23–43.

Matovina, Timothy. 2002. "Companion in exile: Guadalupan devotion at San Fernando Cathedral, San Antonio, Texas, 1900–1940." In *Horizons of the Sacred: Mexican Traditions in U.S. Catholicism*, ed. Timothy Matovina and Gary Riebe-Estrella, 17–40. Ithaca: Cornell University Press.

Matovina, Timothy, and Gary Riebe-Estrella. 2002. *Horizons of the Sacred: Mexican Traditions in U.S. Catholicism*. Ithaca: Cornell University Press.

Maume, Patrick. 1998. "Nationalism." In *The Oxford Companion to Irish History*, ed. S. J. Connolly, 378–381. Oxford: Oxford University Press.

McAvoy, Thomas T. 1969. *A History of the Catholic Church in the United States.* Notre Dame: University of Notre Dame Press.

McCaffrey, Lawrence J. 1996. "Forging forward and looking back." In *The New York Irish,* ed. Ronald H. Bayor and Timothy J. Meagher, 213–233. Baltimore: Johns Hopkins University Press.

———. 1997. *The Irish Catholic Diaspora in American.* Washington, D.C.: Catholic University of America Press.

———. 1999. "Catholicism, Irish-American." In *The Encyclopedia of the Irish in America,* ed. Michael Glazier, 128–137. Notre Dame: University of Notre Dame Press.

McCauley, Deborah Vansau. 1995. *Appalachian Mountain Religion: A History.* Urbana: University of Illinois Press.

McDonald, Forrest, and Ellen Shapiro McDonald. 1980. "The ethnic origins of the American people, 1790." *William and Mary Quarterly* 37:179–199.

———. 1984. "Commentary." *William and Mary Quarterly* 41:129–135.

McGloin, John Bernard. 1978. *San Francisco: The Story of a City.* San Rafael, Calif.: Presidio Press.

McGowan, Mark George. 1999. *The Waning of the Green : Catholics, the Irish, and Identity in Toronto, 1887–1972.* Montreal: McGill-Queen's University Press.

McGrath, Thomas G. 1991. "The Tridentine evolution of modern Irish Catholicism, 1563–1962: a re-examination of the devotional revolution thesis." *Recusant History* 20: 512–23.

McGreevy, John T. 2003. *Catholicism and American Freedom: A History.* New York: W. W. Norton.

McKee, Matthew. 2001. "'A peculiar and royal race': creating a Scotch-Irish identity, 1889–1901." In *Atlantic Crossroads: Historical Connections between Scotland, Ulster and North America,* ed. Patrick Fitzgerald and Steve Ickringill, 67–83. Newtownards, Northern Ireland: Colourpoint Books.

McWhiney, Grady. 1988. *Cracker Culture: Celtic Ways in the Old South.* Tuscaloosa: University of Alabama Press.

Meagher, Timothy. 2005. *The Columbia Guide to Irish American History.* New York: Columbia University Press.

Meyers, Albert, and Diane Elizabeth Hopkins. 1988. *Manipulating the Saints: Religious Brotherhoods and Social Integration in Postconquest Latin America.* Hamburg: Waysbah.

Miccoli, Giovanni. 1974. "La storia religiosa." in *Storia d'Italia,* vol. 2. Turin: Giulio Einaudi.

Miller, David W. 1975. "Irish Catholicism and the Great Famine." *Journal of Social History* 9:81–98.

———. 2000. "Mass attendance in Ireland in 1834." In *Piety and Power in Ireland, 1760–1960: Essays in Honour of Emmet Larkin,* ed. Stewart J. Brown and David W. Miller, 158–179. Notre Dame: University of Notre Dame Press.

———. 2005. "Landscape and religious practice: a study of mass attendance in pre-Famine Ireland." *Eire-Ireland* 40:90–106.

Miller, Kerby A. 1985. *Emigrants and Exiles.* Oxford: Oxford University Press.

———. 2000. "Scotch-Irish, Black Irish, and Real Irish emigrants and identities in the

Old South." In *The Irish Diaspora*, ed. Andy Bielenberg, 139–157. Harlow, England: Pearson Education.

Miller, Kerby A., David N. Doyle, and Patricia Kelleher. 1995. "'For love and liberty': Irish women, migration, and domesticity in Ireland and America, 1815–1920." In *Irish Women and Irish Migration*, ed. Patrick O'Sullivan, 41–65. London: Leicester University Press.

Miller, Kerby A., Arnold Schrier, Bruce D. Boling, and David N. Doyle. 2003. *Irish Immigrants in the Land of Canaan*. Oxford: Oxford University Press.

Mitchell, Arthur. 1999. "The American Revolution." In *The Encyclopedia of the Irish in America*, ed. Michael Glazier, 15–23. Notre Dame: University of Notre Dame Press.

Mitchell, B. R. 1998. *International Historical Statistics: The Americas, 1750–1993*. London: Macmillan.

Moore, Joan. 1994. "The social fabric of the Hispanic community since 1965." in *Hispanic Catholic Culture in the U.S.: Issues and Concerns*, ed. Jay P. Dolan and Allan Figueroa Deck, S.J.. Notre Dame: University of Notre Dame Press.

Mormino, Gary R., and George E. Pozzetta. 1987. *The Immigrant World of Ybor City: Italians and Their Latin Neighbors in Tampa, 1885–1985*. Urbana: University of Illinois Press.

Nelli, Humbert S. 1970. *Italians in Chicago, 1880–1930*. New York: Oxford University Press.

———. 1980. "Italians." In *Harvard Encyclopedia of American Ethnic Groups*, ed. Stephan Thernstrom, 545–560. Cambridge: Harvard University Press.

Nicolson, Murray. 1983. "Irish Tridentine Catholicism in Victorian Toronto: vessel for ethno-religious persistence." In *Canadian Catholic History: A Survey*, vol. 2, 415–436. Ottawa: Historia Ecclesiae Catholicae Canadensis Publications.

———. 1985. "Peasants in an urban society: the Irish Catholics in Victorian Toronto." In *Gathering Place: Peoples and Neighbourhoods of Toronto, 1834–1945*, ed. Robert F. Harney, 47–74. Toronto: Multicultural History Society of Ontario.

Nolan, Charles E. 1993. "Louisiana Catholic historiography." In *Cross, Crozier and Crucible*, ed. Glen R. Conrad, 584–634. New Orleans: Center for Louisiana Studies.

Noll, Mark A. 1992. *A History of Christianity in the United States and Canada*. Grand Rapids, Mich.: William B. Eerdmans Publishing.

Novak, Michael. 1972. *The Rise of the Unmeltable Ethnics: Politics and Culture in the Seventies*. New York: Macmillan.

Nunn, Tey Marianna. 1993. "Santo Niño de Atocha." M.A. Thesis, Department of Anthropology, University of New Mexico, Albuquerque.

O'Brien, Michael. 1914. "Some examples of the Scotch Irish in America." *Journal of the American Irish Historical Society* 14:269–79.

———. 1919/1971. *A Hidden Phase of American History*. Freeport, N.Y.: Books for Libraries Press.

———. 1923. "Shipping statistics of the Philadelphia Custom House, 1733 to 1774, refute the Scotch-Irish theory." *Journal of the American Irish Historical Society* 22:132–141.

———. 1925. "The Scotch-Irish myth." *Journal of the American Irish Historical Society* 24:142–153.

———. 1927. "The Irish in the American colonies." *Journal of the American Irish Historical Society* 26:21–29.

O'Donnell, Edward. 1997. "The scattered debris of the Irish nation: the Famine Irish and New York City, 1845–55." In *The Hungry Stream: Essay on Emigration and Famine,* ed. E. Margaret Crawford. 49–60. Belfast: Institute of Irish Studies, Queen's University of Belfast.

Olson, Daniel V. A., and Paul Perl. 2001. "Variations in strictness and religious commitment within and among five denominations." *Journal for the Scientific Study of Religion* 40:757–764.

———. 2005. "Free and cheap riding in strict, conservative churches." *Journal for the Scientific Study of Religion* 44:123–142.

Orsi, Robert A. 1985. *The Madonna of 115th Street: faith and community in Italian Harlem, 1880–1950.* New Haven: Yale University Press.

———. 1996. *Thank You, St. Jude.* New Haven: Yale University Press.

———. 2003. "Is the study of lived religion irrelevant to the world we live in?" *Journal for the Scientific Study of Religion* 42:169–174.

———. 2004. "A new beginning again." *Journal of the American Academy of Religion* 72:587–602.

———. 2005. *Between Heaven and Earth: The Religious Worlds People Make and the Scholars Who Study Them.* Princeton: Princeton University Press.

Orsi, Robert A., ed. 1999. *Gods of the City.* Bloomington: Indiana University Press.

Ownby, Ted. 1990. *Subduing Satan: Religion, Recreation, and Manhood in the Rural South, 1865–1920.* Chapel Hill: University of North Carolina Press.

Peña, Milagros. 2002. "Devising a study on religion and the Latina experience." *Social Compass* 49:281–294.

Peréz, Arturo. 1994. "The history of Hispanic liturgy since 1965." In *Hispanic Catholic Culture in the U.S.: Issues and Concerns,* ed. Jay P. Dolan and Allan Figueroa Deck, S.J., 360–408. Notre Dame: University of Notre Dame Press.

Perl, Paul, Jennifer Z. Greely, and Mark M. Gray. 2006. "What proportion of adult Hispanics are Catholic? A review of survey data and methodology." *Journal for the Scientific Study of Religion* 45:419–436.

Pistella, Domenico. 1954. *The Crowning of a Queen.* New York.

Pope, Barbara Corrado. 1988. "A heroine without heroics: the Little Flower of Jesus and her times." *Church History* 57:46–60.

Posen, I. Sheldon, and Joseph Sciorra. 1983. "Brooklyn's dancing tower." *Natural History* 92:30–37.

Post, Lauren. 1990. *Cajun Sketches from the Prairies of Southwest Louisiana.* Baton Rouge: Louisiana State University Press.

Pozzetta, George E. 1995. "Italian Americans." In *Gale Encyclopedia of Multicultural America,* vol. 2, ed. Rudolph J. Vecoli, 765–781. New York: Gale Research.

Primeggia, Salvatore. 2004. "La Via Vecchia and Italian folk religiosity." In *Models and Images of Catholicism in Italian Americana: Academy and Society,* ed. Joseph A. Varacalli, Salvatore Primeggia, Salvatore LaGumina, and Donald D'Elia, 15–39. Stony Brook, N.Y.: Forum Italicum Publishing.

Primeggia, Salvatore, and Joseph A. Varacalli. 1996. "The Sacred and Profane among Italian American Catholics: the Giglio Feast." *International Journal of Politics, Culture and Society* 9:423–449.

Prodi, Paolo. 1989. "Controriforma e/o riforma cattolica: superamento di vecchi dilemmi nei nuovi panorami storiografici." *Romishe historische mitteilungen* 31:227–237.

———. 1994. *Disciplina dell'anima, disciplina del corpo e disciplina della società tra medioevo de età moderna.* Bologna: Società editrice il Mulino.

Purvis, Thomas L. 1984a. "Commentary." *William and Mary Quarterly* 41:119–125.

———. 1984b. "The European ancestry of the United States Population, 1790." *William and Mary Quarterly* 41:85–101.

Quigley, Michael. 1997. "Grosse Île: The most important and evocative Great Famine site outside of Ireland." In *The Hungry Stream: Essays on Emigrants and Famine,* ed. E. Margaret Crawford, 25–40. Belfast: Institute of Irish Studies, Queen's University of Belfast.

Quinlan, Kieran. 2005. *Strange Kin: Ireland and the American South.* Baton Rouge: Louisiana State University Press.

Rameau de Saint-Père, Edme. 1889. *Une Colonie féodale en Amérique, l'Acadie (1604–1881).* Paris: Librairie Plon.

Raynal, Abbé. 1812. *A Philosophical and Political History of the Settlements and Trade of the Europeans in the East and West Indies,* vol. 3. Glasgow: D. M'Kenzie.

Reed, John S. 1988. "A 'female movement': the feminization of nineteenth-century Anglo-Catholicism." *Anglican and Episcopal History* 57:199–238.

Reed, John Shelton. 2005. "Our Celtic fringe: the American mainstream has Scots-Irish blood." *Weekly Standard,* August 15–22, 2005, pp. 36–38.

Reinhard, Wolfgang. 1989. "Reformation, Counter-Reformation and the early modern state: a reassessment." *Catholic Historical Review* 75:383–404.

Rischin, Moses. 1978. "Introduction: the classic ethnics." In *The San Francisco Irish, 1850–1976,* ed. James P. Walsh, 1–8. San Francisco: Irish Literary and Historical Society.

Robbins, Thomas. 2001. Review of *Acts of Faith. Review of Religious Research* 42:334–336.

Robichaud, Norbert. 1955. *L'esprit religieux chez les anciens Acadiens,* vol. 14. Québec: Département de l'Instruction Public.

Roche, James Jeffrey. 1899. "The 'Scotch-Irish' and 'Anglo-Saxon' fallacies." *Journal of the American Irish Historical Society* 2:89–91.

Rodechko, James P. 1970. "Michael J. O'Brien, Irish-American historian." *New York Historical Quarterly* 54:173–192.

Said, Edward W. 1978. *Orientalism.* New York: Pantheon Books.

St. John's Manual: A Guide to the Public Worship and Services of the Catholic Church and a Collection of Devotions for the Private Use of the Faith. 1856. New York: James B. Kirker.

St. Patrick Benevolent Society (Philadelphia, Pa.). 1804. "The constitution of the St. Patrick Benevolent Society." Retrieved Oct. 1, 2005, from Readex database, Early American Imprints, Series II: Shaw-Shoemaker, 1801–1819, Record No. 10440514DD7123DO.

St. Vincent's Manual. 1859. Baltimore: John Murphy and Company.

Salpointe, J. B. 1898. *Soldiers of the Cross.* Banning, Calif.: St. Boniface's Industrial School.

Salsman, John M., and Charles R. Carlson. 2005. "Religious orientation, mature faith, and psychological distress: elements of positive and negative associations." *Journal for the Scientific Study of Religion* 44:201–209.

Sánchez-Walsh, Arlene M. 2003. *Latino Pentecostal Identity: Evangelical Faith, Self, and Society.* New York: Columbia University Press.

Sandoval, Moises. 1990. *On the Move: A History of the Hispanic Church in the United States.* Maryknoll, N.Y.: Orbis Books.

Schmidt, Leigh Eric. 2001. *Holy Fairs: Scotland and the Making of American Revivalism.* Grand Rapids, Mich.: William B. Eerdmans Publishing.

Schneider, A. Gregory. 1991. "Social religion, the Christian home, and Republican spirituality in antebellum Methodism." In *Perspectives on American Methodism: Interpretive Essays,* ed. Russell E. Richey, Kenneth E. Rowe, and Jean Miller Schmidt, 192–208. Nashville, Tenn.: Abingdon Press.

Schroeder, Rev. H. J. 1950. *Canons and Decrees of the Council of Trent.* St. Louis, Mo.: B. Herder Book Company.

Shanks, Cheryl. 2001. *Immigration and the Politics of American Sovereignty, 1890–1990.* Ann Arbor: University of Michigan Press.

Shannon, James P. 1960. "The Irish Catholic immigration." In *Roman Catholicism and the American Way of Life,* ed. Thomas T. McAvoy, 204–210. Notre Dame: University of Notre Dame.

Shelley, Thomas. 2001. "'Only one class of people to draw upon for support': Irish-Americans and the Archdiocese of New York." *American Catholic Studies* 112:1–21.

Sigur, Alexander O. 1983. "The Acadian faith odyssey: impressions of an Acadian parish priest." In *The Cajuns: Essays on Their History and Culture,* ed. Glen R. Conrad, 127–132. Lafayette: Center for Louisiana Studies, University of Southwestern Louisiana.

Skerkat, Darren E., and Christopher G. Ellison. 1999. "Recent developments and current controversies in the sociology of religion." *Annual Review of Sociology* 25:363–394.

Slater, Will, Todd Hall, and Keith J. Edwards. 2001. "Measuring religion and spirituality: Where are we and where are we going?" *Journal of Psychology and Theology* 29:4–21.

Smith, Jonathan Z. 1990. *Drudgery Divine: On the Comparison of Early Christianities and the Religions of Late Antiquity.* Chicago: University of Chicago Press.

Society of the Friendly Sons of St. Patrick, in the State of New York. 1786. "Rules to be observed by the Society of the Friendly Sons of St. Patrick, in the State of New York." New York: Printed by Hugh Gaine, at the Bible in Hanover-Square. Retrieved Oct. 1, 2005, from Readex database, Early American Imprints, Series 1: Evans, 1639–1800, Record No. OF2F821004C16070, vol. 2005.

Sorrentino, Joseph M., S.J. 1914. "The Italian question." *America* 12:193–194.

Soulé, Frank, John H. Gihon, and Jim Nisbet. 1855. *The Annals of San Francisco; containing a summary of the history of . . . California, and a complete history of . . . its great city: to which are added, biographical memoirs of some prominent citizens.* New York: D. Appleton and Company.

Speroni, Charles. 1955. "California fisherman's festivals." *Western Folklore* 14:77–91.

Starbuck, Edwin D. 1907. "The child-mind and child-religion," part 3 "The method of evolution of consciousness and of religion." *The Biblical World* 30:191–201.

————. 1912. *The Psychology of Religion: An Empirical Study of the Growth of Religious Consciousness.* New York: Walter Scott Publishing.

Stark, Rodney. 2001a. "Gods, rituals, and the moral order." *Journal for the Scientific Study of Religion* 40:619–636.

————. 2001b. *One True God: Historical Consequences of Monotheism.* Princeton: Princeton University Press.

————. 2003. *For the Glory of God.* Princeton: Princeton University Press.

————. 2004. "SSSR presidential address, 2004: putting an end to ancestor worship." *Journal for the Scientific Study of Religion* 43:465–475.

Stark, Rodney, and Roger Finke. 1988. "American religion in 1776: a statistical portrait." *Sociological Analysis* 49:39–51.

————. 2000. *Acts of Faith: Explaining the Human Side of Religion.* Berkeley: University of California Press.

Stark, Rodney, and Laurence Iannaccone. 1991. "Sociology of religion." In *Encyclopedia of Sociology,* vol. 4, ed. Edgar Borgatta, 2029–2037. New York: Macmillan.

Starr, Dennis. 1985. *The Italians of New Jersey: A Historical Introduction and Bibliography.* Newark: New Jersey Historical Society.

————. 1994. "La festa: survival or extinction?" In *To See the Past More Clearly: The Enrichment of the Italian Heritage, 1890–1990,* ed. Harral E. Landry, 191–197. Austin, Tex.: Nortex Press.

Steele, Thomas J., S.J. 1994. *Santos and Saints.* Santa Fe, N.Mex.: Ancient City Press.

————. 2000. *Archbishop Lamy: In His Own Words.* Albuquerque, N.Mex.: LPD Press.

Steensland, Brian, Jerry Z. Park, Mark D. Regnerus, Lynn D. Robinson, W. Bradford Wilcox, and Robert D. Woodberry. 2000. "The measure of American religion: toward improving the state of the art." *Social Forces* 79:291–318.

Steinberg, Stephen. 1989. *The Ethnic Myth: Race, Ethnicity, and Class in America.* Boston: Beacon Press.

Stevens-Arroyo, Anthony M. 2003. "Correction, si; defection, no: Hispanics and U.S. Catholicism." *America* 189:16–18.

Swanson, Guy. 1967. *Religion and Regime.* Ann Arbor: University of Michigan Press.

Sweet, William W. 1930. *The Story of Religions in America.* New York: Harper and Brothers.

Tamney, Joseph B. 2005. "Does strictness explain the appeal of working-class conservative Protestant congregations?" *Sociology of Religion* 66:283–302.

Tarango, Yolanda. 1995. "Women." In *Perspectivas: Hispanic Ministry,* ed. Allan Figueroa Deck, S.J., Yolanda Tarango, and Timothy Matovina, 40–45. Kansas City, Mo.: Sheed and Ward.

Taves, Ann. 1986. *The Household of Faith.* Notre Dame: University of Notre Dame Press.

Thompson, Robert Ellis. 1895. *A History of the Presbyterian Churches in the United States.* New York: Christian Literature.

Thorne, Barrie. 1999. *Gender Play: Girls and Boys in School.* New Brunswick, N.J.: Rutgers University Press.

Timberlake, James H. 1963. *Prohibition and the Progressive Movement, 1900–1920.* Cambridge: Harvard University Press.

Tomasi, Silvano M. 1975. *Piety and Power: The Role of the Italian Parishes in the New York Metropolitan Area, 1880–1930.* Staten Island, N.Y.: Center for Migration Studies.

Tracy, David. 1981. *The Analogical Imagination: Christian Theology and the Culture of Pluralism.* New York: Crossroad.

Treviño, Roberto R. 2006. *The Church in the Barrio: Mexican American Ethno-Catholicism in Houston.* Chapel Hill: University of North Carolina Press.

Trigger, Rosalyn. 1997. "The role of the parish in fostering Irish-Catholic identity in nineteenth-century Montreal." M.A. thesis, Department of Geography, McGill University, Montreal.

Trinterud, Leonard J. 1970. *The Forming of an American Tradition: A Re-examination of Colonial Presbyterianism.* Freeport, N.Y.: Books for Libraries Press.

Tweed, Thomas A. 1997a. *Our Lady of the Exile: Diasporic Religion at a Cuban Catholic Shrine in Miami.* Oxford: Oxford University Press.

———. 1997b. "Introduction. " In *Retelling U.S. Religious History,* ed. Thomas Tweed, 1–23. Berkeley: University of California Press.

Tweed, Thomas A., ed. 1997. *Retelling U.S. Religious History.* Berkeley: University of California Press.

Urick, Mildred. 1969. "The San Rocco festival at Aliquippa, Pennsylvania: a transplanted tradition." *Pennsylvania Folklife* 19:14–22.

Usner, Don J. 1995. *Sabino's Map: Life in Chimayó's Old Plaza.* Santa Fe: Museum of New Mexico Press.

Varacalli, Joseph A. 1986. "The changing nature of the 'Italian Problem' in the Catholic Church of the United States." *Faith and Reason* 12:38–73.

———. 2006. *The Catholic Experience in America.* Westport, Conn.: Greenwood Press.

Vecoli, Rudolph J. 1964. "Contadini in Chicago: A critique of *The Uprooted.*" *Journal of American History* 51:404–417.

———. 1969. "Prelates and peasants: Italian immigrants and the Church." *Journal of Social History* 2:217–268.

———. 1977. "Cult and occult in Italian-American culture." In *Immigrants and Religion in Urban America,* ed. Randall M. Miller and Thomas D. Marzik, 25–47. Philadelphia: Temple University Press.

———. 1996. "Are Italian Americans just white folks." In *Through the Looking Glass: Italian and Italian-American Images in the Media,* ed. Mary Jo Bona and Anthony J. Tamburri, 3–17. Staten Island, N.Y.: American Italian Historical Association.

Vidal, Jaime R. 1994. "Towards an understanding of synthesis in Iberian Hispanic American popular religiosity." In *An Enduring Flame: Studies on Latino Popular Religiosity,* ed. Anthony M. Stevens-Arroyo and Ana María Díaz-Stevens, 73–95. New York: Bildner Center for Western Hemisphere Studies.

von Arx, Jeffrey Paul. 1998. *Varieties of Ultramontanism.* Washington, D.C.: Catholic University of America Press.

Walsh, James P. 1976. "Varieties of Irish America: a new home in San Francisco." In *Varieties of Ireland, Varieties of Irish-America,* ed. Blanche M. Touhill, 41–54. St. Louis: University of Missouri.

————. 1978. "The Irish in early San Francisco." In *The San Francisco Irish, 1850–1976*, ed. James P. Walsh, 9–25. San Francisco: Irish Literary and Historical Society.

Walter, Paul A. F. 1916. "A New Mexico Lourdes." *El Palacio* 3:2–27.

Ward, Greg. 1997. *Southwest USA: The Rough Guide*. London: Penguin Books.

Warner, Harry S. 1928. *Prohibition: An Adventure in Freedom*. Westerville, Ohio: World League Against Alcoholism.

Warner, R. Stephen. 1993. "Work in progress toward a new paradigm for the sociological study of religion in the United States." *American Journal of Sociology* 98:1044–1093.

Webb, James H. 2004. *Born Fighting: How the Scots-Irish Shaped America*. New York: Broadway Books.

Weber, Max. 1905/1996. *The Protestant Ethic and the Spirit of Capitalism*. Los Angeles: Roxbury Publishing.

————. 1946. "The Protestant sects and the spirit of capitalism." In *From Max Weber: Essays in Sociology*, ed. H. H. Gerth and C. Wright Mills, 302–322. New York: Oxford University Press.

Weigle, Marta. 1976. *Brothers of Light, Brothers of Blood: The Penitentes of the Southwest*. Albuquerque: University of New Mexico Press.

————. 1983. "The first twenty-five years of the Spanish Colonial Arts Society." In *Hispanic Arts and Ethnohistory in the Southwest*, ed. Marta Weigle, 181–204. Santa Fe, N.Mex.: Ancient City Press.

Weigle, Marta, and Peter White. 1988. *The Lore of New Mexico*. Albuquerque: University of New Mexico Press.

West, Mary Allen. 1889. "Domestic service." *Our Day, A Record and Review of Current Reform* 4:401–415.

Westerkamp, Marilyn J. 1988. *Triumph of the Laity: Scots-Irish Piety and the Great Awakening, 1625–1760*. New York: Oxford.

————. 1999. *Women and Religion in Early America, 1600–1850*. London: Routledge.

Williams, Phyllis H. 1938. *South Italian Folkways in Europe and America*. New York: Russell and Russell.

Wilson, Chris. 1997. *The Myth of Santa Fe*. Albuquerque: University of New Mexico Press.

Wilson, John F. 2003. *Religion and the American Nation: Historiography and History*. Athens: University of Georgia Press.

Wittke, Carl. 1956. *The Irish in America*. Baton Rouge: Louisiana State University Press.

Wulff, David M. 1997. *Psychology of Religion: Classic and Contemporary*. New York: John Wiley and Sons.

Wuthnow, Robert J. 1988. "Sociology of religion." In *Handbook of Sociology*, ed. Neil Smelser, 473–509. Newbury Park, Calif.: Sage Publications.

————. 2003. "Studying religion, making it sociological." In *Handbook of the Sociology of Religion*, ed. Michele Dillon. Cambridge: Cambridge University Press.

Wuthnow, Robert, and Wendy Cadge. 2004. "Buddhists and Buddhism in the United States: The scope of influence." *Journal for the Scientific Study of Religion* 43:363–380.

Young, John Howard. 1988. "The Acadians and Roman Catholicism: in Acadia from 1710 to the expulsion, in exile and in Louisiana from the 1760s until 1803." Ph.D. diss., Dedman College, Southern Methodist University.